MEDICAL LEGAL VIOLENCE

Medical Legal Violence

Health Care and Immigration Enforcement
Against Latinx Noncitizens

Meredith Van Natta

NEW YORK UNIVERSITY PRESS
New York

NEW YORK UNIVERSITY PRESS
New York
www.nyupress.org

© 2023 by New York University
All rights reserved

References to Internet websites (URLs) were accurate at the time of writing. Neither the author nor New York University Press is responsible for URLs that may have expired or changed since the manuscript was prepared.

Please contact the Library of Congress for Cataloging-in-Publication data.
ISBN: 9781479807390 (hardback)
ISBN: 9781479807420 (paperback)
ISBN: 9781479807444 (library ebook)
ISBN: 9781479807437 (consumer ebook)

New York University Press books are printed on acid-free paper, and their binding materials are chosen for strength and durability. We strive to use environmentally responsible suppliers and materials to the greatest extent possible in publishing our books.

Manufactured in the United States of America

10 9 8 7 6 5 4 3 2 1

Also available as an ebook

To my family

CONTENTS

PREFACE

This was not the book I thought I would be writing when I began this project in 2015. Back then, I had just transitioned out of my job as a surgical case manager at a nonprofit organization that served low-income, uninsured people living in the San Francisco Bay Area—many of whom were undocumented immigrants from Latin America. Their legal status meant that they were excluded by law from most forms of health insurance, and my job as case manager was to match uninsured patients who needed an outpatient surgical or diagnostic procedure to a surgeon who was willing to provide that procedure for free in a hospital that would write off the costs as charity care. I also served as a health care interpreter for our Spanish- and Portuguese-speaking patients in medical offices and hospitals, a role I would continue even after I left case management. My colleagues and I coordinated a wide range of services that allowed patients to get on with their lives with less pain or disability, as well as diagnostic services like colonoscopies and breast or thyroid biopsies to diagnose cancer.

Sometimes the biopsies came back inconclusive or positive for cancer, and I especially dreaded those cases because comprehensive cancer treatment was beyond the scope of our partnered "charity care" programs. For undocumented patients living in areas where county hospitals had robust safety nets, this was a devastating but relatively manageable situation. Such counties had universal health care coverage programs available to low-income residents regardless of their immigration status, and patients could take their diagnostic records to the county hospital to arrange the coverage and care they needed. It was by no means a perfect system, but it was something. Other counties, usually in more rural areas, lacked such health plans or safety net infrastructures. When a patient came from a county with no public hospital and no health plan for undocumented immigrants, the road ahead was much less clear.

Several years have passed since I was a case manager, but I still remember apologetically explaining to patients who just received a serious diagnosis that we were closing their case and referring them back to their community clinic to follow up with their primary care provider. Patients were upset and wanted answers to the many questions running through their mind as they contemplated not only their diagnosis but also the uncertain path forward. What were they supposed to do? Who was going to help them? What was going to happen now? The truth was that I had no idea. I, too, wondered what would happen to those patients whose cases I closed.

I decided to design a research program that would start where my case management ended. I wanted to know what happened when I closed a case, and what obstacles to and opportunities for care such patients might encounter when grappling with a serious medical condition. I sought to describe the challenges while identifying opportunities to expand care, and in the wake of recent health reform and immigration reform proposals emerging at the time, there was reason for cautious optimism. Yet, over the course of my fieldwork from 2015 to 2020, the policy environment for both spheres became more exclusionary rather than less so. My questions about expanding health care receded in importance as the people I encountered struggled to make sense of increasingly anti-immigrant rhetoric and more aggressive immigration enforcement activities.

When I set out on this project, I had a poor understanding of the political battlefield that the intersection of immigration and health politics would become. I had hoped to unearth locally inclusive policies and practices that enhanced noncitizens' health chances and that could be scaled up as federal immigration reform took a more inclusionary turn. That was naïve, and by an accident of timing I happened to bear witness to a period of intense uncertainty and anxiety as the Trump administration accelerated the punitive immigration enforcement measures that had existed already in some form in the United States for decades.

While this was not the story I imagined I would be telling when I set out in 2015, I found myself in a unique position to observe and reflect on how this remarkable transition, and the policies that preceded and followed from it, affected Latinx noncitizen patients and the clinic workers who provided their care. I also had the privilege of whiteness and institutional affiliations and resources that enabled me to observe the impacts of rhetoric and policies that did not directly affect me in the ways they impacted my friends, family, and colleagues who did not have those advantages. My relative power has afforded a platform whereby I might shed light on stories that are not my own, stories that are still very much unfolding. This book represents a first step toward understanding the lived consequences of contemporary health and immigration policies and how they might endure in the absence of more humane politics in the future, and it exists because of the collective effort of those who have shared their time and expertise with me over the past several years.

Finally, the coronavirus pandemic that struck at the tail end of my research has made this book more urgent than I ever anticipated. The stories that follow are the stories of those we now call "essential workers," of those whose livelihoods our society often values more than the lives behind that labor. Their work—in fields, factories, service industries, health care institutions, and beyond—is essential by definition, and yet through the pandemic we have seen that those who undertake such work are often treated as disposable. And the *medical legal violence* I describe here normalizes that disposability in often slow and subtle ways. In this book, I shed light on the histories, policies, and practices that have made such disposability seem natural and inevitable. I explain some of the reasons that have made the pandemic so disproportionately deadly in immigrant communities, and I ask how things might be different if we begin to learn from this history rather than continuously repeat it.

Introduction

Anti-Immigrant Politics and Medical Legal Violence

On September 26, 2016, I shadowed a clinic worker named Elizabeth at one of the largest clinic networks in a politically progressive county where I was carrying out fieldwork for this book.[1] I sat across the desk from Elizabeth in a small, fluorescent-lit room where donated diapers, baby clothes, and other infant-care items were stacked against one side of the unadorned wall. An empty chair beside me awaited clinic patients seeking Elizabeth's aid in navigating their health care and social service needs. As I watched Elizabeth go about the wide variety of tasks on that September morning—tasks that included a mix of social work, medical case management, and insurance eligibility counseling—a woman named Maribel entered the office with her daughter and told Elizabeth she needed to see an attorney. Maribel, who was originally from Central America, said she had an asylum hearing coming up in a few months and was confused about the process. The hearing had been scheduled in another state thousands of miles away (where Maribel had first settled), and she expressed concern about updating her address and hearing location. Maribel understood little about the asylum process and worried that she was already being processed for deportation. Elizabeth explained that the first step was for Maribel to pass her credible fear interview; if she did not pass, she might then be subject to a removal order.[2]

Maribel expressed skepticism over the process Elizabeth described and asked to be disenrolled from all services that she was receiving through the clinic. "I came [here] fleeing," she explained imploringly to Elizabeth as she rationalized her disenrollment request. Maribel feared that because she had moved to another state, immigration agents would, as she put it, "come to my house and catch me as a fugitive." She understood that she needed to update her address for the court hearing, but she also worried that once she did, immigration agents would discover that she was receiving benefits through the clinic.

I had heard such concerns before, both directly from clients when I was a case manager and indirectly through my research with clinic workers, but this was the first time I observed it in person in the clinic. Even though she had every right to seek asylum in the United States and access health care at a community clinic that provided services irrespective of legal status, Maribel could not confidently disentangle the punitive potential of immigration enforcement from the more humanitarian arm of state-adjacent social service agencies. As Elizabeth and Maribel spoke, I recalled a conversation I had with Dr. Lee, the clinic's medical director. He explained that whereas some parts of the state had universal county-based health care safety nets that included noncitizens with varying legal status, noncitizen patients in this county had to rely more on hospital-specific charity care and emergency or state-funded Medicaid support. These were the very programs for which undocumented, liminally legal, and recently arrived immigrants like Maribel often hesitated to apply. (Emergency Medicaid allows income-eligible noncitizens without a qualifying legal status to temporarily enroll in Medicaid coverage, but only for emergency care.)

"The fear is that they're going to be reported to some sort of immigration or governmental agency," Dr. Lee explained to me when I asked why patients were reluctant to enroll for care for which they were legally eligible. "[They fear] their status here is going to be jeopardized, [that] they'll be sent back." He continued, "I tell them that [these resources are] *made* for these cases and that, yes, you're getting some sort of governmental aid with the insurance. But it—there's no feedback loop that once you get that aid, it goes into another pool where immigration is going to come after you."

Elizabeth was attempting to make a similar argument to Maribel now. She explained that although she was not an expert in immigration law, from what Maribel had told her, her presence in the United States was already registered with immigration agencies, and she had presented a request for asylum based on fear of returning to her country of origin. Elizabeth added that even though Maribel was a "person without a formal status," she still had rights in this country and needed to have patience with the process. Maribel remained skeptical but agreed to share her updated address with Elizabeth. When Elizabeth compared the address against Maribel's clinic records, she remarked that the clinic had been sending letters to a different location. Maribel replied that she was using an acquaintance's address for mail, and she did not want to give the clinic the address of the place where she was actually living in case Immigration and Customs Enforcement (ICE) agents came looking for her there. Elizabeth reiterated that she understood why Maribel felt fearful, but she already had a case pending, so ICE had no reason to come looking for her. Plus, she added, they already knew that she was living in the United States while awaiting her hearing.

Elizabeth seemed to sense that this line of reasoning was not persuading Maribel to trust her or the process. She took a figurative step back and suggested that Maribel wait to make any decisions until after she met with a lawyer, which—based on her understanding of Maribel's situation—she had until December to do. "This [change of address] form isn't going to put you at any risk," Elizabeth added. She reminded Maribel that she was already registered in "the system" (she did not specify whether she meant the immigration system or the health care system) and that they just needed to verify her whereabouts. "This is something more administrative," Elizabeth continued. "If you haven't committed any crime, they won't come looking for you because they are giving you an opportunity to fight your case." Elizabeth paused and asked how Maribel was feeling. "It's that I'm afraid that this would go directly to immigration," Maribel replied, "and that they'll arrest me, or . . ." She trailed off, and Elizabeth explained that, on the contrary, if necessary, Maribel could now show immigration agents her paperwork to prove that she had an asylum case pending and that all her information was up to date. Elizabeth then added that she would follow up directly with a lawyer to check on Maribel's case.

Later in the day, I overheard Elizabeth telling Jacqueline, an immigration lawyer, about Maribel's case over speakerphone. She asked whether updating Maribel's records might trigger any immigration enforcement consequences. "It's not gonna put her at any risk?" she asked candidly. Jacqueline paused for a long time before replying that it would be a minimal risk, but that immigration agents might still come for Maribel. Jacqueline asked for more information about Maribel's case, and Elizabeth explained what she could while also considering that Maribel might be missing some of her paperwork. Given this lack of clarity, Jacqueline seemed decidedly more guarded in her response than Elizabeth had been when speaking with Maribel. She emphasized that Maribel needed to apply for asylum as soon as possible because her one-year window to complete her paperwork was almost up. Completing the proper bureaucratic steps was essential to securing legal authorization to remain, and also work, in the United States. If she did not do so within the appointed window, Maribel would likely become undocumented and at risk for deportation and separation from her US-born child.

Jacqueline asked Elizabeth to find out more about who was giving Maribel legal advice about her case right now and why she had not hired an immigration attorney yet. "Can she not afford it?" Jacqueline wondered. Elizabeth replied that Maribel had indeed reached out to lawyers, but they were not returning her calls. Jacqueline responded bleakly that this did not surprise her. Everyone was overwhelmed with cases lately— this was in 2016, after Deferred Action for Parents of Americans and Lawful Permanent Residents (DAPA) had been struck down, but before the Trump administration largely dismantled asylum and Temporary Protected Status (TPS) programs. "She needs to apply for asylum," Jacqueline repeated. "She has a legitimate fear, right?" Elizabeth responded affirmatively, adding that more than one of Maribel's children had been killed in Central America already. "She needs to get on that asylum," Jacqueline reiterated. Without such status, however precarious, Maribel's ability to live and work in the United States would be consigned to the realm of illegality. Like many of the people I describe in later chapters, such a situation would likely expose her to more exploitative economic conditions and narrower health care access than if her presence were legally authorized. Her fears of surveillance and deportation were more likely to materialize, thus justifying in some ways her reluctance to seek the kinds of health and well-being services Elizabeth's clinic offered.

That evening, after I had left the clinic, I watched the first presidential debate between candidates Hillary Clinton and Donald Trump on television. Anti-immigrant rhetoric had been on the rise already during the party primaries (particularly among Republican candidates), and the enhanced gravity of the situation—that one of these two individuals would become president in a matter of months—did not seem to temper the message. "We have gangs roaming the street," candidate Trump declared to the record-breaking eighty-four million people watching the debate, "and in many cases, they're illegally here, illegal immigrants. And they have guns. And they shoot people. And we have to be very strong. And we have to be very vigilant" (M. Kennedy 2016). I thought about Maribel, who fled her home country because of violence that the United States played a large role in fomenting, and recalled how she felt like a "fugitive" being relentlessly pursued by immigration agents—even inside the space of the clinic itself.[3] I remembered her asking Elizabeth to remove her from clinic services and keep her real address off the record until she could get legal aid to adjust her status—a process stymied by the fact that the lawyers she reached out to were already overburdened. She was running out of time in a nation that every day seemed more out to get her, and at this moment her security mattered more to her than her health.

Anti-Immigrant Politics and Medical Legal Violence

Maribel's story emphasizes the anxiety that many noncitizens experience when weighing the benefits they might receive through government (and government-adjacent) agencies against the possibility that doing so might make them more visible to federal immigration enforcement agencies (Asad 2020; Jimenez 2021). Whereas sometimes medical or other social needs may tip the balance in favor of enrollment, Maribel clearly felt that the risks outweighed the advantages. In this book, I describe how anti-immigrant politics in the United States increasingly undermine health care for Latinx noncitizens in ways that deepen health inequalities while upholding economic exploitation and white supremacy.[4] I also argue that the surveillance and criminalization of Latinx immigrants that have been expanding for decades increasingly target not only individuals but their families, communities, and the institutions that promote their health and well-being. When the research for this book began in 2015, the national political landscape seemed primed for incremental immigration and health reforms. While this by no means portended a substantial shift away from a still overwhelmingly punitive immigration governance regime, the time nevertheless seemed right to examine whether emerging opportunities for health equity in the United States might ever reach people whose legal status excluded them from social benefits programs. As the research unfolded between 2015 and 2020, the limitations of federal immigration and health reforms became clear. In the absence of comprehensive reforms and amidst the resurgence of nationalist, nativist discourses across the country, the possibility of health equity for noncitizens faced tougher odds and higher stakes than ever.

This book tells the story of what that looked like on the ground as Latinx immigrant patients and health care workers navigated political tumult in three different states across the United States in those years. It is a story that, at one time, might have been about how more inclusive, less punitive policies could improve health equity for immigrant communities. Instead, it soon became a testimony to one of the most explicitly anti-immigrant periods in US history and foreshadowed the human costs of disenfranchising noncitizen "essential workers" that the COVID-19 pandemic would later lay bare. While such a statement may seem hyperbolic for a nation that at its inception made whiteness a fundamental criterion for citizenship and passed several pieces of legislation that explicitly discriminated against immigrants on the basis of their race, ethnicity, and national origin, recent events have only underscored how much that history endures today.[5] The nation's relationship to immigration, past and present, is inseparable from the legacies of the intertwined forces of white supremacy and capitalist production that brought the country into being and stratified the life chances of those who have resided here. More than just a question of individual bigotry, white supremacy in the United States took root with the racial classification schemes that justified European colonial expansion and evolved to become a "fundamental organizing principle" of the nation's contemporary social systems—including and especially its capitalist economic order (Omi and Winant 2014, 3). When I write about "white supremacy" throughout this book, I am referring to the racist beliefs and actions of individuals as well as to this enduring, systematic, and institutionalized phenomenon of racialized social stratification.

The questions driving this work initially emerged during the Obama administration as I sought to explore possibilities for expanding health care coverage to undocumented immigrants following the implementation of the Affordable Care Act (ACA) and the announcement of expanded Deferred Action for Childhood Arrivals (DACA) and DAPA programs in 2014.[6] Would these moves represent a step toward real inclusion, or would they further entrench health inequities by elevating full legal membership as a minimum prerequisite for comprehensive health care? Before I could gauge the degree to which reformist rhetoric matched the reality of immigrants' health care experiences, however, the Trump administration came to power and sparked uncertainty in health and immigration policy. The negative characterizations of the ACA and immigrants that several Republican candidates espoused during the 2016 election cycle transformed into immediate policy priorities on January 21, 2017, and my professional and academic positions gave me a front-row seat to witness many of the consequences play out in real time.

Following President Trump's inauguration, health and immigration policies in the United States magnified the already "punitive turn" in immigrant health care restrictions that began decades before he ever came to office (Stuart, Armenta, and Osborne 2015). The Obama administration had continued to build upon this punitive infrastructure—enacting intensive immigration enforcement activities, overseeing record numbers of deportations, and perpetuating noncitizen exclusions from health and well-being services—while at the same time proposing moderately inclusionary measures such as DACA and DAPA (González-Barrera and Krogstad 2016). Yet whereas the Obama administration strategically projected a relatively (if often superficially) humane health and immigration governance regime through the ACA and deferred action programs, respectively, the Republican Party unapologetically campaigned on a platform that decried the ACA as a "catastrophe" and boldly embraced anti-immigrant, anti-refugee, and racist rhetoric. Looking back on debates over immigration and health policy over the past few years, one can see that the political polarization of these policy contestations clearly created a hazardous landscape for the noncitizens and their families who sought health care in communities across the United States.

This book describes how increasingly punitive federal immigration policies have enabled what I call *medical legal violence* that unites criminal law, immigration enforcement, and health care law and policy in ways that disproportionately harm Latinx immigrants. This type of violence enlists health care institutions as potential sites for surveilling and penalizing noncitizen immigrants as they seek care while also implicating health care workers as either *agents* or *targets* of that violence. This dynamic is *violent* because it results in direct and indirect injury to noncitizens and mixed-status families, and it is *medical* because it attempts to enlist clinical systems and personnel that are meant to heal people into practices that might instead put certain patients in harm's way.

Of the approximately 25 million noncitizens currently living in the United States, nearly half (10.5 million) are "unauthorized" or "undocumented"—that is, they lack definitive legal permission to do so (Budiman et al. 2020). Federal and state laws exclude these undocumented immigrants, as well as many authorized immigrants, from many public benefits, including health care coverage (Kaiser Family Foundation 2015). Programs that under the ACA reduced the numbers of uninsured Americans by thirteen million (especially through Medicaid expansion and the subsidized health care marketplaces) explicitly excluded undocumented immigrants and recent immigrants (Kaiser Family Foundation 2016). While thousands of noncitizens might have become eligible for limited state-level (not federal) health coverage through DAPA and expanded DACA, legal challenges at the state and federal level overturned DAPA and temporarily suspended DACA enrollment (Wiley 2014). During the course of writing this book alone, DACA was variously rescinded, temporarily reinstated, suspended, and revived, and the future of DACA and other deferred action programs under the Biden administration remains to be seen.[7]

While the punitive turn in immigration was already well underway and persisted through the Obama administration, both health and immigration reform efforts faced new, major challenges under the Trump administration. Noncitizen patients, their health care providers, and policy makers had to make sense of these complex, changing, and overlapping policy arenas, often at the very moment urgent medical decisions had to be made. A growing body of research has drawn attention to immigration status as a social determinant of health (e.g., Davies, Basten, and Frattini 2010; Castañeda 2009; Quesada, Hart, and Bourgois 2011; Zimmerman, Kiss, and Mazeda 2011; Castañeda et al. 2015; Marrow and Joseph 2015), but there is less evidence of the effect of recent political turmoil on noncitizens' health decisions.

In this book, I examine the shifting terrain of noncitizens' health potential in the United States and advance existing scholarship through the lens of contemporary policy upheaval. To do so, I rely on ethnographic observations and interviews to identify how noncitizens have negotiated access to state-provisioned health services amidst confusion about health and immigration policy. I also evaluate the role of safety net health care workers who have helped noncitizen patients navigate an unstable political landscape. Their experiences provide timely insights into ever-narrowing public pathways to health care and the restriction of citizenship and public benefits opportunities in an age of enhanced immigration enforcement. They also show what resistance to that criminalizing exclusion can look like.

White Nationalism and the Criminalization of Immigration

Before anti-immigrant sentiment helped secure victories for many Republican politicians in the contemporary United States and culminated in the Trump administration, the renewal and steady rise of anti-immigrant politics throughout the end of the twentieth century and into the twenty-first century were already well underway. Much as they have done during previous moments of nationalist fervor, these contemporary movements aim to put citizens first by invoking an imagined, cohesive past in which the nation-state protected the well-being of its patriotic citizens from threats at home and abroad. This was the ethos behind President Trump's campaign slogan, "Make America Great Again." This message both explicitly and tacitly signals the erosion of that shared historical imaginary, one that might be restored to glory for proper Americans—that is, white people—and safeguarded against those who have supposedly eroded it—that is, people (especially immigrants) of color.[8]

While other factors, such as the economic dispossession of low-income and working-class white people and/or affiliation with certain religious traditions (especially Evangelical Christianity), are certainly at play here, it would be a mistake to overlook the central force of white supremacy and systemic racism in driving this political movement. Importantly, these nationalist movements both implicitly and explicitly frame citizenship in racial terms, wherein white European ancestry is the default determinant of legitimate national belonging. It is no secret that nationalist parties in the United States (and Europe) very much construct the "nation" in terms of a homogeneous white imaginary in juxtaposition to "invading" outsiders of color. Politicians from these parties generally rely upon criminalizing tropes of Latin American migrants (in the US case) and migrants from African, Middle Eastern, and Asian countries (in the case of Europe, but also the United States) to vilify such migrants and exclude them from the formal benefits that citizenship makes possible.[9]

These are not merely rhetorical moves; they have become codified in the very fabric of federal, state, and local laws and institutions in this country. In particular, immigration scholars have long drawn attention to the growing sphere of illegality and criminalization that bars noncitizens—especially nonwhite noncitizens—from legitimate social and political inclusion. Legal scholars (including Miller 2003; Stumpf 2006; and Kurzban 2008) have traced the process by which criminal law and immigration law have become ever more intertwined, and many refer to this phenomenon as "crimmigration" (Stumpf 2013; García Hernández 2015). "Crimmigration" delegitimizes particular noncitizens—running the gamut from those without papers to those with temporary legal status to lawful permanent residents—by inscribing the rhetoric of immigrant criminality in increasingly punitive laws, and it especially targets immigrants from Mexico and Central America (De Genova 2014). While the term denotes the *over*-criminalization of immigration in the United States, Chacón (2012) cautions that the union of these rhetorical and legal devices creates a "self-perpetuating phenomenon" wherein increasingly punitive laws construct a "criminal" immigrant to justify the existing exclusionary narrative (Chacón 2012, 629). Thus while "crimmigration" helps explain how this happens, in this book I use the term selectively and with caution so as not to further naturalize this dynamic (see also Melossi 2015, 39).

Immigration federalism (Varsanyi et al. 2012; Gulasekaram and Ramakrishnan 2015) also naturalizes this convergence of criminal and immigration law across different political geographies and jurisdictions throughout the United States—a question I explore in detail throughout this book. The US Constitution grants the federal government exclusive power to create immigration law in the United States. In recent decades, however, much of the work of enforcing these federal laws has devolved to the state, county, and local level. This immigration federalism enlists local law enforcement agencies—including state highway patrols, county sheriff's departments, and local police departments—and deputizes their agents to carry out immigration enforcement activities. The 1996 Illegal Immigration Reform and Immigrant Responsibility Act (IIRIRA), a massive immigration reform bill passed by a Republican-led Congress and signed into law by Democratic president Bill Clinton, added section 287(g) to the 1965 Immigration and Nationality Act.[10] This amendment allows the attorney general to enter into agreements enabling state and local agencies to perform immigration enforcement activities, including apprehending, investigating, detaining, and transporting noncitizens (8 U.S.C. §1357(g)).[11]

This lawmaking was followed by the Bush administration's Secure Communities program in 2008, which enabled noncitizen arrestees' fingerprints to be uploaded to both the Federal Bureau of Investigation (FBI) and Department of Homeland Security (DHS) databases.[12] The Obama administration eventually replaced Secure Communities with the Priority Enforcement Program (PEP), with the stated aim of focusing on "criminal" noncitizens while maintaining the biometric dragnet of previous programs.[13] At the same time, sanctuary policies—such as refusing to honor ICE detainers—also proliferated as many local jurisdictions became frustrated with bearing the economic and political costs of immigration enforcement by proxy. The Trump administration ended PEP and reinstated Secure Communities (with a promise to reinvigorate 287(g) agreements) by executive order within the first days of assuming the presidency, and the administration also vowed to punish jurisdictions that refused to cooperate by withholding federal funding and pursuing more federal immigration raids in those areas.[14] On January 20, 2021, President Biden repealed the previous executive order that had revived the Secure Communities program—ostensibly to prioritize criminal immigration enforcement.[15]

Regardless of changing administrations or program names, the conflation of criminal law and immigration law that sparked these various devolutions of immigration enforcement to local officials highlights bipartisan promises to focus on "criminal" immigrants when, since 1996, the very act of entering the United States without proper documentation is a criminal, not merely civil, offense (IIRIRA; Fragomen 1997). This "legal production of migrant 'illegality'" (De Genova 2002) underscores how the exclusionary nature of immigration laws has constantly and subtly evolved since the mid-twentieth century and has gained momentum through the present. The gradual acceleration of ever more discriminatory and criminalizing laws, which particularly affects immigrants from Mexico and Central America, makes "illegalization" seem natural and inevitable. As I discuss throughout this book, perceiving law in this way results in *symbolic violence* that disproportionately falls upon those who apparently fail to "play by the rules" that seem intrinsic to society (see Bourdieu 2000).

Taken together, the immigration reforms, law enforcement reforms, and social welfare reforms of the late twentieth and early twenty-first centuries ultimately created the vast space of illegality and "liminal legality" (Menjívar 2006) that exists in the contemporary United States, suffusing each of the local contexts I researched. Despite the drawing down of Secure Communities and piecemeal immigration reforms like DACA, immigration policies at the tail end of the Obama administration signaled a perpetual state of exclusion from full social and political participation. Many immigrants who receive DACA protections or other forms of conditional relief from immediate deportation remain caught in legal limbo, where "they will continue to live inside the country but in spaces of illegality, in a gray zone of nondeportability but also exclusion" (Menjívar and Kanstroom 2014, 12). Thus, while deportation of ostensibly "criminal" immigrants accelerated, so did the apparatuses of exclusion for liminally legal immigrants.

Furthermore, this "gray zone of nondeportability" is a fickle space, prone to changing with the political agenda of whoever is in charge at any given time. With this long-standing infrastructure of illegality already in place, the Trump administration specifically targeted protections such as DACA and TPS as a practical starting point for the hardline immigration enforcement environment it promised to create (Cohn, Passel, and Bialik 2019). Immigrants who had sought a modicum of safety by turning themselves in, so to speak, to the federal government in exchange for temporary deportation relief during the Obama administration expressed fear that they might become easy targets for removal precisely because they were already "in the system" (Asad 2020). In this book, I highlight how noncitizen patients weighed these risks within the health care context and emphasize the efforts of clinic workers to work within those systems—and sometimes against them—on behalf of those seeking care.

Citizenship and Neoliberal Social Welfare under Racial Capitalism

Understanding the changing state of immigration policy provides an essential foundation for grasping how these changes specifically interact with the health of noncitizens who are variously categorized as legal, liminally legal, and "illegal." Also crucial to this foundation is understanding how the particular citizenship regime of the contemporary United States shapes—and is shaped by—health and social welfare policies. To begin with, citizenship itself is a multifaceted and dynamic process rather than a fixed state, and it is contingent upon history and geography. This is especially true for those who find themselves perpetually outside its formal reach (see, e.g., Bosniak 2006; and Motomura 2007). Citizenship can be understood partially as the ability to enact certain rights within a given society—such as traditional conceptualizations that link formal citizenship to participation within the civic, political, and economic spheres (Marshall 1950) or those relating to more contemporary expressions of legal, social, and cultural membership (Bloemraad et al. 2019) that "can surpass or supersede legal membership" (Castañeda 2019, 11).

When I talk about citizenship in this book, I mean both formal legal membership in the nation-state and the dynamic, relational processes that construct the boundaries of social and political belonging. These various forms of citizenship can exist simultaneously, but very often they do not—as I demonstrate by comparing distinct local sites within one nation. Many US-born citizens, especially those impacted by systemic racism and the criminal legal system, are unable to participate fully in social and political life in their communities. And many noncitizens, including undocumented immigrants, take active roles as social and political actors within the societies they join.

This was certainly the case with some of the patients and clinic workers I spoke with while writing this book, and this variability emphasizes different kinds of *legal consciousness* and how legal notions of citizenship are both shaped by society and shape that society in turn. Legal consciousness refers to both how ordinary individuals experience and understand the law (Merry 1985) and how they participate in making meaning around the concept of "legality" in the first place (Silbey 2005). It is a dynamic rather than static condition in that people may exist "before," "with," and/or "against" the law depending on their social position and situation (Ewick and Silbey 1998). Focusing specifically on the case of undocumented migrants, for example, Abrego (2011) and Sigona (2012) illustrate how shifting immigration laws, legal interpretations, and enforcement activities across time and geographies make particular kinds of legal consciousness possible and shape how migrants exercise agency and resistance to oppressive structures and practices. This distinction impacts how differently situated groups experience being "with" and/or "against" the law and shapes the relative possibility of collective mobilization.

Despite this variability, because legal citizenship is a necessary prerequisite for the kinds of health care benefits I describe in this book, it is also important to understand where these *de jure* (in the law) and *de facto* (in practice) forms of citizenship diverge and what this means for noncitizens' agency and resistance. In the first place, citizenship-based health entitlements in the United States exist within a neoliberal system that conceptualizes health as a commodity rather than a right (Light 2000), and social welfare discourses are highly racialized at the same time that they invoke legal citizenship as a measure of deservingness (Willen 2007, 2012b; McAdam and Kloos 2014; Patel 2015; Bloemraad et al. 2019). Patel emphasizes how the trope of "deservingness" enacts a "form of racialized legitimacy" that upholds the privileges of whiteness in settler states (2015, 11, 12), and Asad and Clair (2017) suggest that ostensibly color-blind legal citizenship classifications have the *de facto* consequence of discrediting racial and ethnic minority groups' social position through what they refer to as "racialized legal status." As illustrated by my conversations with clinic workers who are from the same immigrant communities that they serve, this can particularly affect Latinx citizens in the United States, who experience the spillover effects of being associated ethnically with a discredited (il)legal status in ways that may have chilling consequences on their actual benefits use.

Such racialized depictions also fault particular groups for failing to embody neoliberal values of personal responsibility and economic productivity. A key example of this is the 1996 Personal Responsibility and Work Opportunity Reconciliation Act (PRWORA), also known as welfare reform. At the same time that the 1996 IIRIRA accelerated the criminalization of many immigrants, PRWORA created new restrictions for many noncitizens—including many lawful permanent residents who had been in the country for less than five years—against accessing federal public benefits that included health, nutritional, and cash assistance (Viladrich 2012). Social policy scholar Diane Sainsbury has referred to these intersecting pieces of immigration and welfare legislation as "one of the largest disentitlements in welfare history" (2012, 152). The particular problem for Latinx immigrants living in the United States is that civil and political rights correspond to US citizenship, a designation that is becoming ever more difficult for many immigrants from Latin America to attain. Given the increasing pace of migrant criminalization and the reality of racialized legal status, the exclusion of many Latinx noncitizens from citizenship opportunities disqualifies them from benefits that only citizens (and only a certain kind of citizen at that) "deserve." These trends also perpetuate their exclusion from political participation and from "the moral community of people whose lives, bodies, illnesses, and injuries are deemed worthy of attention, investment, or concern" (Willen 2012a).

Such exclusions reproduce health inequalities on the basis of legal status while enlisting American citizenship values to uphold white supremacy under contemporary neoliberal capitalism. Indeed, these two structural forces—racism rooted in white supremacy and economic exploitation fundamental to neoliberal capitalism—are inseparable from one another. According to Cedric J. Robinson, racism was essential to the evolution of capitalism as a global economic system. Robinson coined the term "racial capitalism" to describe how "the development, organization, and expansion of capitalist society pursued essentially racial directions, [and] so too did social ideology" (1983, 2). Even though neoliberal capitalism in the contemporary United States looks different now than when it emerged at the nation's inception, it nevertheless retains the central feature of extracting social and economic value from people who are racialized as "people of color" within white supremacist racial classification schemes. This extractive relationship often involves dangerous working conditions that harm Latinx noncitizens, while neo-liberalized welfare systems and criminalizing laws increasingly exclude them from health and social support programs to remedy those harms.

State Variation in Noncitizens' Safety Net Access

Despite myriad barriers to naturalization, especially for people migrating from Latin America (Bergeron 2013), legal citizenship remains a nonnegotiable prerequisite for many of the provisions of health care reform. While Medicaid—a federally subsidized insurance program for low-income individuals and families—does exist in every state for its low-income residents, variability in state-level Medicaid enactment results in radically different material consequences for citizen and noncitizen residents alike.[16] This variation in Medicaid enactment is one of the key differences for noncitizens' health access among the three states I discuss in this book, and understanding this is crucial to grasping the dynamics at each of the clinic sites I observed. Because states have so much flexibility in implementing Medicaid on their own terms, what the program actually looks like on the ground depends largely upon where someone lives. States can use their own funds to supplement Medicaid and make it more accessible to groups who are federally ineligible. For example, six states (California, Illinois, Massachusetts, New York, Oregon, and Washington) use state funds to cover income-eligible undocumented children who would otherwise not meet federal residency eligibility criteria (Artiga and Diaz 2019; Salami 2017). On the other end of the spectrum, however, twelve states rejected federal Medicaid expansion funds. In these states, which include Texas, some midwestern states, and almost all the US Southeast, fewer US citizens and no undocumented immigrants qualify for Medicaid (Kaiser Family Foundation 2020c).

The one key exception is Emergency Medicaid, which is available to income-eligible undocumented immigrants and recently arrived lawful residents in all states. The 1986 Emergency Medical Treatment and Active Labor Act (EMTALA) requires that emergency departments at hospitals receiving federal funds must treat any patient experiencing a medical emergency, regardless of immigration status or ability to pay.

The definition of "medical emergency" is open to interpretation, however, and therefore Emergency Medicaid is frequently reserved for cases that are immediate matters of life and death (Sontag 2008; Sommers 2013).[17] Again, geography often determines how this threshold is measured.[18] Unsurprisingly, in the more politically conservative states that I observed, noncitizen Medicaid eligibility was among the narrowest in the country, whereas in the progressive state it was much more expansive. This mattered greatly for the relative health chances of those I met throughout this research.

Beyond Emergency Medicaid, there are other ways that undocumented immigrants can access the health care they need. For primary care, they often rely on community clinics like the ones where I conducted fieldwork. Accessing specialty care, on the other hand, can be extremely challenging. Like Medicaid eligibility, eligibility for specialty care varies widely by institution, medical condition, and geographic region. Some county departments of health, like San Francisco and Los Angeles, have expansive health care programs that provide primary *and* specialty care to immigrants who are ineligible for regular (full-scope, non-Emergency) Medicaid. Additionally, some noncitizens who are ineligible for comprehensive health care can receive treatment on a case-by-case basis through hospital charity care programs.

When I was a case manager, this was the kind of care I helped coordinate. Essentially, this involved hospitals donating their time, equipment, and services to low-income, uninsured patients. Such programs were an important lifeline for patients with medical conditions that did not necessarily fall under the acute, life-and-death situation covered by Emergency Medicaid. In my experience, these ran the gamut from screening and diagnostic procedures (like colonoscopies and breast biopsies) to surgical procedures like hernia repair, eye surgery for conditions like cataract removal and diabetic eye complications, gallbladder removal, and gynecological procedures. For many low-income, undocumented, and uninsured patients, charity care (also known as hospital financial assistance) programs are the only way that they can access the care they need without going into staggering medical debt.

Each of these points of health care access—state-funded Medicaid, Emergency Medicaid, and institution-specific charity care/financial assistance—involve particular bureaucracies to determine a patient's eligibility and document their care. This typically includes verifying a patient's income using pay stubs, ascertaining their household income and composition (how many kids, how many adults contributing to household finances, and so on), confirming local residence using a utility bill addressed to the patient's home, documenting medical need through medical records, and reviewing the immigration documents of patients and their sponsors. To put it simply, there is a lot of paperwork involved. In the era of electronic health records (EHRs), that information circulates among all parties: the community clinic that refers a patient for care, the health institution or agency that approves that care, and the funding institution or agency that reimburses and/or charges the patient for that care. If Medicaid or Emergency Medicaid is involved, this means that a patient's health record may be under review by both federal and state government agencies.

During my professional and academic career, I have observed many of these *assemblages*—the dynamic collision of policies, bureaucracies, and people in particular places and times—of immigrant health care access play out in real life. In this book, I disentangle some of these assemblages in a state-by-state accounting while simultaneously considering the national context as a whole. I specifically examine these dynamics across three states with distinct state-level political landscapes—"red" (Republican), "blue" (Democrat), or "purple" (mixed)—based on which party dominated the 2016 presidential and relevant gubernatorial and congressional races.[19] In the red and purple states I observed, noncitizens' options for advanced care were often limited to Emergency Medicaid and charity care programs. In the blue state, noncitizen patients at the clinic I observed were able to access a combination of state-funded Medicaid, Emergency Medicaid, and charity care.

While the red and blue states were most alike in terms of their noncitizen demographics (both are "traditional" Latinx immigrant destinations with high degrees of immigrant integration) and their statewide Medicaid expansion following the ACA, the red and purple states aligned more in terms of immigrant criminalization and noncitizen public benefits exclusions.[20] Despite fears of federal surveillance and penalty in blue state clinics that I describe in chapter 3, the blue state was still the best place to be for an undocumented immigrant with complex health needs. If a patient decided to prioritize their health over their security concerns in the face of mounting federal immigration enforcement threats, they did indeed have a pathway to care through state-funded Medicaid and a relatively well-funded health care safety net compared to the other sites. No such pathway existed in the red or purple state.

I point out this distinction here because, as the following chapters illustrate, federalized immigration policies routinely collide with state variation in noncitizens' access to the health care safety net to create an uneven health care landscape for many immigrants. This situation makes the intersection of serious illness and illicit or liminally legal status a dangerous one. In places where health systems do not have a mechanism to specifically include people with such statuses in primary or specialty care, "managing" a complex illness is impossible. Acute symptoms may warrant emergency treatment under EMTALA, but the components of so-called "responsible" disease management—medication, durable medical equipment, diet and exercise changes, and regular primary and specialty care visits—remain out of reach. It is often only when medical conditions get out of control that a claim to treatment becomes available for noncitizens.

Legal Violence Enters the Clinic

To think through some of these complicated questions, I take up Menjívar and Abrego's (2012) concept of "legal violence" and extend it to the clinical sites I observed during fieldwork. "Legal violence" refers to the practices whereby the "increasingly fragmented and arbitrary field of immigration law has gradually intertwined with criminal law," and it impacts immigrants and immigrant communities in spaces such as schools, workplaces, and families (Menjívar and Abrego 2012, 1381). Two theoretical frameworks underpin their concept of legal violence. The first is *structural* violence, whereby structural inequalities like institutionalized racism, poverty, sexism, and nationalism harm individuals and groups through socially embedded arrangements that mask the sources of that violence (Galtung 1969; Farmer 2003; Pinderhughes, Davis, and Williams 2016). Unlike direct interpersonal violence, structural violence is not a matter of one person injuring another, and so it is impossible to hold any one person accountable for its harms.

The second kind of violence underlying legal violence is *symbolic*, which normalizes and reproduces the social harms that, in the context of this book, undermine Latinx noncitizens' well-being. Symbolic violence happens when unequal power relations become so embedded in social structures and interactions that they come to seem natural or inevitable—even to the people who are disadvantaged by them (Bourdieu 2000, 170). Symbolic violence is insidious and powerful because both those who benefit from and those who are harmed by existing power relations misrecognize them as innate and immutable. The depersonalized nature of both structural and symbolic violence can make it hard to imagine that the world could be otherwise, that the distribution of power could look different than it does. Moreover, rather than the law being viewed as a source of that violence, the culpability for its harms lands upon undocumented and liminally legal immigrants themselves as a "generalized belief that these immigrants deserve such suffering because they 'broke the law'" (Menjívar 2013). This is how symbolic and structural violence become constitutive aspects of legal violence.

In addition to legal violence, throughout the book I also implicitly engage with Foucault's (1978, 2004) notion of "biopolitics" to analyze noncitizens' health negotiations in the neoliberal regime of the contemporary United States. Biopolitics is part of a mutually reinforcing kind of social control that subjugates individual human bodies while also regulating populations according to increasingly rationalized, scientific techniques (Foucault 1978, 139–40). In this book, I focus on how the biopolitics of US immigration and health aims to regulate particular noncitizen populations according to highly bureaucratized criteria. I highlight several cases in which contemporary immigration and welfare laws have effectively disqualified noncitizen patients from comprehensive health care on the basis of their racialized legal status and by instilling fear that they will be punished for using services meant for only the most deserving citizens.

Additionally, as immigration enforcement and public health care administration increasingly rely upon electronic databases that include individuals' biographic and biometric information, interoperability across agencies becomes more likely. This means that as technological governance expands and increasingly automates immigration enforcement and health care eligibility determinations, individuals within agencies have less discretion as frontline bureaucratic agents over the information they collect and what might happen to it once it is collected (see, e.g., Kalhan 2013; and Eubanks 2018). Indeed, Maribel feared this very interoperability when asking Elizabeth to disenroll her from services, and lawyer Jacqueline by no means dismissed these concerns. And, as I describe throughout the book, Maribel is not the only one disciplining herself out of services under the panoptic gaze of interconnected government agencies that have long criminalized people like her.[21]

With respect to the United States of the twenty-first century, the "coercive bureaucracies" of US immigration agencies, particularly Customs and Border Protection (CBP) and ICE, ideologically construct "illegality" as a category to be enacted not only in legislation, but in everyday bureaucracies (Rodríguez and Paredes 2014). Such coercion often relies on the social and material "bureaucratic inscription" whereby individuals' personal information and immigration status become embedded in official state registers (Horton 2020). This happens at multiple levels of governance in ways that enable street-level actors to exert biopolitical control over migrant populations even well beyond the governmental agencies where they are first recorded. Throughout the book, I depict situations in which frontline workers in a variety of spaces may become, as Menjívar (2017) has observed, "de facto immigration enforcers, expanding the reach of the state and doing the governmentality work that state agencies normally do" (39).

These dynamics become especially harmful when immigration enforcement seeps into, and is at times reinforced by, biomedical bureaucracies. Some forms of state-funded Medicaid, for example, work like DACA in that they demand that the patient provide proof of *legitimate illegality* to public benefits authorities, which is of course a risky move as it makes noncitizens legible to federal immigration bureaucracies (Asad 2020; Jimenez 2021). Rather than deportation deferral, work permits, or educational benefits, however, medical benefits often carry an added urgency that results in fraught life-and-death decisions. And medical providers and institutions sometimes find themselves caught between the imperative to manage health risks and the technologies that perpetuate the overcriminalization of immigration. As Sontag's *New York Times* exposé on hospital-initiated deportations reveals, noncitizen patients often come to embody "the collision of two deeply flawed American systems, immigration and health care" (Sontag 2008; see also New York Lawyers for the Public Interest 2012).

Throughout the following chapters, I explore how noncitizens with serious health conditions navigate this complex, contingent, and continuously changing sea of *de facto* and *de jure* rights and responsibilities. In doing so, I build upon the robust body of existing scholarship in the spheres of sociolegal immigration studies and immigrant health that helps me make sense of the stories I encountered over the years this project unfolded. In this book, I derive particular insights from excellent qualitative research that has illuminated the human impacts of criminalizing immigration. Works like Golash-Boza's *Deported* (2015), Macías-Rojas's *From Deportation to Prison* (2016), Armenta's *Protect, Serve, and Deport* (2017), and García's *Legal Passing* (2019) use one-of-a-kind ethnographic and interview data to reveal various ways the criminalization of immigrants plays out in the everyday life of immigrant individuals and families. While each work represents a distinct lens on the topic, these scholars excel at connecting the legal violence that criminalizes immigration in the United States to the lived experiences of those who are its targets.

This book adds to the ongoing conversation these scholars and others have begun, but it focuses on a distinct space: the clinic. Medical anthropologists in particular have long examined the relationship between power and health, and several have drawn attention to how this dynamic plays out in the context of migration and immigrant communities in the United States. Notable examples include Holmes's *Fresh Fruit, Broken Bodies* (2013), Horton's *They Leave Their Kidneys in the Field* (2016), Kline's *Pathogenic Policing* (2019), and Castañeda's *Borders of Belonging* (2019). These powerful ethnographic and interview-based works highlight how neoliberalism and the overcriminalization of immigration intersect to harm (im)migrants' health across a variety of social spaces that span migration itself through exploitative working conditions, interactions with law and immigration enforcement agents, and everyday life in families. As Kline aptly summarizes, immigrant policing is "a form of health policy" that not only impacts immigrants' health, but also has the potential to criminalize health care professionals who provide certain types of care by "making medical personnel agents of documentation status surveillance" (Kline 2019, 4–5).

In this book, I tackle these same questions from a somewhat different approach—and, importantly, at a rather different time—than the aforementioned sociological, sociolegal, and medical anthropological scholarship. Much of the strength of existing work is the deep ethnographic detail that authors have conveyed by intensively studying one specific context. While scholars such as Golash-Boza (2015) and García (2019) take a comparative approach to illustrating the human consequences of global capitalism (Golash-Boza) and the legal consciousness of immigrants, immigrant families, and immigrant communities (García), many others zero in on one location over an extended time to provide profound, highly contextualized examples of the harms of criminalizing migration. Like García, who argues that more work is needed to understand the effects of state and local immigration measures on the ground (2019, 3), I use a comparative strategy to illustrate how the convergence of criminalization and immigration federalism plays out in different subnational jurisdictions.

Additionally, unlike other scholars who focus on *structural vulnerability*—that is, the way someone's location within a stratified social order can disproportionately expose them to various harms (Quesada, Hart, and Bourgois 2011)—here I fix my lens on a particular kind of *violence* that impacts people who occupy somewhat *distinct* social positions. For example, whereas medical anthropologists such as Holmes (2013) and Horton (2016) illustrate how the concept of structural vulnerability can draw much-needed attention to "the bodily, material, and subjective states that [unequal social] structures produce" (Horton 2016, 5), they focus primarily on the social locations and experiences of Latinx (im)migrants who are made vulnerable by these social and structural arrangements.

In concentrating on *medical legal violence*, I account for similar dynamics while also capturing how such social and structural arrangements implicate those who are located within health care institutions as health care workers. These workers occupy an essential and relatively privileged position in relation to their "structurally vulnerable" patients, and yet they, too, must contend with medical legal violence in their everyday routines. Through their work, health care practitioners in the safety net must often walk a fine line between enacting anti-immigrant practices through federalized bureaucratic procedures and facing censure for rejecting such practices. Experiencing this violence from a position of marginally greater power than their patients often sparks *medical legal consciousness* that engages workers' collective agency toward resisting that very violence on behalf of their patients—for example, by collaborating with legal experts to challenge intimidation and misinformation in government agencies.

In the chapters that follow, I introduce new details into ongoing conversations in the sociology of immigration, law and society, and the medical humanities and interdisciplinary social sciences by providing unique evidence of how accelerating legal violence has gained momentum and expanded through health care institutions. Throughout the book, I illustrate how increasingly aggressive federal immigration enforcement has turned medical legal bureaucracies into a potential tool for immigrant surveillance through *medical legal violence*. This kind of violence involves the expansion of anti-immigrant laws through health institutions that disproportionately surveil and penalize immigrants of color as they seek health care, while enrolling health care workers as either agents or targets of that violence. Medical legal violence serves to maintain a disenfranchised, exploitable source of racialized laborers without disrupting a political-economic situation that benefits white supremacy. In other words, medical legal violence perpetuates Latinx noncitizens' economic inclusion alongside their sociopolitical exclusion in ways that harm their health, compromise clinical care, and maintain the current balance of power in the United States. It also creates opportunities for a kind of medical legal consciousness in clinics that can foster resistance to that violence while promoting health as a human right.

Documenting Noncitizen Patients' and Clinic Workers' Stories

As immigration and health policies transformed during the 2015 to 2020 period when I carried out research, I conducted ethnographic observations and in-depth interviews with eighty participants in community clinics across three different states in the United States. I selected these states based on their differing state-level political governance as well as which clinics were willing to open their doors to me. (For details on each fieldsite, please refer to appendix 1.) Part of the bargain I struck in securing ethics approval, adhering to guidance I received from immigration law experts, and protecting the trust and security of the clinics I observed was to avoid identifying the specific states and clinic sites where I conducted research. For this reason, I use the "red," "blue," and "purple" designations I described earlier. This choice means that I lose some of the nuance that a detailed historical contextualization of each state and county could provide. Given the real fear and anxiety spiraling through immigrant communities at the time, however, I did what I thought necessary to safeguard the information participants shared with me. I also secured a Certificate of Confidentiality from the National Institutes of Health to further protect data. Additionally, I did not solicit any identifying information—including name, age, race/ethnicity, or immigration status—from any of the participants. Whatever information I have regarding these categories emerged organically during the observations and/or interviews.

In each state, I conducted in-depth interviews with immigrant (mostly noncitizen) patients, clinic staff and providers, and community partners to understand how they responded to changing health and immigration policies at the local, state, and federal level. I also undertook ethnographic observations in which I shadowed clinic workers and attended public meetings where these policies were discussed. Understanding the perspective of clinic workers (both administrative and clinical) alongside the experiences of some of the patients they served enabled me to draw a more complete picture of the unique and collective challenges these groups faced, as anti-immigrant rhetoric accelerated and later became codified in anti-immigrant policies over the years that my research unfolded. This nuanced perspective also provided important insights into how the clinics I observed related to other bureaucratic agencies, such as public benefits and immigration and law enforcement agencies. The stories of participants situated in a variety of social and institutional positions spoke to an insidious yet quotidian sense of surveillance and potential sanction that shaped patients' and clinic workers' experiences and conditioned possibilities for exercising agency and resistance.

The symbolic violence of anti-immigrant rhetoric that the Trump administration espoused interacted synergistically with existing structural violence to keep Latinx noncitizens in a "state of exception" (Agamben 2005). The resulting medical legal violence produced participants' experiences of being indispensable yet disposable labor and facing both immediate and compounded injury. In the first chapter, I reflect on examples from multiple sites to demonstrate how accelerating legal violence enabled the continued sociopolitical exclusion of racialized noncitizens, especially those from Latin America. I focus specifically on the discursive and material "state of emergency" as a form of legal violence that typified the Trump administration's approach to immigration law. This chapter addresses this condition as both the result of historically continual processes in the global political economy of capitalism, and historically specific to the contemporary United States.

I follow this comprehensive overview by zooming in on a "red" state fieldsite to illuminate a key aspect of medical legal violence: the *assemblage* of colliding state- and federal-level bureaucratic obstacles, punitive immigration laws, and restrictive health policies that subjected Latinx immigrants to disproportionate harm. I illustrate these dynamics through observational and interview data to analyze how local and federal immigration policies have collided with exclusionary health policies to trigger serious health consequences for noncitizens and their families. Participants described the challenges of balancing risks of illness and injury against the risks of detention, deportation, and family separation. I conclude that newly converging US medical legal bureaucracies have forced noncitizen patients in the red state county to make agonizing decisions that often destabilize their own health and the well-being of their families.

In chapter 3, I turn my attention to a "blue" state to describe how the federalized nature of US health and immigration policies enabled medical legal violence in a place with relatively progressive, immigrant-inclusive politics, and I reflect on how this changed over time during the transition from the Obama to the Trump administration. I specifically focus on another aspect of medical legal violence—the threat of federal biopolitical surveillance and penalty—to understand how community clinics tried to maximize Latinx noncitizens' inclusion in the local safety net system despite a growing wariness that the federal immigration enforcement and subsidized health care programs like Medicaid might subject noncitizen patients to unwanted government attention. In this chapter, I argue that the 2016 election eroded patients' and clinic workers' confidence in navigating federal immigrant benefits exclusions without risking immigration enforcement penalties. In the absence of more inclusionary federal reforms, clinics had created strong networks among community organizations and government agencies that maximized resource availability for liminally legal and undocumented immigrants and mixed-status families. While originally intended to optimize resources for noncitizen patients, such collaborations increasingly discouraged some patients from pursuing care for which they were eligible and put clinics in the difficult position of resisting federal immigration priorities without compromising the security of their patients.

As the Trump administration entered what would be its final year, I turned my focus to a "purple" state in a relatively new immigrant destination to bring nuance to what otherwise might have been a rather dichotomous story. Chapter 4 therefore departs from the red state/blue state binary to explore the delicate situation of a politically polarized state in the US South. In a place that has become a social policy battleground, the tension between state-level resistance to immigrant criminalization and city- and county-level collaboration with federal immigration enforcement agencies has increasingly politicized the provision of health care to noncitizens and mixed-status families. This, in turn, has elevated another aspect of medical legal violence that I highlight in this chapter: criminalization. The potential criminalization of both noncitizen patients and clinic workers was more readily apparent in the purple state than I had observed elsewhere, and it further stratified health care access in an already resource-strapped area. These dynamics expanded medical legal violence in ways that directly affected both immigrant patients and the clinic workers who provided their health care.

After describing the experiences of patients and health care providers and staff in three distinct state contexts, in chapter 5 I zoom back out to focus on the perspectives of nonmedical clinic workers across all three fieldsites and explore how changing policies have shaped their *medical legal consciousness*. This refers to an awareness of the law in health care negotiations and a feeling of being alternately "with" or "against" the law as health care facilitators who are also often members of communities impacted by the overcriminalization of immigration and medical legal violence. As US health and immigration laws increasingly fixated on the perceived potential of noncitizen patients to commit fraud to the detriment of citizens and long-term lawful permanent residents, frontline clinic workers subtly mobilized to advocate for their patients and communities and resist the expansion of medical legal violence.

The book concludes with a snapshot of the coronavirus pandemic's arrival when I was finishing fieldwork in the purple state in the spring of 2020 and a discussion of how the virus's stratified impact in the United States emphasizes the human consequences of medical legal violence in immigrant communities. As I finish writing this book while the pandemic is still very much underway, I conclude that the same racist, anti-immigrant laws that have long excluded Latinx noncitizens from health care and undermined clinics' efforts to provide that care have led to a tragic but predictable humanitarian disaster in immigrant communities throughout the country and beyond its borders. The harms of medical legal violence have accelerated and intensified at a staggering magnitude in the wake of the COVID-19 crisis, most of all in the spaces of racialized economic exploitation where many Latinx immigrants work and reside. As the nation looks ahead to recovery and a new post-pandemic reality, comprehensive immigration reform alongside a serious reckoning with white supremacy must be at the top of the agenda to dismantle this violence and rebuild more equitable structures in the future.

1

States of Injury

Exception, Emergency, and Exclusion

On a mild afternoon in April 2017, I met patient Esteban at one of the blue state clinic's nondescript administrative offices. Although I had never met him in the clinic, Esteban greeted me warmly and patiently answered my cursory questions before beginning to narrate his health saga. He explained that he had been living and working in the United States for more than three decades and seldom interacted with the health care system until suffering a relatively recent injury. He had fallen while working on a job (he did not specify the task, but it sounded like a construction job), and the impact broke his ribs and "split his spleen in two." After he was treated at the emergency department, support staff at the community clinic helped him apply for state-funded, full-scope Medicaid (an option not available to his red state and purple state counterparts) to cover ongoing treatments. These were necessary because—as Esteban understood the situation—the injury had damaged his circulation and seriously impaired his liver. When possible, Esteban did whatever day labor he could manage to earn a little extra money for himself and his US-born son, but he was barely getting by. He hoped rather than believed that he would recover soon so that he could get back to work, but he could not count on any disability or income assistance to spur that recovery or ease his situation if recovery proved impossible.

Esteban had first come to the United States almost four decades ago and worked in a restaurant until he was arrested during a workplace raid in 1981 and deported to Central America. The experience shocked him deeply because he had supposed that if he worked well and kept his head down, he would be sure to get a good salary and go on with his life. "But sometimes it doesn't matter," he said, and he described being treated "as if we [Latinos] were extraterrestrials." He recalled the dehumanizing shame of his immigration arrest and the consequences it had for his future, saying, "They put shackles on your feet, all as if you were a grand assassin. . . . Because of this they've denied me everything, all the opportunities to get my residency, my citizenship, everything."

That Esteban's life had been destabilized by an on-the-job injury and chronic illness is not in itself unique. US citizens and noncitizens alike experience similar strife in the face of injury and illness. A key difference, however, is that the socioeconomic decline that accompanied Esteban's physical fall was exacerbated by his illicit status and recent wave of anti-immigrant sentiment—both of which he expressed as threats to his well-being. "That [anti-immigrant rhetoric] hurts because we're human beings," he asserted, "and didn't come here to do bad things. I came here to work, to do what the American won't. Because Americans won't do the type of work that we do." Esteban spoke with pride of how hard he had worked in the United States, and he seemed to have internalized the idea that the role of Latinx immigrants was to shoulder the work that Americans would not. "Sometimes they have us demolish houses when it's not good for your health," he remarked. "The Latino does that. The American doesn't do that." He explained that it was in their nature (the nature of "el latino" or "los latinos," as he put it) to do physical labor at the behest of American supervisors who carried out the intellectual and managerial labor.

Esteban seemed resigned to the fact that he was valuable in US society only as a source of manual labor, even while he articulated the exploitative nature of this relationship. Only when he reflected on the discrimination he had faced, and when he considered that he may not be able to return to work because that same work had worn his body down, did he express his profound disappointment. Just as he resigned himself to his perceived position within the US political-economic system, he also accepted the possibility that his health issues might be irreparable. What Esteban did not say explicitly, but what his present situation starkly illustrated, was that he was simultaneously included in US society on the basis of his economic potential and excluded from it as a so-called criminal alien who could no longer sustain that economic activity once it broke him. Even though legal violence barred him from becoming a full political member of US society, he nevertheless found ample opportunities for economic inclusion (in restaurants, in construction, or doing odd jobs as a day laborer) when he was healthy. There was a place for someone like him, and he internalized his role as a manual laborer who must contribute through physical exertion. Once that labor became untenable, however, he believed that there was no place for him in that system and—except for the community clinic—nowhere to turn for relief.

In this chapter, I argue that accelerating legal violence in the contemporary United States represents a reactionary effort to ensure the continued political exclusion of noncitizens who are racialized here as "people of color," especially those from Latin America. I focus specifically on a form of legal violence that typified the Trump administration's approach to immigration law, the *state of emergency*, which makes possible the medical legal violence that harms people like Esteban. This happens by expanding discrimination on the basis of legal status in the name of national security, and it extends beyond the border and into clinics across the country.

While the Trump administration's place within the broader historical arc of US political economy was not unusual, there has been a generalized sense—in the country, the world, and among those I spoke with— that its specific tactics of legal violence were remarkable. The symbolic violence of anti-immigrant rhetoric and policy that the Trump administration harnessed to dehumanize immigrants and keep them in a state of exception (Agamben 2005), and its codification into medical legal violence, produced participants' experiences of being indispensable yet disposable labor, and facing both immediate and compounded injury. Furthermore, millions of noncitizens of color contribute to economic production without the prospect of commensurate political representation (because of barriers to naturalization, criminalization and incarceration, and the constant threat of deportation). This perpetuates a dialectical relationship between economic inclusion and sociopolitical exclusion (De Genova 2013) that ensures a relatively captive pool of racialized labor for the United States while undercutting opportunities for political participation.[1]

This phenomenon predates the United States' existence as a nation and endures today, and in this chapter I draw attention here to the twin phenomena of *injury* and *disposability*. De Genova (2013) describes an inclusion/exclusion dialectic that uses the spectacle of the US-Mexico border and the rhetoric of "invasion" to divert attention away from the mundane political economy of migrant labor and the more subtle expansion of legal violence that increasingly criminalizes immigrants as they build their lives in the United States, in spaces well beyond the border. And deportability serves as a prime mechanism for this subjugation, which disciplines the labor of authorized and unauthorized immigrants alike. As De Genova and others (e.g., Park 2011; Brotherton and Barrios 2011; Golash-Boza 2016; and Asad 2020) have made clear, protracted deportability is the definitive condition of noncitizens in the United States, and it is a definitively racialized condition at that.

One way that governments can maintain this kind of dialectical relationship in support of racial capitalism is through the "state of exception": a condition determined by a representative of the state (typically the executive) in a time of apparent emergency or crisis that enables the suspension of rights and the suppression of public law. It is *exceptional* in that it should, theoretically, be a temporary condition that will subside when the threat to the state is neutralized. Yet many scholars (e.g., Agamben 1998; Mbembe 2003; De Genova 2013; and Weheliye 2014) emphasize that this state of exception, once conceived, tends to continue indefinitely. For example, Mbembe (2003) highlights examples like occupied Palestine to illustrate how today's states of exception owe much to slavery, colonialism, and apartheid, which kept people "alive but in a *state of injury*" (21; emphasis in original). This injury accompanies the stratification of people within the same geographical space along axes of socioeconomic and political inequality. It also reinforces the head of state's unrivaled authority to "define who matters and who does not, who is *disposable* and who is not" (27; emphasis in original).

The relationship between the state of exception and the definition of "who is disposable and who is not" is key to understanding how medical legal violence comes to harm people like Esteban and others whose stories I highlight in this chapter and throughout the book. The space that many noncitizen immigrants occupy amidst expanding legal violence—whether as "undocumented," liminally legal, or lawfully present immigrants—represents a state of exception. What I observed in the field and heard from participants draws attention to the ways that laws have shifted toward greater or lesser social inclusion by treating noncitizens as exceptional. At the national scale I also began to notice, as many did, the ways that the Trump administration expanded legal violence against particular groups—namely, Latinx migrants and residents of Muslim-majority countries—through heightened symbolic violence. The point of actions like the Muslim travel ban or family separations at the border was not really to uphold existing law nor forge new laws through collaborative processes, such as congressional legislation.[2] The point was to suspend rights quickly and dramatically, and the power of executive order enabled President Trump to do so. With this tool he could declare crises and create spectacles that demanded constant attention.

While every president in the nation's history has possessed this power of executive order, the particular way that President Trump wielded it in relation to migration was remarkable by contemporary standards. For example, on February 15, 2019, President Trump declared, "by the authority vested in me by the Constitution and the laws of the United States of America," that there was a national emergency at the southern border. This fixation on the "border crisis" and the rhetorical—and lately operational—"state of emergency" revealed an almost medieval preoccupation with sovereign territorialism and government by spectacle and fiat (Foucault 2004). In other words, the kind of nationalist fervor evinced by Trump's executive border policies reinforced a sense of nation-as-citadel to be protected against "invading" outsiders. Such rhetoric led to grave material consequences that endure today, including increased visibility of border militarization (which began in the mid-1990s, accelerated after 9/11, and gained renewed attention under the Trump administration), the effective suspension of asylum at the southern border, and a humanitarian crisis as COVID-19 struck migrants trapped on the wrong side of multiple states of emergency.

In this chapter, I focus on this state of exception, buttressed lately through a "state of emergency" and the narrative of protracted crisis, to illustrate how this spectacle deflects attention away from the everyday violence inflicted on the many noncitizens who work under dangerous and exploitative conditions without being able to count on the social or political benefits that might be available to citizens. These examples underscore both the direct and compounded harms that often render Latinx immigrants disposable in ways that are difficult to remedy given the expanding medical legal violence of immigrant health in the United

States. While I am by no means the first to observe this inclusion/exclusion dialectic, I highlight a historically specific shift during the end of the Obama administration and beginning of the Trump administration that enables new insights into how this violence unfolds slowly and methodically in even the most disparate local political environments. And, as I look back on my fieldwork through the lens of the pandemic, it is abundantly apparent that this story of injury and disposability is precisely what the pandemic has laid bare. By this point in the pandemic, it is clear that the inclusion/exclusion dynamic that enabled the noncitizen state of exception in the United States also enabled the disproportionate toll the pandemic would take on immigrant communities. It accelerated and compounded injuries and made this disposability visible in real time.

Defining the Enemy

One of the most straightforward ways to suspend human rights in a representative democracy like the United States is to criminalize those who must be excepted, thereby designating their behavior and existence as illegal or extralegal. Such criminalization enables the expansion of medical legal violence, and several of the patients whose experiences of economic exploitation and physical harm I describe below spoke to me of feeling increasingly criminalized since the Trump administration took control. Their comments illuminate their feelings of being constructed as an enemy while inhabiting a state of exception, and they especially highlight how these dynamics can result in embodied harms through medical legal violence.

For example, during our long conversation, Esteban told me that he was witnessing the greatest surge in discrimination that he had experienced since he arrived in the United States in the early 1980s. Back then, immigration agents had arrested him during a workplace raid—an experience that humiliated and dehumanized him. President Trump's anti-immigrant rhetoric reignited this humiliation, and Esteban believed that this distressing political turn and heightened racism were reducing economic opportunities for Latinx immigrants. "Since [Trump's presidency] the American isn't offering much work anymore to Latinos," he explained in a frustrated tone. "Now that this Mr. Trump arrived, I see that he opened the doors to those who don't like Latinos, many who are—who I'd consider Nazis, right?"[3] Esteban also said he believed that there were a lot of people in the county where he lived who agreed with President Trump on this, and they were starting to assert themselves with more confidence. Esteban supposed that this was because they wanted "more benefits" for themselves, and perhaps they thought that kicking out Latinx immigrants would ensure this.

Felipe and Tomás, two migrant workers I met at a farm in the red state county I studied, recalled similar surges in anti-immigrant senti-ment following the turbulent political changes at the state and federal levels in recent years. Both Felipe and Tomás had been working in the red state during the years of an omnibus immigration bill I refer to as "Law X." Among its many provisions, this bill authorized law enforce-ment agents to check a driver's immigration status during traffic stops, mandated federal identity verification technology in employment set-tings, and required schools to verify students' legal status (National Con-ference of State Legislatures 2012). This led to racial profiling of Latinx people, and Felipe and Tomás experienced the anti-immigrant senti-ment behind this legal violence despite having "papers" to protect them. They were frustrated that the Trump administration seemed to have revived this state-level discriminatory trend just as it had been dimin-ishing in the county where they lived and worked. As Felipe lamented, "They don't leave you in peace anymore. People are already scared [in this red state], but they were feeling pretty good because [those laws were] about to go away. And now they haven't gone away because this government that entered sheltered [that bigotry] again, and it's the same again." When I asked which level of government Felipe was referring to, Tomás broke in to clarify. "Trump, federal," he said flatly. Felipe repeated that this was a frightening situation, especially for people who did not have papers—which, as he had reminded me—was harder to achieve these days. "[Those without papers] don't leave the cave, because if they leave the shadows, the force [ICE] will catch them."

Roberto, a landscaper with diabetes living in the same county as Fe-lipe and Tomás, expressed similar frustration but uniquely drew a con-tinuous thread between the days of state-level anti-immigrant laws, the Trump administration, and the US political economy.[4] He described how the state declined economically in response to statewide anti-immigrant legislation but had started to recover a bit before Trump came to office. "But with all this with the new president [Trump], things aren't so normal," he remarked.

> If it were up to [President Trump], he'd throw out eleven or twelve million [undocumented Latinos] that are here. He'd already have thrown them out. But, if he threw them out . . . the US would go down. . . . Because there'd be no more workforce. Right now, the United States, everyone, all the big industries, the big companies, they know perfectly well that the Mexican laborer, or the Hispanic laborer, is the cheapest. And we're the battle horses, because we're always at the foot of the cannon. . . . We almost never miss work, we're not problematic, we're really hardworking. Here we are, holding out. . . . Sometimes I wish that [Trump] would just keep things stable and let everybody work.

Like many patients I spoke with, Roberto articulated a sense that he represented essential yet easily exploitable value to the US economy. He also emphasized the docility and diligence of fellow Latinx immigrant laborers, a refrain I heard frequently in conversations with clinic patients in each state. Such rhetoric underscores the symbolic violence of the ingrained sense of disposability that Roberto articulated, which kept him fixated on economic inclusion even as he decried that very exploitation.

Even Víctor, a blue state resident who lived in a more progressive region than Roberto and had gained legal permanent residence around the time that he was diagnosed with colon cancer, described a similar observation when we spoke in April 2017. Víctor had hoped to bring his wife and children to the United States from South America, but after President Trump took office, he believed it would be impossible. He hoped that Trump would not be reelected and that whoever took his place would have a different approach to immigration. "With this guy [Trump], nothing can be done. He's got a lot of laws. They've changed, they've taken away a lot of laws from us," Víctor lamented. When I asked which laws he meant, Víctor specified that the president was especially targeting sanctuary sites. Víctor was less worried about how this would affect him—"that's why I have my papers"—but was troubled by how such threats would affect his friends and family in the area. He warned them not to get into trouble and to drive carefully because a simple traffic ticket would be enough to detain and deport them. That's why, Víctor said, "I always go around with my immigration papers here." He showed me all the copies of immigration documents he kept on his person, a practice Víctor started after Trump's election, just in case "they [law/immigration enforcement agents] stop me on the street and don't believe that I have my residence." After nearly three decades living and working in the United States, and after finally obtaining his green card, Víctor still took precautions because he believed chances were high (and getting higher) that he would be seen as a criminal and treated as such unless he "took care" in this way.

Each of these participants resented the rising tide of vilification and discrimination that the Trump administration's anti-immigrant rhetoric seemed to have intensified and legitimized in recent years. As Esteban and Víctor (in the blue state) and Roberto, Felipe, and Tomás (in the red state) made clear, this sentiment was not new; they had experienced it before under other immigration policy regimes. The difference now was that the sentiment was federally justified in ways they had not experienced in the many decades they had lived and worked in the United States. The sweeping categorization of Latinx (im)migrants as the enemy of the United States—rather than a fundamental engine of economic productivity and social cohesion—seemed both remarkable and unjust to them. The examples that follow demonstrate how this recent remarkable expansion of existing legal violence—of an exclusionary framework decades (even centuries) in the making—deftly leverages the criminalizing potential of immigration law in injurious ways that maintain Latinx (im)migrants' economic inclusion and sociopolitical exclusion.

States of Injury

Nearly all the patients I spoke with across my three fieldsites had been living and working in the United States for several years, if not decades. Occasionally I spoke with individuals who had recently arrived in the United States or continued to migrate periodically for work, but the majority had built lives and families in the United States and planted deep roots here. Many came specifically to work here to create opportunities for their families in the United States and in their countries of origin. Collectively, they worked in a variety of jobs, including landscaping, construction, sanitation, dry cleaning, restaurants, and agriculture. Most worked in physically demanding jobs without health benefits or worker protections. They all contributed to the US economy through their labor and taxes, but few were able to secure adequate social benefits from the government when their bodies buckled under the strain of that labor. They put everything into the system, they produced and they consumed, but they were unable to rely on that system as US citizens could. They also had fewer opportunities to exercise political agency than many US citizens possessed, and they faced higher stakes regarding the potential consequences of resisting that system. In this sense, they were particularly vulnerable to exploitation and criminalization.

Some of the patients I spoke with, like Esteban, experienced direct bodily harms from their extended residence in the state of exception and were effectively discarded as disposable once they could no longer fulfill their economic role. Red state patient Cristina, whom I met in June 2018, had lived and worked in the United States for more than three decades before facing a work-related disability. For most of that time, she had actually lived in the same state as Esteban (the blue state), but she eventually left to escape neighborhood violence and give her children a safer life in the red state. While she appreciated the relative tranquility of her new community, Cristina regretted losing the full-scope Medicaid that she and her US-citizen children were able to access when they lived in the blue state. Cristina had been diagnosed with diabetes nineteen years ago when she lived there, and she explained that her Medicaid helped her keep the disease in check during that time. When she came to the red state, however, she struggled to get and keep adequate health care coverage. As an authorized worker with a tax ID, she was sometimes able to get jobs that provided health insurance, yet she could never seem to make enough money to afford her premiums, deductibles, or copays with private insurance through her employers. Once Cristina finally did manage to get on top of her insurance payments, she got septicemia (serious blood poisoning), which she believed was due to her work in sanitation. She was hospitalized for three days, and the doctor told her she could not work for a month and a half. Because she was no longer working, she lost her insurance and received a bill for $30,000 for her hospital stay.

Cristina worried that going back to her old job would put her back in the vicious cycle of inconsistent insurance and potential injury.[5] In an effort to boost her income a little without getting locked into that spiral, Cristina took a part-time job that paid two dollars more per hour than anywhere else she had worked previously. This job as a dishwasher required her to wear plastic boots that were often soaked by the spray from whatever she was washing, and this led to a bone infection in one of her feet. Since she had been living with poorly controlled diabetes for some years, this bone infection became life-threatening and required amputation of one of her toes. "I think that because of that job, I am how I am now," she said mournfully. "Without feet, what am I good for anymore? . . . You say, 'It's two dollars more.' You think it's a little more, but it cost me my toe."

Having lived in two politically divergent states, Cristina experienced the gamut of immigrant inclusion and exclusion, and she dearly wished to become a citizen. And although she was technically eligible for citizenship, she could not pass the exam nor afford a consultation with a civil surgeon (the physicians who oversee immigrants' medical examinations for entry) to confirm that she had cognitive impairments that limited her ability to pass the exam. Cristina's record was good, but realistically she was locked out of naturalization—a situation that struck her as deeply unfair. She explained that the difference between citizens and noncitizens was the ability to demand one's rights. "[We] also have rights because I work and I pay my taxes," Cristina argued, "but they don't see it that way." She described feeling belittled because she was asking for support now, which hurt because she knew she had paid taxes for years and supported the state the whole time she was working. "I haven't stopped working since I arrived here," Cristina remarked, describing how even her medical record was bursting with papers from all the jobs she had done over the years. "I've been really hardworking," she said. "But my body can't anymore; it's tired now."

Cristina's description of herself as a productive worker aligned with the archetype of a legitimate neoliberal subject of the United States—one who may earn social deservingness through their economic productivity—even if she was not technically a citizen of the country in which she had lived and worked for decades. Like Esteban, she found ample opportunities to work—probably even more than Esteban could, given her work authorization—but she similarly suffered an on-the-job injury that rendered her disposable. And whereas Esteban was permanently excepted from citizenship because of his prior deportation, Cristina was functionally excluded from the US body politic because of her low income, limited English proficiency, and lack of cultural capital. Despite their distinct positions on what Joseph (2020) refers to as the "documentation status continuum," neither Esteban nor Cristina was immune from the legal violence that left them permanently injured. And given how their protracted state of exception subjected them to this ongoing legal violence, both found it nearly impossible to remediate that harm through timely, effective, and affordable medical intervention.

Injury, Illness, and Illegality

When I met Jorge at a free clinic in the purple state in January 2020, he caught my attention for several reasons. For one thing, he was the first (and, as I would realize later, only) male patient who would speak with me in an interview in the purple state.[6] He was also relatively young, probably in his late thirties or early forties. Like Esteban, who injured his spleen and liver when he fell at work, Jorge had first entered care after suffering a debilitating on-the-job injury. Jorge, who at one point during our conversation casually referred to himself as "una persona ilegal" (an illegal person), had worked a lot of different jobs since he came to the purple state from Central America in 1999, and he told me that he preferred working outdoors to the poultry plants where he once worked and where most of his Latinx neighbors had been employed. One day when he was working as a furniture mover, however, the driver of the delivery truck accelerated without realizing that Jorge was inside hoisting a chair into position. Between the jolt and the heavy load, Jorge felt something give. He felt intense pain, and a doctor later diagnosed him with slipped vertebral discs in his neck.

Jorge's pain persisted, and he struggled to keep working for the furniture company. To make matters worse, his employers claimed that he had actually suffered the injury at home, and they could not be held liable for his recovery costs. Jorge spoke with a lawyer, who told him he would probably lose the case if he tried to fight for compensation. He was able to qualify for financial assistance through the hospital to cover some of the costs, and—for reasons he still does not understand—the employer ultimately agreed to cover $3,000 of his rehabilitation costs.

Despite physical therapy, however, the pain continued. Jorge gestured at an invisible timeline between us in the small exam room where we had been chatting and invited me into the memory as he relived it aloud. "Listen, the accident happened today," he began, tracing his hands through the air and transporting us to the day of the injury:

> From this day until now, my life changed too much. Because I was cry-
> ing from the pain, I couldn't sleep. If I was sitting down, it hurt. If I was
> standing up, it hurt. If I lay down, it hurt. There wasn't a position in which
> I could calm my pain, just pills, just pills, just pills. And I cried because I
> couldn't sleep, and I'd get out of my bed and go to the sofa, which was the
> only place I might sleep sometimes for an hour, an hour and a half. And
> then I'd go to work. Because you know that if you don't work, there's no
> way to pay the bills, the rent and all that.

Jorge eventually found another job preparing lots for construction, which involved less heavy lifting on his part. The accident left him physically and emotionally broken, however, because the chronic pain and nerve damage that followed also made him nervous and depressed. He had come to the clinic on the day we met to refill a prescription for an antidepressant and to discuss follow-up care after having recently gone to the ER for what might have been a severe migraine. He was unsure of the diagnosis, but he had an allergic reaction to whatever medication they gave him to treat the pain, and his arms were covered in bruises from the various intravenous treatments he had received. When I asked whether the doctors had given him any explanation for his symptoms, he said they told him it was all stress. He was not sure what to believe, but he agreed that he felt stressed and wanted to work with the clinic to find ways to manage his chronic stress and pain.

Jorge expressed feeling conflicted about the treatment he had received, both at the hands of his employers and by doctors at the hospital. When he talked about his experiences with people he knew, they urged him to take legal action. He described a shared sentiment that "los hispanos" received worse care at the hands of less-qualified medical professionals, but Jorge felt ambivalent about asking more from the system. "I can't [take legal action] because the hospital has helped me," he explained. "I can't fight. What I want is to get better, not to fight with anybody." Jorge preferred to give the health care workers the benefit of the doubt, and he seemed distressed to have to ask for help at all—even though he had thousands of dollars of medical debt and made less than twelve dollars per hour. "I don't receive help from the government, like [food] stamps or anything like that because I work to provide for my family," he assured me. Jorge explained that it was his duty to care for his family, not the government's, and he meant to own that responsibility. "Because when you come here, the government doesn't say to you, 'You're going to have your family, you're going to have your kids,'" he continued. "I know that I'm going to have my family, and I'm going to have to manage all the costs because it's my family. I'm not going to be waiting for help from anyone else."

Of course, when Jorge came to the United States, he was young and healthy and never anticipated a situation in which he might be unable to provide for his family. As I listened to his story, it was clear that, like most young people, he never expected having to rely on a hospital's financial assistance program or Emergency Medicaid, or that he would be managing chronic pain so long before old age. In that sense, Jorge was like the millions of uninsured US citizens who find themselves in similar straits following sudden medical crises. Yet, as "una persona ilegal," Jorge expressed a sense of being less entitled to financial support, safe working conditions, and quality health care than he might have were he "legal." As we spoke, he alternated between praise for the opportunity to live and work in a place that was generally safer than where he had migrated from and disappointment over both his injury and the rising insecurity that came with the Trump administration.

Jorge articulated his precarious position in great detail, and he described how he felt insecurity on multiple levels. While he described numerous experiences of exploitation and anti-immigrant discrimination, Jorge felt strongly that the United States was his home—indeed, it had been for more than two decades—and that his fate was inseparable from that of the country as a whole. Jorge expressed concern that even as the president demonized Latinx immigrants, he also undermined US security by antagonizing other nations. Jorge dreaded not only the contempt of his neighbors, who increasingly expressed anti-immigrant attitudes, but also reprisals from other nations' leaders who would not distinguish between the president's victims and allies. "If the president makes a bad decision and does something that harms another country," Jorge explained, "that country's not going to come looking just for the president. That country's going to come for all of us who live here. If something happens, it's not going to be like, 'Oh, that's a Hispanic, he doesn't have anything to do with this. I'm just going to go after the Americans.' No, it'll harm everyone. The decisions that someone important makes harm all of us, not just one person." Jorge had experienced harm at the invisible hand of a system of racialized economic exploitation, and he saw few remedies to that harm beyond working harder and enduring persistent pain. Despite his fierce belief that the United States was his home and that he was a responsible contributor to the place where he was raising his family, the chaos of the Trump administration's immigration and foreign policies added another layer to Jorge's anxieties and expanded the terms of his insecurity.

"I don't know why I didn't die."

I met María in January 2020 at a free clinic in the purple state where she had lived for most of the twenty-odd years since she had left Mexico. As was the case with many of the women I spoke with, motherhood had made María familiar with some of the more benevolent aspects of US medical and legal government bureaucracies. She had received restricted Medicaid coverage to deliver her US-born children and enrolled them in full-scope Medicaid to ensure their ongoing health care, and she had successfully supported her eldest daughter in obtaining DACA. Aside from pregnancy, however, María herself was excluded from health care coverage because of her undocumented status and low income.

For the most part, María had managed all right despite these health coverage exclusions by attending community clinics when she could afford it, but she only felt really well treated once she started attending the monthly free clinic two years ago. She described feeling more comfortable and respected at the free clinic than she ever had elsewhere. Here, María did not have to worry about speaking Spanish or how she would pay for care: "They take care of that [here] because, being Hispanic, sometimes you really battle a lot with things like doctors and all that. . . . Sometimes, before it was [a question of] if they speak Spanish, or if it's expensive, or what if you don't have enough [money] to see a doctor? You wait."

María knew the cost of having to wait. She described frustration over having suffered for a year with debilitating pain in her side and trying to persuade doctors that she was seriously ill. "Sometimes you wait such a long time. I had a really bad experience, because of the doctor, who, sometimes you don't . . ." María paused, searching for the words. She had been suffering from severe gallbladder pain, but the doctors at the community clinic she attended then had dismissed her symptoms. For several months, she felt that they were just giving her random medications and not attending to the source of her pain. She could no longer sleep, and she described the pain as if she were giving birth every day:

> I started feeling worse each time. It was because of my gallbladder, that I already had stones. It was already about to burst, with one big stone stuck like this. I had to go to the ER because every day it hurt. It was horrible. But at the same time, you can't just be spending money here and there. You'd wait to see what [the doctors] say, and you took the medicine. "Take this for three months." And in the last three months, I couldn't take it anymore, and I went to the ER, and they had to do emergency surgery on me. They removed my gallbladder.

This experience left María shaken because her aunt in Mexico had died of a burst gallbladder. It also left her with bills that she was still working to pay off, even though she was able to qualify for Emergency Medicaid to defer some of the costs. "[Medicaid] helped me pay part of it, even though it was an emergency," she explained. "When it's an emergency, they help you, but it has to really be an emergency."

While María was still paying the bills for one near-death experience, she stumbled into another. Already strapped for cash, and feeling lately dismissed and misdiagnosed by medical professionals, María was now working two jobs to make ends meet. She worked long hours at a restaurant, but she also managed to squeeze in work cleaning houses between shifts. "A while ago I had another really awful emergency," María began. She described how she was running late and decided to speed things up by mixing together some of the cleaning products she used. Between the cleaning job and the restaurant work, she was shut indoors for hours. "I do one job right after my other job," María explained, "because you come [to the United States], and you work really hard." She started feeling strange while she was cleaning but rushed back to the restaurant anyway to start her shift there. "My whole face swelled up," she remembered, "my tongue fell asleep, all of this [head/neck/chest] hurt, and I couldn't stop coughing." She began retracing her steps, clearer now with the benefit of retrospect:

> I mixed [those liquids] to finish up quickly, and I'd never done that before. . . . I didn't even go for my mask, which I always use, because I didn't want to lose time. I was inhaling bits at a time, and in that place there's no ventilation. I felt really bad. My head hurt. I said, "Ay, why do I feel like this? I feel horrible." . . . My tongue began to fall asleep; I began to see everything like [*gestures unsteadily*], red welts all over my body. All of this hurt, and I was coughing and coughing. I began to look up what I had inhaled, and I knew what I had inhaled. I thought it was fatal, that it produces a gas. When I got to the hospital, the doctor told me that guerrilla fighters used to mix those liquids to kill people. I was surprised. I don't know why I didn't die, because she [the doctor] says that people die while cleaning the bathroom, that's how they figured out that this was what produced that gas.

Fortunately, María made it to the ER in time and responded well to the respiratory treatments they gave her. It probably went without saying that neither of María's jobs offered health insurance, but I asked her anyway, and she confirmed this. She also confirmed that she continued to clean houses between shifts, although she took more precautions now to avoid poisoning herself in the process. Even so, the conditions that resulted in her latest emergency persisted. This left María vulnerable to future injury—whether through the systemic neglect that conditioned her to mistrust health care workers or through the economic exploitation and sociopolitical exclusion that kept pushing her body to its limit while making it difficult for her to access and afford remedies to that injury.

Compounded Harms and Slow Death

While some patients I spoke with suffered injuries directly while working, the majority embodied a more cumulative and compounded kind of harm, one exacerbated by decades of being economically included under exploitative conditions but socially excluded from remedies to that exploitation. Being excepted from protective social institutions and treated as disposable harmed their bodies in subtle ways that are impossible to pin on an isolated event, but taken together they slowly disabled and disintegrated them nonetheless. This "slow death" (Galtung 1969; Berlant 2007) happens when structural violence inflicts ongoing, insidious harms through embedded social institutions and arrangements rather than overt interpersonal injury. This is, of course, a relative term. Slow death is "slow" only in that it is less immediate than death stemming directly from acute illness or injury, but it is faster than that which inevitably comes about through the process of aging. The cases below illustrate how irreversible injuries result from the compounded consequences of harms that are embodied over decades of living within the state of exception. And while death itself is inevitable, the conditions that compress the precious interval that delimits a human life are not. These conditions emerge from structural power dynamics—namely, racial capitalism—that could be otherwise.

I met Roberto in December 2017 while observing an eligibility encounter in which he was renewing his sliding-fee-scale discount at one of his red state county's largest federally qualified health centers (FQHCs).[7] He and his wife both had diabetes but were undocumented and therefore could not qualify for insurance, so they relied on the clinic for their regular lab work and medication discounts. Roberto explained that he had been living in the red state since about 2003 and had witnessed the transformations in immigrant policies there over the past several years. Roberto had been a licensed welder back in his native Mexico, but without papers he could not get a similar license in the United States. Even so, he found related work in a metalworking shop and made good money there for one year before the statewide anti-immigrant legislation took hold. After that law was implemented, the company began checking everyone's work papers, and Roberto had to seek employment elsewhere.

Roberto found a job as a landscaper and settled into his new role relatively well. Slowly, however, over the twelve years he worked for the same boss, he found he could no longer manage the physical effort of his work. He got dizzy and had trouble standing, and he was thirsty all the time. Roberto felt exhausted and struggled to carry the gasoline-powered leaf blower on his back day in and day out. One day he looked in the mirror and scarcely recognized the person staring back at him. "Oh no," he said to himself. "What a horror. . . . What do I want to live like this for? What am I good for? . . . I'm not even going to be able to work."

This physical decline, and the fear of losing work, finally brought Roberto to the clinic a year before our meeting, where he was diagnosed with advanced diabetes and immediately placed on an insulin regimen. Roberto had not realized that his situation was so grave, but the doctor told him that he had been flirting with a coma and was in bad shape. She also diagnosed him with high blood pressure and advised him to avoid undue stress at work—advice Roberto found difficult to follow because he was always rushing not to fall behind on his jobs. Roberto took these diagnoses hard, and at his lowest point he considered suicide. With his family's and the clinic's support, however, Roberto began to get his blood sugar and hypertension under control and was delighted that he had the energy to work hard again. So much of Roberto's life was wrapped up in his economic activity, and he was desperate at the thought of chronic illness rendering him useless. True, he would have preferred a job with better wages and health benefits, but after the statewide immigration enforcement laws went into effect, he had discounted such possibilities. Given this reality, and that he—a low-income, undocumented immigrant living in a place with anti-immigrant policies—felt he could do nothing to change it, Roberto held fast to the one job he could count on. And he relied on the clinic to keep him fit enough to do so for as long as possible.

A few months after I met Roberto, I accompanied some nurses and medical assistants from his clinic to a remote watermelon farm where they conducted free blood pressure and glucose checks for migrant workers and enrolled anyone who was interested in the clinic's sliding-fee-scale program. The oppressive heat of the day radiated through the concrete mess hall where we set up shop, and I overheard a nurse react with alarm to one of the worker's blood pressure readings. The nurse told patient Tomás that his blood pressure was dangerously high and warned that if it did not reduce before they left, she would send him to the emergency room. Tomás brushed aside these concerns and chalked up his acute hypertension to a tough day at work. He acknowledged that he had a history of high blood pressure, but he rarely felt the symptoms of it. "Now I feel a little fatigued," he allowed, "but later [my blood pressure] will calm down from its agitation on the job. We spent the day out there crouching and jumping in an oven [under the blazing sun] with our sacks, that's all."

Later, I spoke with him and fellow worker Felipe at one of the long tables in the mess hall, where the men discussed the terms of the arrangement that authorized them to work in the United States legally, with certain limitations. Felipe explained that everyone working in the fields alongside them had a work permit. Everyone was given six months for the season and had to return to their home countries at the end of that time. He stressed that this was work permission only, and that they had no liberty of movement beyond what the *patrón* who arranged for that permission allowed. Felipe added that everyone carried a card that their *patrón* gave them, which indicated how far from the farm they were allowed to wander. (This was about a sixty-mile radius, enough to include the nearest urban center where they could do shopping and run minor errands.) If immigration agents demanded identification, they were to present that card—with its travel restrictions—as proof that "they came to work." "They can't leave from here, from the job, they just have to stay here," Felipe explained. "Once they leave here, they've lost, and immigration grabs them and takes them away."

According to what Felipe and Tomás understood, their work authorization did not include health care coverage, and therefore the two were eager to avoid the emergency room. It is possible that Felipe and Tomás were indeed eligible for health insurance but did not realize it—for example, if they had H-2A visas (visas for temporary agricultural workers). The FQHC workers I accompanied to the watermelon farm might have been aware of such programs, but when I joined them, their focus was on assessing immediate health needs and getting people enrolled in the clinic for ongoing care. Anyone who made it to the clinic from the farm would have been able to meet with an eligibility counselor, but the window for H-2A visa holders to enroll in health care coverage is relatively narrow. This means that many eligible workers are effectively excluded from coverage, through lack of awareness and insufficient time and support to enroll.

Felipe, who did not know his exact age but believed he was somewhere around eighty-two years old, recalled one occasion when he thought he was having a heart attack and had to be rushed to the hospital in an ambulance. Fortunately, it was not a heart attack, but unfortunately it left Felipe with a $1,500 bill for the ambulance (which is not uncommon for uninsured patients) and $3,000 for the emergency department visit.[8] Because he had no insurance in the United States and because he made too much as a migrant worker to qualify for Emergency Medicaid, Felipe was ineligible for health insurance. He intended to pay the bills in full, and he was hoping to work out a payment plan with the hospital and ambulance company. "It doesn't matter," he said blandly. "I owe it, and I have to pay it. The trick now is not to get a black mark. Because if I don't pay it, they'll send it to collections, and I'll be in trouble." Felipe's principal concern now was not his health, but his credit. This preoccupation with his credit in the United States underscored his position as a neoliberal subject in a perpetual state of exception: Felipe could work in the United States, contribute to its economy, consume on its financial terms and within its systems of credit and debt, but he was barred from broader social or political inclusion and confined within the sixty-mile radius of the watermelon farms where he worked.

Tomás listened to Felipe's cautionary tale about the ambulance and hospital bills and assured the nurses and me that he would not be going to the emergency room today. He supposed aloud that all this crouching down, springing up, and burying heavy things in the ground had wrought some havoc with his blood pressure today by "agitating" his heart. He assumed that after all these years, the physical demands must be taking their toll. That was just the way it was. "I don't feel sick," Tomás said simply. "I don't feel anything."

Like Roberto and Tomás, blue state clinic patient Víctor—the lawful permanent resident who began carrying his immigration papers on him after Trump was elected—had also worked to the edge of his physical limits for many years. "Out of necessity, because I didn't have papers, I worked too much. I felt bad, and I came to this clinic." For twenty-five years, Víctor had been working as a cook and delivery driver at a local pizzeria, and he often also had to take care of the owner's children at the restaurant. Víctor resented this because it put him behind with his own work, and he often had to stay late into the night to make up the time. This meant that he could not go to the clinic for checkups or to stay on top of his health issues, like hypertension and high cholesterol. Over the years, Víctor noticed his health declining, but there was little he could do about it. His bosses would not give him time off to go to the clinic, and it was no longer open when he got off work.

In 2017 Víctor was diagnosed with colon cancer and had to quit his job to undergo treatment. He said that his boss came looking for him and demanded that he return to work, but Víctor refused. "My health comes first," he said. Fortunately for Víctor, by the time his boss came looking for him, he had finally been granted permanent residence through his brother's sponsorship. He was able to qualify for Medicaid to cover his cancer treatments and chronic illness management, and he began applying for income and housing benefits until he could get back on his feet. Because of his legitimate legal status, Víctor was one of the few patients I interviewed who was able to push back against the exploitative conditions under which he had been working and seek benefits to soften their physical blow. The damage to his health was done, but the bare life of his economic inclusion was tempered in a small way by his forward movement toward legalization and naturalization—movement that is increasingly difficult for many Latin American immigrants to achieve under current US immigration policies.

"Everything fell upon me all at once."

When I met Sabina in January 2020, she had come to the purple state free clinic to have several teeth removed by one of the dental volunteers from a nearby university medical center. She was in her late fifties and had come to the state about ten years ago from Central America. Sabina was friendly but subdued when she joined me in the makeshift interview space I had set up at the clinic. She had never had regular medical care until very recently, when she began attending the free clinic. When she first came to the state, Sabina worked in one of the handful of poultry plants that dominated the local economy at the time. When I asked whether they had offered health care coverage there, Sabina explained that she had entered the country, like so many, "de mojado" (a racialized slur for someone who crossed the border without authorization) and had risked everything to cross and get the job in the first place. Trying to get health care when she was already living and working under the radar seemed like tempting fate, and she felt healthy enough not to bother.

When the poultry plants closed, Sabina had to rely on her nephew to support her economically while she kept house and managed various domestic tasks. This was hard on her sense of self-worth because, as she said, "Value is money. If you don't work, you don't have any value." She added that being undocumented added to her sense of being less-than. "You know that we're not all really here with papers," she said bluntly. "Because here the main thing is that whoever has papers matters, and whoever doesn't, doesn't matter." Sabina's comments echo many of the discussions of immigrant deservingness that have long taken place in migration and social welfare scholarship (Horton 2004; Yoo 2008; Marrow 2012; Willen 2012b; Viladrich 2012). For example, Willen (2012b) conceptualizes "health-related deservingness" as a question of both public policy and (im)migrant subjectivity—that is, how a society determines whether (and which) immigrants deserve health care, as well as how immigrants experience rhetoric that constructs them as deserving or undeserving of health benefits. Additionally, Viladrich (2012) highlights the various discursive engagements around "deservingness" that followed the neoliberalizing and criminalizing turns of welfare and immigration reforms in the mid-1990s—both of which have shaped the state of exception I describe in this chapter. Moreover, this "deservingness" rhetoric often becomes internalized as an aspirational subjectivity for immigrants who feel they must distance themselves from those criminalizing tropes and defend their essential worth through hard work (see Menjívar 2016).

In Sabina's case, unemployment exacerbated the sense of worthlessness she felt as an undocumented immigrant, but her nephew encouraged her to "battle on" as they helped support one another. This arrangement seemed to keep Sabina afloat emotionally, and her good health helped her cope with the structural constraints she faced. Unfortunately, that good health was an illusion that shattered a few months before I met her at the free clinic. "I made it to fifty-six years old, thank God, and I never even felt pain in my fingernails. Nothing, thank God," Sabina explained. "And now everything fell upon me all at once." She had been feeling some pain in her leg and had some serious dental issues and so decided to come to the clinic, where a female medical volunteer offered her a free pap smear and blood work. Sabina thought she might as well take advantage of the services, and soon after, she received a handwritten note from Natalia, a clinic volunteer originally from Central America, asking Sabina to call her back immediately. Sabina pulled the note out from her purse, where she carried it around with her daily, and showed it to me as she expressed deep gratitude for Natalia's compassion and care: "I said to myself, 'My God, what could it be? What could be the matter with me?' So, I came around and called. 'Bad news for you,' she [Natalia] said. 'You have cancer. We need you at the hospital on such-and-such date.'" Sabina was overwhelmed and had no idea even where to find the hospital, which caused her to miss her first oncology appointment. Natalia helped her reschedule and provided guidance and encouragement while Sabina struggled with the idea that, as she said, these might be her last days on earth.

At the same time that Sabina was diagnosed with uterine cancer, she was also diagnosed with diabetes and hypertension. On top of that, she still needed intensive dental treatments that would now have to be postponed until she got her cancer, diabetes, and hypertension under control. The whole experience deeply shook Sabina, and she wept as she contemplated aloud what might have happened if it were not for the free clinic. "If I would have waited . . . I would have died," she said. "Yes, because imagine, the diabetes, blood pressure, cancer, and now the thing with my teeth hit me all at once."

Sabina told me that after her diagnoses, Natalia would come to her home to console her while she cried and asked God why this was happening to her. As she wondered aloud about the reasons God might have for thrusting such challenges upon her, I silently reflected on how much Sabina's illness experience resonated with those of other similarly situated patients I had met throughout my career. Even though Sabina felt that everything fell upon her at once, many of her health challenges (like diabetes, high blood pressure, and widespread tooth decay) in fact resulted from years of residing within a state of exception under conditions of structural violence. Sabina expressed explicit alarm at realizing she might suddenly be close to death at only fifty-six years of age, and she asked God to help her make sense of and cope with this realization, but she only obliquely referenced the social determinants that also had contributed to the possibility of a slow death.

Fortunately, Sabina's cancer was, in her words, "not one of the bad ones." This was why, after emergency treatment and only months after her diagnosis, she was back at the free clinic awaiting multiple tooth extractions. When I asked her about her experience receiving care at the hospital, she explained that she had to verify that she was not working and have her nephew sign some forms and provide check stubs on her behalf. She said this in a matter-of-fact tone and, since she never had health care previously, had no way of knowing whether this was typical or unusual. Sabina did say, however, that she had noticed that few public or private clinics were willing to help the Hispanic community in the way that the free clinic had helped her when she desperately needed support. "Because there really are a lot of us Hispanics that, like I said, there are some with value and without value," Sabina explained, again emphasizing the dichotomized deservingness she had internalized since coming to the United States: "Value is because you have [something], and the ones without value don't have anything. Without that, you're worthless." Through the free clinic's intercession, Sabina was able to receive treatment even despite feeling categorically discounted by the systems of value that prioritized people of means and people with papers. Sabina had never been able to attain legal residence, even though she had worked briefly in the United States, and she had never sought health care until her recent medical saga. She lived most of her life in the United States under the radar and without interacting with medical and legal bureaucracies.

When Sabina finally had to become visible to government-affiliated medical institutions (at the state university medical center) because of her cancer, she did so without a valid photo ID or legal residence but with her faith in God to protect her against the institutions that she believed held her in low esteem. Like others I spoke with across my three fieldsites, Sabina had internalized the notion that as an undocumented, unemployed, and physically unwell Latina immigrant, she had lost what little value her economic productivity might have conferred upon her in a society that otherwise excluded her from full social belonging. Her illness made her residence in the state of exception even more precarious than it had been when she was working, and she looked to her faith and to supportive clinic workers to affirm her sense of worth. While Sabina had not suffered an on-the-job injury, having "everything fall upon her at once" when she finally felt compelled to seek health care in the United States caused her to reflect on the precarity of her social position in ways that highlight how "deservingness" is socially constructed and internalized in relation to immigrants' health. For Sabina and many others I spoke with over the course of my research, this precarity meant engaging in health care only once their life was truly imperiled—and even then, while perceiving that others deemed them undeserving of that care.

"When I feel that I'm dying, I'll have to rush back to Mexico."

Like Sabina and María, red state patient Guillermo had no authorization to live or work in the United States. I met Guillermo while doing observations at a free clinic in the red state. He was waiting for the wound clinic to open so he could have a recent amputation debrided (a procedure in which damaged tissue is extracted from a wound), and he was happy to chat with me until that time. He sat on an exam table with a bandaged foot elevated while a vacuum device drained fluid and dead tissue away from his wound. When I asked Guillermo what type of surgery he had recently that required outpatient debridement, he replied that he was not entirely sure. He guessed it had something to do with an infection following an amputation that required another surgery to remove some infected tendons, sixteen days in the hospital, and a postoperative vacuum drain.

Guillermo told me that he did not know all the details, just that they needed to clean out what was dirty. His nonchalance seemed to stem from the fact that he had already undergone several amputations on his feet due to diabetes complications and now also received dialysis treatment regularly, so it was difficult to keep track. He gestured toward his foot as he recounted the experiences. "About around here I don't have toes anymore," he said. "First they cut off one toe and then they cut off another, and then they cut off all three, and then they cut a little bit in the back, just like that." He also showed me on his arm where he had surgery to create a fistula for dialysis. "They take out the blood and put it back in me again," he told me simply. He spoke with friendly openness and in matter-of-fact terms about the grave state of his health, his composure underscoring just how routine this intensive medical care had become in his daily life.

Like all the men I met across the three states, Guillermo only sought health care once he was experiencing grave symptoms of illness that pre-

STATES OF INJURY | 55

vented him from working. Before he fell ill, he worked a variety of jobs, including picking tomatoes in Canada as a migrant agricultural worker and working in factories and construction jobs across nearby states. Over time, however, as legal violence expanded to exclude noncitizens from "normal" social and economic spaces, Guillermo found it difficult to secure work permission or good jobs that would accept him without it. After entering the United States permanently as a self-described "mojado," and despite his unlawful status, Guillermo found work and settled in with a good boss at a flooring company in the red state county where we met, where he stayed for about fifteen years.

Unfortunately, Guillermo had to leave that job when he fell sick. "It's been about seven or eight years now that I can't work," he recalled. "I know how to work in a lot of things, it's just that because of my feet I can't, I don't have the strength, I get tired, I get dizzy, all because of the diabetes and all the cuts on my feet." Guillermo added that he knew he had diabetes and that it was already "a little advanced" by the time he was formally diagnosed but thought there was little he could do about it. He was ineligible for insurance, and his work complicated the situation. Installing floors was hard enough on his body without the diabetes to worry about, but the nature of the work especially damaged his diabetic feet. He spent all day kneeling with his toes against the floors while he measured, cut, and set materials, and this caused irreversible harm. "That's when they went chop, chop, chop," he explained. Without his toes, and with his need for dialysis several days a week, Guillermo could no longer work. He regretted having to leave his boss of fifteen years, but he explained that his boss knew he could no longer meet the physical demands of the job and worried that Guillermo might sue him if he sustained further injury.

As is often the case for noncitizens with complex care needs, Guillermo was able to obtain Emergency Medicaid to cover his emergency hospitalizations and dialysis, but not his medications or follow-up care. Even though he felt lucky to have had continuous work, he wished he had legal status so he could have had health insurance and paid into social security and other government benefits schemes. "Yes, I've wanted [papers]," Guillermo affirmed. "I want them, because what with me being unable to work anymore and everything, with how much I was working, yes, I wanted the government to help me a little bit." Guillermo explained that he spent so many years working in the United States but tried, and failed, to do his income taxes. He believed that maybe if he could have paid into the system in an official way, perhaps he would have been worthy of disability or income assistance (as US citizens would be) now that he needed them.

As it was, Guillermo found himself profoundly incapacitated with no idea of how he would continue to support himself. The man who had once put all his vital energy, almost his whole life, into feeding Canadians and Americans and building their homes now subsisted on donations from a church and Emergency Medicaid for acute diabetes care and regular dialysis. Should that help run out, or should it prove insufficient, Guillermo was prepared to return to Mexico to die. "When the day comes when I feel that I have no strength left, that I'm dying," he explained, "I'll have to rush back to Mexico. Just to reach my mom and dad, to arrive, to grab them and hold them and give them each a kiss . . . That's what I plan to do."

As was true of other patients I interviewed, Guillermo's lack of legal status in the United States made him an easily exploitable source of physical labor—an exceptional laborer whose economic contribution did not correspond to commensurate social or political benefits. He was simultaneously included in the US political economy and excluded from the minimum recognition of humanity that formal US citizenship enables (though does not guarantee). Only when he became an economic liability, by racking up tens of thousands of dollars in emergency and dialysis bills that he could never pay, did he become eligible for Emergency Medicaid. Yet this vital inclusion nevertheless excluded comprehensive care for medication or follow-up visits, meaning that he would remain caught indefinitely in a vicious cycle of diabetic crises, dialysis, and amputations. He was included in federal health care coverage solely to manage the costs of what would otherwise be uncompensated care. Beyond that, he would remain in a state of bare life (Agamben 1998) until he could no longer survive.

Guillermo's situation, though extreme, was not unique. Indeed, it echoed the experiences of other patients I spoke with in the red, blue, and purple states from 2015 to 2020. These stories revealed the iterative and cumulative harm that chronic social exclusion, alongside intensive economic inclusion, wrought on noncitizens' bodies and lives.

Guillermo—like Esteban, Roberto, María, and Sabina—was permanently locked out of citizenship and its corresponding social and political benefits because of his irregular status. This exacerbated the illness and injuries each of these people suffered after decades of working physically demanding jobs in the United States. Felipe and Tomás, who had permission to work in the United States as migrant agricultural laborers, were functionally excluded from health care coverage or political participation. And although Cristina and Víctor benefited in some ways from their relatively comprehensive legal status, it was insufficient to protect them from exploitative working conditions or guarantee them adequate medical coverage. Together, these examples highlight both the acute and compounding injuries that the state of exception inflicts on Latinx noncitizens, regardless of their particular legal status, and suggests the potential "slow death" that such a state enables.

Conclusion

The Trump administration's fixation on building "the wall," promulgating "emergency" measures to remedy constructed crises, and instituting policies like the Migrant Protection Protocols (also known as "Remain in Mexico") sustained a theater of catastrophe that drew international attention to migration at the southern border. The more subtle and insidious corollary of this performative panic, however, is the strategic maintenance of policies that criminalize migrants once they arrive in the United States and make it impossible for them to access social support benefits or be fully incorporated into the nation's political life. As this chapter has demonstrated, this protracted state of exception aims to blunt the potential of Latinx immigrants to become part of the US body politic in ways that might upset the status quo, and the state of emergency reifies the boundaries of exception—underscoring on more aggressive terms who is disposable and who is not.

In the United States, one of the most effective ways to neutralize perceived threats to white supremacy is to criminalize them, and thereby disenfranchise those who are criminalized. The recent state of emergency is a firm symbolic move to bolster the long-standing state of exception and its concomitant criminalization and state of injury that preserve the disposability of people like the patients I discussed here while making it extremely difficult for them to push back against it. In the following chapters, I zoom in on each of the states—red, blue, and purple—to show how this state of exception enables expanding surveillance and criminalization in the form of *medical legal violence*, which compromises noncitizens' ability to navigate health care as well as clinic workers' ability to provide it. I then zoom back out to focus on how clinic workers have mobilized their legal consciousness to resist this medical legal violence and prioritize the well-being of the communities they serve.

2

Hostile Terrain

Shifting Ground and Anti-Immigrant Assemblages

When it comes to noncitizens' well-being, differences in the particular dynamics of state and local institutions, policies, and actors have shaped distinct conditions of possibility for patients' and providers' health care negotiations across the three states I describe in this book. In the red state clinics I observed, the synergy between local law enforcement and federal immigration enforcement agencies had forcefully shaped Latinx noncitizens' well-being and health potential for several years before I began fieldwork there. This local-federal partnership constrained options for Latinx noncitizens and mixed-status families to attend to their health under threat of enhanced surveillance and racial profiling. Additionally, state-funded, full-scope Medicaid was not available to noncitizens in the red state.[1] As participants made clear, Emergency Medicaid eligibility in the red state was reserved for cases "of life or death" (*de vida o muerte*). The assemblages in which life-and-death choices played out for Latinx noncitizen patients there thus included many of the same components as those in the other states I describe in the following chapters—including federal immigration policies, clinical spaces, Medicaid documentation, and so forth—but were arranged differently and in tandem with disciplinary elements that were unique to that red state during recent years. In this chapter, I illustrate the human consequences of this assemblage—the dynamic relationships among government, noncitizens, physical terrain, and medical and legal bureaucracies that coalesced in the red state county—to illustrate how this transformed noncitizens' well-being there.

This chapter focuses on (1) the *assemblage* of dynamically interacting actors, policies, practices, and moments of controversy and uncertainty in contemporary immigration and health policy that enabled a recent expansion of medical legal violence in the red state county I observed;

and (2) how these dynamics have harmed many Latinx noncitizen patients in search of health. By concentrating on the assemblage through which these patients and their providers negotiate health issues in the red state, I demonstrate how medical legal violence forces some immigrants into dangerous spaces of liminality that result in delayed care, medical crises, and life-and-death decisions. In focusing on the active relationships among noncitizen patients, clinic workers, and federal and county agency personnel within a shifting landscape that encompasses geopolitical and bureaucratic borders, I highlight how multilevel immigrant reception politics can reverberate in immigrant families' lives long after someone crosses the physical boundaries between nations. They continue in the ongoing medical legal violence produced by the policies, practices, and infrastructures that often push noncitizen patients into protracted conditions of danger.

To explain how situations of medical legal violence emerge in this red state context, I first consider the various actors, policies, and places that contribute to it as an "assemblage"—a concept that captures how different elements of a phenomenon relate to each other in a dynamic, nonhierarchical way. While I focus here on the red state context, this concept helps illuminate the embedded infrastructures that shape noncitizens' health chances across the sites I observed, and it is particularly useful for trying to understand something that is in constant motion—which health and immigration policies seemed to be during the time I carried out this research. I often casually described this policy confusion as "the ground constantly shifting" under people's feet, so thinking in terms of an assemblage provided an additional analytical handle for something that was hard to pin down.

An assemblage can sometimes be thought of in topographical terms, kind of like a map with elevation markings, which is helpful for tracing the landscape of policies that seemed to shift daily against a nearly invisible background of systems that seem fixed (Bowker and Star 1999). Looking at medical and legal systems as constantly moving, overlapping planes highlights the often invisible work of embedded bureaucracies and infrastructures in constraining human lives. This approach brings into focus particular cases "where the lives of individuals are broken, twisted, and torqued by their encounters" with the systems that classify them (Bowker and Star 1999, 30). Bowker and Star further describe "torque" as "a twisting of time lines" that contorts bodies, lives, and classification schemes in a kind of human and institutional tug-of-war (30). "When all are aligned," they continue, "there is no sense of torque or stress; when they pull against each other over a long period, a nightmare texture emerges, . . . biographies and categories fall along often conflicting trajectories. Lives are twisted, even torn, in the attempt to force the one into the other" (30). The dynamic flexibility of these systems is all the more violent because of how it forces people to contort to fit in spaces meant to exclude them.

For many noncitizen patients in the safety net, medical legal violence "torques" their bodies and lives as their limited eligibility for health care often misaligns with their actual health needs. These exclusions trap people in situations that prevent them from meeting their vital needs while also exposing them to additional harms, including exploitative labor conditions as well as risks of detention and deportation. The legal and medical bureaucracies that noncitizen patients must interact with remain oriented toward ever greater exclusion and ever fewer opportunities to make it through the shifting assemblage in one piece. As I mentioned earlier in the book, local and state policies can either mitigate or amplify the harms of the legal violence that includes Latinx noncitizens in exploitative labor relations while excluding them from the benefits of full social belonging. In this chapter, I describe how local and state laws doubled down on exclusionary federal policies such that clinics in the red state faced an especially hazardous terrain of unevenly overlapping, constantly shifting, and mutually reinforcing ineligibilities that constrained Latinx noncitizens' well-being and exacerbated existing fear and anxiety.

Medical Legal Violence as Cause and Consequence

The story of the overlapping exclusions that torque present-day noncitizen patients in the red state into precarious health situations began in 1994, when the US Border Patrol adopted a comprehensive strategy to embrace "prevention through deterrence."[2] This involved increased Border Patrol funding and personnel and diverting immigrant entry routes through terrain that was so inhospitable that people would not dare cross it (Dunn 2009; De León 2015; Macías-Rojas 2016).[3] Yet the effects of this prevention-through-deterrence strategy do not end once someone crosses the border. They remain very much at play in federal public benefits strategies—such as the 1996 welfare and immigration reforms I mentioned in the book's introduction—once individuals and families try to build their life in the United States. In this way, immigration and health laws increasingly push several classes of noncitizens into dangerous situations by excluding them from health care. In many ways, medical legal violence in the United States functions similarly to the desert borderlands in that it demands that noncitizen patients and mixed-status families traverse an uneven, treacherous bureaucratic terrain with few hospitable points of entry. Sometimes and in some places, these points of entry—such as Medicaid eligibility—broaden to include more individuals (as in more immigrant-inclusive states, especially before the 2016 election), but more frequently they narrow. Whether a noncitizen patient facing a health crisis finds medical help in this metaphorical desert depends largely on the federal immigration climate and local will to aid or hinder these negotiations.

In October 2018 the Trump administration announced a plan to enhance the 1996 welfare and immigration restrictions by expanding the types of public benefits use that would categorize certain immigrants as a "public charge" and thereby disqualify them from an entry visa or permanent residence.[4] Historically, "public charge" has referred to the likelihood that an immigrant will become a burden to American taxpayers through their excessive use of public benefits. Immigrants seeking a visa or permanent residence may be deemed "inadmissible" if they use certain public benefits, like cash assistance or publicly subsidized long-term care. Thus, at the same time that the federal government was garrisoning the southern border and enlisting the desert as an ally to deter migrant entry, federal health and welfare agencies were likewise creating new boundaries to undermine the well-being of noncitizens and mixed-status families already within its borders. The stories of the people I met in the red state shed light on the importance of time and place for shaping the health possibilities of noncitizens and their families in ways that may otherwise go unnoticed because the spectacle of the border deflects attention away from the more everyday harms of ongoing legal violence.

The naturalness and apparent intransigence of US immigration law are what make the law so durable, while they allow policy makers to divert blame for the law's consequences—blame that certainly crosses party lines. Although the fieldwork for this chapter took place during the Trump administration, the groundwork was laid long before by Democratic administrations that developed and expanded some of the most harmful immigration laws on the books, accelerated rates of deportation, and expanded biometric surveillance of migrants (De Genova 2014). The Trump administration, in turn, leveraged those existing laws and cunningly adapted them to a "zero-tolerance" regime. The legal framework has long been in place, and rather than dismantling it, successive federal administrations have expanded it in new ways—often by enlisting local and state agencies to carry out their priorities on the ground through surveillance and enforcement.

In many ways, the red state clinics I visited are an "ideal" case study of expanding medical legal violence because they illustrate the conditions under which noncitizen health exclusions may be maximized through a combination of medical bureaucratic expansion (for example, through ACA implementation), the criminalization of Latinx immigrants through local law enforcement practices, and the magnification of federal anti-immigrant policies through local interpretation and collaboration. First, the red state county I observed, which is in a border state that includes a major urban core as well as several rural and remote areas, was an enthusiastic participant in the 287(g) program I described in the book's introduction. This means that local law enforcement agencies— namely, the county sheriff's office—partnered with federal immigration agencies to undertake immigration enforcement activities at the local level. Second, the county is located in a state that not only favored Trump in the 2016 election, but also engaged in state-level lawmaking that amplified federal immigrant exclusions and led to racial profiling of Latinx residents in the years before I conducted fieldwork there.

Finally, the red state county I observed is intriguing because, unlike several other governors of "red" states, this state's governor somewhat unexpectedly decided to expand Medicaid through federal funds provided via the ACA. Following massive budget cuts that squeezed many residents out of insurance coverage and furloughed many health care workers after the 2008 recession, the ACA revived the state's safety net and expanded Medicaid coverage for nearly half a million residents (Healthinsurance.org 2018). This included thousands of residents of the red state county I observed, the most populous in the state (US Census Bureau 2021). While undocumented immigrants and legal permanent residents living in the country for less than five years remained excluded from this expansion, it nevertheless extended Medicaid's bureaucratic reach throughout the county. Yet while this expansion benefited the county's low-income citizens and bolstered its community clinics, this transformation also penalized undocumented residents and mixed-status families through Medicaid's new federal documentation requirements and growing public benefits exclusions.

Exacerbating such exclusions was the county's location in one of several states that enacted omnibus immigration bills during the first Obama administration (National Conference of State Legislatures 2012).[5] (For the purposes of this chapter, I hereafter refer to the statewide omnibus immigration law affecting the county by the pseudonym "Law X"). Like most of these bills, which were modeled after Arizona's SB 1070, Law X included provisions such as requiring law enforcement agents to inquire about someone's immigration status during a lawful stop; enabling state residents to sue local and state agencies if they did not comply with federal immigration enforcement laws; mandating the use of E-Verify technology for employment; imposing penalties for failing to carry alien identification and registration; and requiring schools to verify students' legal status (Arizona State Senate 2010; National Conference of State Legislatures 2012). Despite these laws' popularity with anti-immigrant hardliners, the US Department of Justice eventually overruled many of these provisions due to their broad unconstitutionality and propensity for racial profiling (US Department of Justice 2012a, 2012b).

In addition to omnibus immigration action at the state level, sheriff's offices at the county level had significant autonomy over the degree to which they interacted with federal immigration enforcement agencies. County and municipal law enforcement agencies were empowered to collaborate with federal immigration enforcement agencies through the 287(g) program and the Secure Communities program, which, as I explained in the introduction, enabled the sharing of biometric data on apprehended immigrants across law enforcement agencies, including DHS and the FBI. While the Obama administration had suspended the Secure Communities program in favor of the Priority Enforcement

Program (which nevertheless left intact the biometric surveillance system of Secure Communities), the Trump administration revived the program four days after Trump's inauguration. In doing so, it sent a firm message regarding the direction immigration enforcement priorities would take in the years that followed (Immigration and Customs Enforcement 2018).

All of this meant that local law enforcement, particularly county sheriff's offices, long had the tools and mandate to participate in federal immigration enforcement. When combined with the state-level Law X, this expanded the conditions for harming noncitizen individuals and their families living in the red state through geographic and bureaucratic "torquing." At the same time, the ACA was expanding health care coverage to US citizens and creating an extensive bureaucratic infrastructure, including new documentation requirements for Medicaid eligibility. Through the collision of anti-immigrant and pro-health policies, the terrain of biopolitical surveillance shifted perceptibly in the red state county I observed. And as this ground shifted underfoot, many individuals and families fled the county or risked being torqued by expanding medical legal violence.

"These are not normal times for us."

In June 2018 I met Dr. Young, the medical director of a free clinic that served a large undocumented immigrant population, located in an urban area of the county. Dr. Young had clinical and research experience in how immigrant health care at the border had changed over the past two decades of US immigration policy. In fact, Dr. Young had done a hospital chart review on the period from the early 1990s through the early 2000s and tracked how trends of cancer and chronic illness treatment gave way to more traumatic injury cases as immigration enforcement ramped up during that time, and people were forced to take more dangerous routes and face extrajudicial anti-immigrant practices, such as trenches dug by the Minutemen opposite high border fences.[6] He brought up all of these points during an interview over lunch in the cavernous cafeteria the clinic shared with an affiliated shelter, saying, "So [the Minutemen] made the fences higher. . . . They dug trenches on our side of the border where the fence was to make it a further drop. . . . I'd be reading a chart and it would be a sixty-five-year-old lady who jumped off this thirteen-foot fence into a five-foot trench and broke both [her legs] that were open [fractures], and now she can't walk or do anything." Dr. Young also recounted how a van had overturned in the desert while being chased by border patrol "in an area where cars really shouldn't be, and the van was not an off-road van, so it tumbled, and eight people ended up with all these orthopedic [issues]." The hardening of the southern border created a new category of immigrant trauma patients arriving in ambulances. Dr. Young stressed that the policy change had "overwhelmed" the emergency rooms now that acute trauma cases were outpacing what had previously been a contained situation of transborder elective procedures and chronic care management.

Dr. Young was one of the few providers I spoke with (in any state) to locate patients' health negotiations explicitly within the broader historical arc of immigration enforcement policy in the United States. But while Dr. Young's experience highlighted the bodily consequences of immigration policies that increasingly forced Latinx immigrants into acutely dangerous situations, many other effects involved injury well beyond spaces of border militarization. Even as the physical boundaries between the United States and Mexico became more treacherous because of prevention-through-deterrence strategies, the boundaries between citizens' and noncitizens' medical eligibility similarly hardened through the 1996 immigration and welfare reforms and subsequent exclusionary health and security laws. Unfortunately for the undocumented residents of the red state county I observed, local lawmakers amplified these exclusions by enabling aggressive immigration enforcement and intimidation that undermined the health and well-being of the county's immigrant communities. Providers and community leaders I spoke with also emphasized more insidious incursions of local immigration enforcement into spaces of immigrant health and well-being far beyond the border. Many argued that the coalescence of localized and federal anti-immigrant policies and practices—for example, county-level 287(g) agreements and the statewide Law X, and enhanced border enforcement following 1994 and post-9/11 legislation—made life in the county riskier for Latinx individuals and families long before the 2016 election.

Several participants (providers and patients alike) recalled how relatively recent state and local anti-immigrant policies forced many Latinx individuals and families out of the county altogether. Leticia, a behavioral health provider specializing in child and family well-being, had been a leader of a prominent Chicano community organization in the state for forty years, but Law X shook her organization to its core. For the first time in her career, she found herself teaching three- and four-year-old children what to do if they encountered an immigration enforcement vehicle in their neighborhood or in front of their house. With a mixture of anger and incredulity, she described the situation to me: "What we sadly had to face was the reality of having to train our children how to manage and navigate [parental detention and deportation]. So we had big sessions with families and their children to show them what a border truck, you know the green trucks, look like. . . . Where do you go when you come home and the bus is dropping you off and you see that there is one of those cars over at your house, what do you do?" Leticia also explained that the broader community organization for which she worked operated about three thousand multifamily housing units in those years, which meant that she witnessed how "overnight we had keys left in the boxes or in the doors or on the counters, and families just fled." Even though her organization never asked for any identifying information from those they supported, clients told the organization workers that they were scared.

Leticia highlighted the role of the sheriff's office in traumatizing the local Latinx community through intimidation and racial profiling. "They were just pulling people over," she said. "The profiling that was denied [by the sheriff] for all those years was evident in our Black and Brown family environment." This meant that Leticia, as a behavioral health provider, was dealing with traumatized children who did not know how to articulate that trauma: "Think of yourself, an adult, right? You have a trauma that affects you, you get an upset stomach, you get a headache, you get anxious. Now visualize that with an eight-, nine-, thirteen-year-old kid, right? The eight- and nine-year-olds probably don't even know how to explain what's going on physically, but the thirteen- and fourteen-year-olds may act out aggressively. That's how they display that anxiety." Like other providers and one state legislator I interviewed in the county, Leticia remembered schools closing during that time, as students disappeared with their families. "In all that time [of Law X], we're thinking to ourselves . . . what's the message? What's the right thing to be saying to our families right now? It was just so over-whelming at the time, and still when I think about it, I can't believe that we lived through it." Leticia stressed that those were "not normal times for us." Without skipping a beat, she added, "And they still [in 2018] are not normal times, federally."

Like Leticia, clinic patient Noemy also vividly remembered when times became "not normal" in the county, and she worried about how federal policies after the 2016 election were beginning to mirror those traumatic times locally. I met Noemy in the summer of 2018 at Dr. Young's free clinic, where she had first come in for a routine pap smear and was now meeting with staff to transition to a more long-term clinic at one of the regional FQHCs. Noemy shivered in the clinic conference room where we met, in part due to the blasting air conditioning and in part, it seemed, because she was recalling a particularly traumatic time for her family. They had been living in the red state county since 2003, when they came from Mexico striving to make ends meet. Things were stable until Law X was passed: "When that [law passed], I returned [to Mexico] because of the fear . . . and I said, 'What if . . . they catch me, and my little girls?' . . . They are so small, if they get me—because with that law, even if they saw you walking in the street and saw that just because you were Latino, they were going to detain you." Noemy could not bear thinking of what would happen if she were detained and separated from her children. Between the sheriff's federally sanctioned collaboration with ICE and DHS through Secure Communities and the clear message from the state legislature that Latinx residents (legally present or otherwise) would not be allowed to go about their lives in peace, she decided to return to Mexico with her whole family.

Realizing that they could not survive economically in Mexico, Noemy and her husband eventually returned to the red state county where I met her. Many of the provisions of Law X had been challenged in court by then, as had local law enforcement leadership, and Noemy hoped that the changes would bring better days for her family. Still, she could not shake the feeling that she had made a huge mistake in leaving the United States in the first place: "We got so nervous that, maybe instead of doing the right thing, we did the wrong thing." Noemy struggled to justify the decisions she had made for her family when uncertainty turned to panic, such as leaving one daughter behind in Mexico because their constant fear and movement had foreclosed her chance for DACA. Looking back, Noemy wondered whether they should have tried to stay through the hard days. As uncertainty surged again after the 2016 election, Noemy wondered what would happen now that—from her point of view—the county's former immigration priorities seemed to have become national policies under the Trump administration. "We'll wait to see what happens," Noemy mused. "It's all that's left for us to do."

Providers and clinic workers also told me that, during the heyday of Law X, local law enforcement sometimes increased their presence near hospitals and mobile clinics to intimidate immigrant patients and prevent them from seeking care.[7] Clinic workers recalled seeing sheriffs' and ICE vehicles parked outside health care facilities. Many remembered patients having to make difficult decisions during Law X's full enactment, as the collision of federal and state immigration laws forced undocumented immigrants into more precarious situations and raised the stakes of everyday decisions—such as what to do in the event of a medical emergency. Liliana, an outreach worker from a large FQHC, described the "huge struggle" the clinic faced during those years. "We lost so many people on [Medicaid], so many children on [Medicaid] . . . when [Law X] came out," she remembered. "It was so horrible. It took some time. It took at least a year and a half to start getting people to start trusting and getting back on it."

One nurse I spoke with, Maya, worked at a county-run emergency department during the peak of Law X and noticed "a lot more hesitancy" among many immigrant patients to seek health care in those years. One case in particular stood out in her mind:

I had a woman come in and was having a heart attack. We didn't know at the time, but she had every other symptom in the book, and she just did not want to step into the ER. She was outside and her daughter, who had citizenship, came in and said this is the situation. I was on triage that day, so I kept telling her, "It's okay." I even went out there to communicate with her, "It's okay. You can come in. We will treat you. We will do what we need to do." "Yeah" [she said], "but what happens if I get admitted and then if I get a doctor that just doesn't support my status . . ." All these worries were preventing this woman who was full-on having a heart attack from coming in.

Maya explained that to persuade the patient to cross the threshold from the parking lot into the emergency room, her supervisor had to come outside and offer to admit the patient as a Jane Doe. "If us putting you in as a Jane Doe makes you feel any different, which for some patients it did, we would do that," Maya recalled. Such a workaround—invoking the protective anonymity of "Jane Doe" for fearful noncitizen patients in crisis—highlights the complexity of navigating the overlapping exclusions of the county's assemblage of immigration enforcement and health care eligibility.

Sandrina, a nurse and county hospital administrator, echoed Maya's memory when telling me they nearly had to close their facility because so many of their patients suddenly disappeared after Law X went into effect. Whether they left the county or state or merely went into hiding locally, Sandrina could not say, but it was clear that they did not feel safe seeking health care. Sandrina also witnessed sheriff's vans parked outside her building during that law's tenure. She remembered that the number of labor and delivery cases dropped as people moved away or went into hiding. She recalled patients' fears vividly, especially when it came to medical paperwork: "[We'd ask] in Spanish or even in English, 'Do you have your papers?' And what we were talking about is their prenatal [labs]. . . . They were thinking we were talking about their legal paperwork. So they would start turning, walking away. 'No, no, no,' we'd have to tell them. 'No, no, no, not those. We don't care about that. We're here to take care of you, we do not care [about your legal status].'"

These nurses' realization that such a seemingly innocuous bureaucratic term—*papeles*—could so terrify patients emphasizes the symbolic violence of the biopolitical assemblage of the red state county in recent years. (Sandrina did not mention whether they changed how they referred to lab paperwork, and our conversation immediately turned back to the law itself, but her astonished tone implied that they had.) While there is nothing inherently charged or noteworthy about the word "papers," this particular assemblage of medical bureaucracy and immigration enforcement practices imbued it with discursive power and injurious potential for noncitizens with urgent health needs.

Dr. García, a mental health professional with a nursing background whom I had met at a local nurses' association meeting, further connected the state's contemporary anti-immigrant politics with health care documentation concerns. We met at a Starbucks café inside a bustling grocery store in December 2017. A television on the wall broadcasted President Trump's speech about plans to move the US embassy in Israel from Tel Aviv to Jerusalem. Just before Dr. García arrived, a white man walked in, looked at the TV, and gleefully shouted, "Yes! I love Trump!" The other café patrons, none of whom outwardly resembled this man, looked up briefly but did not react. When I mentioned this to Dr. García, who arrived and glanced at the TV shortly after the man entered, she seemed displeased but not surprised. Like the others in the café, she was used to this kind of political performance. She also had long experience seeing that performance enacted through the state's anti-immigrant institutions. Dr. García recalled one example from several years ago, when a client missed an appointment because of racial profiling at a traffic stop: "A police car stopped beside them and arrested them because they looked undocumented, . . . and indeed they were, and they confiscated their car. . . . I was living in [another city in the same county] at the time and I remember thinking, 'Man, I wish they had stopped me 'cause I would have sued their ass.' But it was all on appearance. You look undocumented, you must be undocumented, you're gonna be treated like you're undocumented."

Dr. García added that while this racial profiling put everyone on edge in the county's Latinx communities, it also made her think twice about what kind of information she could safely include in noncitizen patients' medical records. She explained that she had learned that many area schools had begun recording information about the legal status of parents and students to deter enrollment of children from undocumented and mixed-status families, and she began to wonder what might happen if such information were recorded in patients' electronic health records.[8] With growing agitation, she explained, "I worry personally as a provider about the electronic record in terms of how much should I put in there. Should I even say they're undocumented? So I've stopped saying that. . . . I'm thinking that with the electronic record it would be very easy to [record clients' legal status], and for us to be required to do that. I get angry that I should even have to worry about shit like that, you know? That has nothing to do with clinical treatment, but unfortunately, it does." Dr. García also said that while her nurse mindset led her to want to "document the hell out of everything because if you didn't document it, you didn't do it," her training in psychology opened her eyes to being judicious about what should be left out of the chart. Compared to nursing, she explained, "In psychology, you document as little as possible. So . . . I find that I'm going into this psychologist way of doing things because in some ways I think it's more protective of my clients."

Unlike the blue state site I describe in the next chapter, where local- and state-level policies buffered some anti-immigrant policies at the federal level in ways that eventually made the state vulnerable to sanction from the Trump administration, the red state had an ongoing history of amplifying legal violence against Latinx noncitizens and their families and embedding it in multiple spaces of everyday life. This included clinics and other affiliated organizations, which had to deal with the fallout of massive disruptions among the Latinx communities they served. Despite federal health privacy laws such as the 1996 Health Insurance Portability and Accountability Act (HIPAA), which protects private health information, and long-standing assurances that immigration enforcement agencies considered health care institutions a "secure location," the widespread trauma of intersecting anti-immigrant efforts like enforcement through deterrence, Law X, and Secure Communities partnerships made medical legal violence a daily reality for patients and health care workers alike.

De Vida o Muerte: Medical Legal Violence and Torquing Bodies

Even though times had been hard before the 2016 election, when I conducted a new round of fieldwork in mid-2018, there was a growing sense that the red state county—and the nation at large—might be returning to darker days of enhanced immigrant surveillance. Two developments primarily drove this perception: (1) a maelstrom in English- and Spanish-language media around family separations at the border in the summer of 2018, and (2) magnified awareness of new bureaucratic hurdles to public benefits and charity care enrollment for noncitizens seeking health care.

In June 2018 I spoke with Dr. Francis, the medical director of a small free clinic similar to Dr. Young's. She described how difficult it had been to get specialty care for undocumented immigrants in the county over the four years that she had worked at this particular clinic. Dr. Francis was used to bureaucratic barriers to noncitizens' health but had noticed new obstacles to care that complicated her efforts to pave pathways to services. Recently, while navigating a noncitizen, uninsured patient through the usual medical legal bureaucratic hoops to get a thyroid biopsy at the county hospital, Dr. Francis discovered that the county was now requiring that all patients apply for Emergency Medicaid before having a financial eligibility interview for charity care. This meant that they could not finance care without making themselves legible to a federal agency.[9] Previously, when non-acute noncitizen patients would meet with a financial counselor at the hospital to finance care, many who were ineligible for Medicaid or reluctant to apply for government benefits would apply for charity care or work out a payment plan in installments. Now, everyone had to apply for Medicaid first. Only once they were denied could they move forward with financing or charity care applications.

Dr. Francis explained that these bureaucratic hurdles were a new development, and that they fit the trend of growing barriers that emerged since the Trump administration began—including the looming rumors of a change in the public charge rule. These barriers were making it much harder for her to get undocumented immigrant patients the care they needed, and the obligatory Medicaid application exacerbated the situation. "I think that undocumented [patients] are scared to do that application," she remarked, "because obviously the government will now know they exist by having that application online." Dr. Francis added that many of her patients were working through their pain and avoiding hospitals, waiting until their conditions got out of control and the emergency room was their only option. Even though many of her patients showed up to her clinic acutely ill and in need of emergency services, they would not risk going to the hospital. "I tell them that they will get treated," she added, "and that they will not be deported for going to the emergency room, but they never go." She recalled a patient whose brother and son had already been deported, "so he won't go near anywhere." Dr. Francis continued, "A lot of our patients will just wait until they're on death's door, and they don't realize that when they go to the emergency room, that they will actually get treated, and that there's the possibility of getting on Emergency [Medicaid] there. So, they just don't ever go to the hospital because in their mind they can't get treated because they're undocumented."

While many of the patients I spoke with across the three states did have some experience with Medicaid in some form—most often in cases of pregnancy and acute emergency—Dr. Francis made a compelling point about the anxiety that doing so often provoked. And even when undocumented immigrant patients did overcome their hesitation to apply for Medicaid and/or qualify for Emergency Medicaid in a "life-or-death" case, this by no means guaranteed adequate treatment. Nurse practitioner Marie, a wound care specialist I met at Dr. Young's clinic, told me that most of the noncitizen patients she treated were people who came in shortly after surgical hospitalizations. They needed follow-up care but were unable to afford it because they were either uninsured or covered by Emergency Medicaid for only the "life-or-death" portion of their care. Marie expressed frustration that many of her patients' conditions were a direct result of delays in care due to lack of health access. She described how cancer patients, for example, usually received a late diagnosis when their cancer was already at a more advanced stage. And only when that cancer created an acute emergency—such as a bowel obstruction in the case of colon cancer—would Emergency Medicaid cover immediate treatment. "Of course [they] get their colon taken out and the cancer gets removed, but then they never get the post-op chemo or radiation. That doesn't get done," she explained.

Such incomplete clinical engagement is precisely how biopolitical surveillance in the form of enhanced local and federal immigration enforcement intersects with health eligibility exclusion in the red state county to harm many Latinx immigrants in health crises. These overlapping features perpetually force them into narrow spaces of eligibility that require patients to forgo or delay care in ways that twist and contort them until bodily injury is all but inevitable. Yet, because they are the result of ongoing, compounded inequities codified in the law and embedded within exploitative labor relations rather than immediate trauma, the structural nature of these harms obscures the source of their violence.

When I met Marie at the wound clinic, she was attending to Guillermo, whom I had just interviewed. Guillermo embodied Marie's frustration with the way the county's biopolitics disproportionately harmed the county's Latinx immigrant patients. Guillermo had undergone several toe and tendon amputations due to complications from diabetes, and he qualified for Emergency Medicaid because of his low income and need for regular dialysis following diabetic kidney failure.[10] With the exception of dialysis, however, Emergency Medicaid covered only acute hospitalizations, thus trapping Guillermo in a vicious cycle of chronic and acute illness. Without comprehensive insurance, Guillermo could not afford the prescriptions necessary to keep his diabetes in check, so he only received medication and insulin when he was hospitalized for grave diabetes complications. He also had to resort to ad hoc follow-up care at the free clinic rather than with a primary care provider or his surgeon. Guillermo's inability to achieve a stable medication regimen or postoperative care meant he was frequently hospitalized, and his disability increased as this vicious cycle eroded his health.

Like some of the patients whose situations I describe throughout this book, Guillermo had to weigh the risk of illness and injury against the risk of detention and deportation when he became gravely ill. He was undocumented and had limited his visibility to federal agencies for most of his life, and he was willing to apply for Medicaid not because he was not afraid of getting "in the system" but because he had a $210,000 hospital bill and no way to pay it. And the assemblage of immigrant-exclusionary policies at the local and state level, overlaid by the federal terrain of noncitizen exclusions from economic and health spheres, violently torqued Guillermo's body. While he was able to fit within the financial and bodily eligibility requirements for Emergency Medicaid once his advanced diabetes brought him to the edge of death, the limitations of that coverage meant that he was literally and continually torn to pieces in the process.

"It's all in limbo . . . It's something that's a little unstable."

One key feature of the assemblage I have described in this chapter is that it is not static but dynamic and always shifting. While the general federal trend over the past twenty years has been toward greater exclusion of noncitizens from "normal" social spaces, there have been brief moments when the avenues to inclusion have broadened rather than narrowed. This was especially true when President Obama announced deferred immigration action through the 2012 DACA and 2014 DAPA executive orders. These programs signaled a symbolic aperture in federal priorities toward some classes of noncitizens, and—in the case of DACA—hundreds of thousands of immigrants chose to come "on the radar" to reap the benefits of work authorization and deportation protections.

There are parallels between DACA and Medicaid in terms of the kind of risk-benefit decisions that DACA recipients and noncitizens facing health crises have had to make in recent years. Depending on the landscape of federal immigration priorities at any given time, noncitizens who fear punitive immigration action must determine the conditions under which they are willing to become visible to federal immigration agencies (Asad 2020; Jimenez 2021). These decision-scapes are visible through examples of undocumented immigrants navigating a shifting federal topography of immigration policy that destabilized immigrant health in the red state county. The cases described here exemplify the difficult decisions participants had to make not only for themselves, but also for their family members, with consequences that reverberated beyond the clinic. They illustrate how immigrants' well-being is often temporally and spatially determined in ways that sometimes seem cruelly capricious as they change from moment to moment, administration to administration.

I met the first of these patients, Javier, while conducting ethnographic observations at Dr. Young's free clinic. He had accompanied his eighty-two-year-old father, Jacinto, to the clinic for prostate, heart, and blood pressure issues. Jacinto lived primarily in Mexico but had fallen ill while staying with family in the red state. Although I had initially intended to speak with Jacinto, Javier interrupted frequently to explain things his father said and to add his own perspective. Soon Javier was speaking at length about his own experiences as an undocumented immigrant negotiating Emergency Medicaid services for himself and DACA for his three children. For example, when he injured his legs in the past, Javier had to receive emergency care at the county hospital, which is where he was enrolled in Emergency Medicaid. He described what happened when he showed up in the emergency department with unspecified leg injuries. "They made me fill out some forms in which they tell you, 'You're going to take [Medicaid], yes? Okay,'" Javier recalled. "They fill out your forms . . . but you already took [Medicaid]," he continued. "Possibly it will cover [your treatment]. . . . But if you don't get it, obviously they'll send you a bill or they'll say, 'You owe however much. How can you pay it?'"

Despite Javier's wariness and lack of legal status, he was willing to engage with certain federal agencies when he perceived that the immediate benefit justified the potential risk. This included his use of Emergency Medicaid, as well as his decision to enroll his three children in DACA before they graduated high school. The latter decision was made during the Obama administration at a time when aggressive anti-immigrant policies governed the red state, and his county in particular. Emergency Medicaid protected Javier's earning potential while helping him avoid medical debt, and DACA bolstered his children's security in a space where it took very little to detain Latinx individuals (regardless of their legal status), so the risk-benefit calculation fell in favor of engaging with federal protections. Such calculation reflected a nuanced consciousness of the shifting assemblage that delimited noncitizen well-being according to policy, timing, and geography. In Javier's case, this awareness reflected the need to simultaneously account for immigration and health laws and leverage favorable opportunities to protect the health and livelihood of his family while remaining circumspect about the limitations of such opportunities.

Our conversation took place in June 2018, at a moment when DACA's future was very much in doubt. This destabilization emphasized the temporary nature of federal benefits and conditional gratitude that Javier expressed, and it threw their capriciousness into relief as he and his family continued to live under the threat of the benefits being taken away. When I asked Javier about his children's status, he replied that things had gotten "a little complicated" under what he referred to as Trump's "political reforms." He expressed gratitude for the Obama administration's "benefits" but explained that it was hard to know what President Trump was planning to do or what his vision was for immigration. "Because he says one thing and then later another," Javier said. "One day the president might announce immigration reform, but the next, 'You know what? Everybody out.' It's all in limbo," Javier continued. "That [Trump] could wake up tomorrow on the right side of the bed, or he could wake up on the wrong side and make one decision or make another decision—it's something that's a little unstable."

I asked Javier whether things had also been unstable before the Trump administration or whether he viewed it as a new development. "You've lived it," Javier replied brusquely. "I did, but as a citizen," I replied. "Yes, you live it as a citizen, but it must affect you, too. Because it affects you, for example, with tuition payments. That affects you as a citizen." I agreed, but added that I lived and studied in California, where statewide policies resisted and buffered the impact of some of the Trump administration's policies. "One question," Javier interjected candidly. "[Are you a] Republican or a Democrat?" Taken aback by the bluntness of the question and the implicit suggestion that I might be a Trump supporter, I replied that I had always considered myself a Democrat. Without saying explicitly that I personally found the standard Democratic platform insufficiently progressive, I added frankly that I lately questioned the usefulness of traditional two-party designations in the current political context. "It's complicated," Javier agreed, but he soon returned to the blue-red divide, saying, "The thing is that here is Republican, and you all [in California] are Democrats." When I remarked that California had Republicans, too, and some areas were pretty similar to the red state county where the clinic was located, Javier highlighted the impact of Law X to emphasize his point.

Like others I spoke with, Javier said that the state had been doing well economically, and people like him lived well, mostly unbothered by authorities. After Law X, he explained, the state economy suffered, and things became truly difficult for immigrants. This baffled Javier, who asserted that much of the financial and cultural wealth of the United States came from people who emigrated from elsewhere. But the state law scared people, and some left. Javier thought about leaving, too, but he had risked much to get his family to the United States and believed that God had brought them safely here for a reason. They endured the fear and insecurity during the tenure of Law X and felt some relief when it ended and a new governor came into office, but the Trump administration brought them right back to a similar state of uncertainty.

Javier expressed his frustration at this turn of events, saying, "You can't make plans. . . . You [Meredith, a US citizen] can make plans, you can construct, build your plans, but [we] can't because you don't know what will happen to you tomorrow, and it's something that makes you powerless, because you can't reach your potential, you don't give what you should, because you're afraid." Unlike fellow clinic patient Noemy, whose family was displaced by fear over immigration law uncertainty, Javier wagered on trusting the federal government during the Obama administration over risks at the state level to secure temporary legal and medical relief. Now that the state's former politics seemed to have become national priorities under the Trump administration, however, Javier felt his family's precarious position even more acutely.

Like Noemy, Javier felt paralyzed by doubt over how to proceed or what would happen now that his children were on a government register. He knew that whatever aid he received through benevolent arms of federal agencies, for example through Emergency Medicaid and his children's DACA, could just as soon be used against them as the political tides likewise turned. While Javier had gambled on the law when he perceived it to be on his side and necessary for his family's well-being, he sensed the torque of policies reversing course and felt "powerless" in the face of that backward motion. Although he did not say so explicitly, Javier's experiences made him keenly aware that the synergistic assemblage of place, policies, time, and institutional practices had once again narrowed the conditions of possibility for his family to thrive.

"When it's an emergency, then we take that risk."

The unpredictability of shifting immigration policy and health policy landscapes made it difficult for the red state county's undocumented immigrants and mixed-status families to determine how to balance their health needs against the fear of becoming visible to the punitive arms of immigration enforcement agencies. As I described earlier, local law enforcement practices had long undermined the perceived safety of health care centers as "sensitive locations" by intensively promoting federal immigration enforcement to intimidate the county's noncitizens. This aggressive criminalization spurred many eligible undocumented immigrants—like Javier's children—to pursue DACA when it became available, but it also made them feel vulnerable when the Trump administration delegitimated the program. And the symbolic shift away from inclusion toward enhanced enforcement against all so-called "illegal" and liminally legal immigrants complicated the decisions of noncitizens in health crises.

The perceived overlap between punitive immigration agencies and federal health benefits made some patients fear health care institutions as potential sites for surveillance and exclusion. This raised the stakes of risk calculation among Latinx noncitizens already conscious of their constructed illegality and begged the question, How sick is sick enough to warrant possibly becoming visible to immigration agencies? Here I describe the case of Sebastián and Laura to illustrate this tension. The assemblage of local and state anti-immigrant practices and policies, alongside the Trump administration's threats of enhanced immigration enforcement and a crackdown on benefits use, produced intersecting fears of detention, deportation, disability, and death for this family in crisis. In this case, only when death seemed imminent were they willing to take the risk of detention/deportation that they feared most.

I first noticed patient Sebastián when I saw him hobbling through the free clinic with his beleaguered adult daughter and caregiver, Laura, close behind him. A mechanical drain funneled a red viscous liquid away from Sebastián's groin and into a plastic receptacle. It turned out that Sebastián and Laura (both undocumented) had a long wait before the urologist would be available to see Sebastián, so they had some time to kill and did not mind spending it talking to me. As we settled into the clinic's conference room, I learned that Sebastián had recently left the hospital after a month and a half of inpatient treatment. He was now staying at a charity respite center for what I gathered was congestive heart failure and liver and kidney failure. He was in terrible shape, scooting his walker forward miserably and wearing a vacant and defeated expression. I suspected that Sebastián would not be particularly chatty, and I was right, but Laura seemed to have a lot she wanted to get off her chest. She also received medical care in the red state county and was going through her own health issues, so she was able to speak about her own and her father's struggles (of which there were many) while they waited.

Laura and Sebastián began by describing his recent plunge into grave medical crisis. Sebastián had never really gone to the doctor because he had always been healthy, as far as he knew. He only agreed to go to the emergency room once his genitals had become so swollen (Laura gestured to indicate something between the size of a large grapefruit and a small melon) that he felt he no longer had a choice. By then, he was in crisis and had to be admitted to control the fluid overload that was, he would learn, destroying his organs. Laura explained that they had agreed to enroll her father in Emergency Medicaid to cover his emergency care costs, but this did not include his follow-up care or rehabilitation. That was why he was coming now to the free clinic for specialist appointments and was staying at a charity respite center while he recovered. Laura regretted having waited so long to get her father into care, saying that maybe if they had acted sooner, he would not have ended up so ill and on dialysis now. But Laura explained that there were so many reasons for people like them to be afraid to seek help. It was not just the diagnosis they feared, she told me, but also the cost and the possibility of deportation.

For her part, Laura had been getting health care through the county hospital and a local community clinic. She knew she had diabetes, but she had been without medication for months because—as a low-income, uninsured, and functionally uninsurable, undocumented single mom— she could not afford it. Now that her father's health was declining, however, she feared that her own condition could also deteriorate rapidly or get so out of hand in the time it took to decide that the consequences would be irreparable—as had been the case for her father. Laura had only found out the previous winter that she had diabetes, and she already suffered from foot pain and numbness. She had gone to the emergency room last December when she could no longer bear her discomfort, and there she was diagnosed with diabetes. Now Laura worried about what would happen if she could not keep the disease in check. Yet with the outstanding bills for her own emergency visit and with her father's declining health, she was even less able to afford medication.

When I asked Laura whether she had thought about applying for Emergency Medicaid for her own emergency care costs, she explained that she was too afraid under the Trump administration to apply for anything through the government. She had enrolled in Emergency Medicaid several years ago to give birth to her US-born children, but she said that now the idea of applying for Medicaid even on behalf of her citizen children made her stomach churn. While she was willing to enroll her father in Emergency Medicaid because he was, as Dr. Francis put it, "at death's door," she was not willing to do the same for her own relatively slow-moving health crisis. The risks were similar—becoming visible to the federal government and potentially vulnerable to deportation through that visibility—but Laura did not feel that her own situation met the threshold of urgency to warrant such a gamble. And given Emergency Medicaid's definition of "emergency" as a "life-or-death" situation, it was likely that county Medicaid administrators would have agreed with her on that count, even if she did risk applying. Because the eligibility systems that classified noncitizens' federal and statewide health care eligibility were designed to squeeze out people like Laura, it is no wonder she denied for herself what she reluctantly accepted for her father. The risk of being deported and separated from her children was greater than her current health concerns. Because of this, Laura was willing to literally sacrifice her feet and her health to diabetes to avoid the possibility of getting caught and squeezed in those narrowing eligibility passageways that would not guarantee her health but might put her in the path of immigration enforcement.

Laura began shaking visibly when she thought about what might happen to her children if she were deported, and she started to cry. Things were tough under Law X, she explained, but she took "precautions" and tried to stay out of trouble so that she could support her family as a single mother. As cautious as she was back then, however, she was nevertheless arrested once at a routine traffic stop. The police told her that she had a problem with one of her car's lights. When they discovered that Laura was undocumented, she was taken to jail and shackled at the wrists and ankles. Laura was frightened and humiliated, but she felt fortunate that she had to spend only one night in jail and that the people from "immigration" were kind to her. They asked whether she wanted to see a judge, and she said she did, but they released her without her ever seeing an immigration judge or explaining any follow-up to her. "The truth is that in that moment they told me I could go," she recalled, "I left running to see my children."

Laura did not want to tempt fate with another encounter with immigration agents, especially now that things had, from her point of view, gotten much worse than the days when the state anti-immigrant law was in full force. Ever since "the new president" (as she referred to Trump) came to office in 2017, she felt that everything had become much harsher for immigrants. At least, that was what the news and everyone around her was saying. "Now they're saying so many things," Laura remarked, "and yes, you get scared, you take your precautions." When I asked what type of precautions Laura had to take, she reiterated that she must avoid driving or asking for help from service agencies because she feared being deported without her children:

> You don't ask for help, because they already said they're going to report you or something. That's the fear, asking for help. Maybe there are places like [this clinic] where they don't, but not like at the hospital where they ask if you have insurance or not, that's the fear. . . . When they ask that, I tremble. . . . Like now when we were at the hospital [with my dad]. . . . When you finally reach that limit, when it's an emergency, then we take that risk . . . that once they give us [medical] attention, they can report us. And now lately times are more difficult; the truth is for me things are more difficult today than a few years ago. . . . You don't look for help, but when it gets to be an emergency, sometimes I get to thinking, maybe if [my dad] had seen a doctor sooner, maybe now he wouldn't be going to dialysis.

Like Javier, who had accepted Emergency Medicaid for himself and DACA for his children, Laura's family had been living only partially in the shadows over the past decade in the red state county where we met. Laura had enrolled herself in Emergency Medicaid and her US-citizen children in full-scope Medicaid prior to the beginning of the Trump administration, and her father was enrolled in Emergency Medicaid during the time of our interview in June 2018. But as Laura said, these days only an emergency as grave as her father's would warrant such a risk. Her own diabetes complications and her children's regular health care were harder to justify than her father's near-death experience. Even Laura's twenty-seven-year-old younger sister, who also had diabetes, feared using any health care services because she believed that doing so would prompt the government to take away her DACA. Ironically, even though the more "legal" members of Laura's family were eligible for health care and entitled to it, she worried that their accepting it would enable the federal government to use health care as a justification to penalize her family. And with the future of DACA in doubt and the looming possibility of a change in the public charge rule, this fear seemed well founded.

Medical legal violence happens when people like Laura and her family avoid health care until moments of crisis because exclusionary immigration and health laws have forced them into dangerous spaces of liminality. Laura's arrest under Law X made her even more fearful, and uncertainty over DACA kept her sister out of the clinic despite her own serious illness. Only when Laura feared for her father's life was she willing to risk their exposure to government surveillance, but she worried that asking for help left them vulnerable to deportation. Like nurse Maya's heart attack patient, Laura's family was forced by anti-immigrant laws into dangerous situations that might have been avoided if they had felt secure enough to seek care before a health crisis. Yet the particular constellation of state and federal immigration and health laws that existed in the red state county over the past several years constrained their options for care until they reached the life-or-death decision threshold that outweighed their deportation fears.

Conclusion

On January 8, 2019, President Trump addressed the nation in primetime regarding a "crisis" that he argued warranted $5.7 billion for a border wall and potential state of emergency (Trump 2019). He spoke of physical barriers and security personnel to delineate the boundaries between US citizens and Latinx migrants, and clearly this bold posturing resonated with a sizable portion of the US population. Yet the visibility of the immigration stalemate staked in terms of such concrete boundaries risks overlooking the many subtle ways in which boundaries of belonging are also being forged in vital spaces where noncitizens' and mixed-status families' lives unfold. By connecting punitive immigration laws at state and federal levels with complex federal health bureaucracies, noncitizen patients at times come to perceive health care institutions as potential sites for surveillance and exclusion. To prevent noncitizens from full social inclusion, the contemporary assemblage of immigrant health in this red state county expands medical legal violence and deters noncitizens from prioritizing health in favor of security.

The red state county I observed represents a near archetype of the kind of prevention-through-deterrence strategies that inflict medical legal violence on many Latinx immigrant individuals and families living in the United States. Well before the 2016 election, local 287(g) agreements and Law X in the red state funneled Latinx immigrants into the path of local and federal law enforcement. It made it impossible for many to go about their daily life, closing down opportunities for education, employment, housing, and health care. It confined many, like Laura, to their homes and encouraged others, like Noemy, to "self-deport." That was the idea, after all: to make life so unbearable that the individuals and families whom state leaders found undesirable would not just keep to the shadows but disappear entirely.

The Trump campaign took this same message and gave it a national platform, and that platform was realized in federal immigration policies. Even though several provisions of state anti-immigrant laws were struck down by federal courts, the Trump administration consistently took a firm stance against migration (both legal and "illegal") into the United States by rejecting visa applications, separating families, altering family reunification precedents, and denying asylum opportunities (National Immigration Law Center 2018). It promised to build a wall and continued to funnel immigrants through the harshest, most unforgiving terrain while blaming cruel nature and incorporeal policy for the fate of ill-fated, irresponsible immigrants.[11]

Yet as our collective attention increasingly turned to the battle over the wall and the legitimate humanitarian crisis of migrant deaths at the border, the insidious bureaucratic violence unfolding through the bolstering of existing laws and increasing scrutiny of public benefits documentation played out offstage. A topographical approach to immigrant health in the twenty-first-century United States demands tracing the specific, dynamic relationships among the people, time, and place that shape how boundaries were contested and possible futures enabled or foreclosed. The physical boundaries that captured the nation's attention during the Trump administration—the desert, the border, the wall— acted in close association with the less visible but no less important moments when the parameters of the contemporary immigration debate emerged: the 1994 prevention-through-deterrence strategy, the 1996 immigration and welfare reforms, and present-day health and immigration lawmaking—including the ACA and the public charge rule change.

When an undocumented immigrant in the red state county I observed shows up at the emergency room in a medical crisis that finally tips the balance of fear from deportation to disability or death, that patient has also traversed an uneven terrain of medical legal violence that has made such a choice both possible and necessary—less of a crossroads than a dead-end. This assemblage expands legal violence through health care bureaucracies and institutions to maximize the exclusion of noncitizens and mixed-status families from US society. It also benefits from these excluded groups' awareness of their own constructed illegality—their consciousness of being increasingly on the wrong side of shifting laws and policies—to perpetuate that very exclusion.

The Trump administration did not create all these laws, but it artfully constructed new blockades from existing legislative infrastructure that optimized their exclusionary potential. Including vital services—such as health care, nutrition, and housing assistance—in federal immigration governance subtly forced many noncitizen patients and mixed-status families toward heart-wrenching decisions that played out in the shadows, beyond the drama of the border "crisis" or the associated battle lines of the government shutdown. In these ways, the newly converging boundaries of US immigration and health exclusions raised the stakes of illness and injury for thousands of immigrants living in the red state and beyond. The following chapter examines how these same federal dynamics played out in a distinct state context, one where opposition to those dynamics created its own opportunities and hazards for immigrant health. It emphasizes the insidiousness of medical legal violence despite local institutions' and actors' attempts to resist it.

3

Immigration Federalism and Health Care Surveillance in a Progressive Jurisdiction

On a warm October afternoon in 2015, I searched for a parking spot beyond the orange traffic cones that demarcated the weekly health fair of the blue state clinic I would be observing. The health fair itself consisted of various event tents and several tables in the clinic's parking lot and alongside one of its walls. A crowd of raucous blonde teenagers blaring pop music presided over some food bank tables, and several attendees formed a line around the perimeter of the one-story clinic building. I noticed more joining on foot from nearby neighborhoods, some pushing shopping carts ahead of them in anticipation of carrying food back home without the aid of a car or bus. As the sun blazed over the festive scene, I searched for Isabel, a certified enrollment counselor and outreach worker I had arranged to shadow for the day. When I introduced myself, Isabel greeted me warmly before promptly disappearing back into the crowd to continue orchestrating the assorted health fair activities.

Not wanting to be underfoot while Isabel worked, I circulated through the parking lot, taking in the scenes at the various stations. Outreach workers sat beneath one tent offering to enroll curious passersby as clinic patients, while a nurse in an adjacent tent provided free blood pressure and blood sugar checks. Some of the health fair attendees seemed to be regulars—especially those who had come prepared with bags and carts for the food bank table—but some were definitely new to the spectacle and approached the tents hesitantly. Aside from the teenagers in the food bank sector, almost all the people at the health fair were Latinx. While the clinic staff under the tent spoke to these attendees in Spanish, and they answered in Spanish, many also spoke to each other in indigenous languages and inconspicuously interpreted for those whose Spanish was less fluent.

While I was able to observe Isabel's ebullient energy and warm de-meanor with members of the small crowd, I realized that we would have little time to speak one-on-one during the fair itself. Instead, we agreed to meet her at her office two days later. Without preamble, and before I could even begin recording our interview, she told me with an exasper-ated smile that yesterday's health clinic (in a different city than the one I had observed two days before) had gone terribly. Sometimes that hap-pened, she said dismissively, before immediately recalling another re-cent health fair that was "the worst" she could remember. Isabel ran her fingers through her curly hair, which cascaded over her shoulders and the shawl she was wearing, as she summoned the unpleasant memory. She described how a white man had come to the health fair to gather items from the food bank table. As he approached, he began screaming at the other people in line and telling them that they needed to go back to Mexico. He admonished them for leeching off the system and told them to get lost. Isabel, a Latina immigrant from Central America who had lived in the area for more than a decade, firmly warned the man that he could not speak so disrespectfully to the group and reminded him that there were children present.

The man disappeared for a moment but quickly returned with an American flag he had retrieved from his truck to continue his tirade. Isabel then explained to him that he was going to be banned from the health fairs in the future if he continued this behavior, which only an-gered him more. Isabel eventually de-escalated the situation (she didn't say how), but as we spoke, she expressed surprise at the man's overt ex-pression of racism. She explained that in all the time she had lived in the area, the discrimination she and others in the Latinx community faced was usually more "between the lines." It was a generally progres-sive region, at least on the surface, and much of the discrimination she would describe later in the interview tended to be more veiled—if no less hurtful. Isabel wondered aloud whether Donald Trump's presiden-tial campaign, which had officially launched only a few months before our October meeting, was emboldening people to be more explicit about their feelings toward Latinx immigrants and their presence in the country.

As the months and years went by, and even now as I finish writing this book in 2022, such tensions have pushed us collectively to reckon with who we are as a country. National politics are noticeably polarized, and violent expressions of white supremacy and anti-immigrant sentiment have surged. As Isabel's experiences suggest, however, this phenomenon did not suddenly come into being during the last few years. Rather, the rise of more overt white supremacist governance further legitimated and institutionalized the kind of rage that people like the flag-waving health fair attendee longed to express. Even though Isabel knew from personal experience that these sentiments lurked beneath the surface, among her neighbors and within institutions that excluded people like her, she found their renewed explicitness—and their impact on her clinic work—distressing.

In this chapter, I acknowledge these dynamics while also emphasizing how the relatively progressive immigrant politics at the *state* and *local* level that aimed to resist medical legal violence at the *federal* level drew explicit threats from the Trump administration to surveil and punish such resistance. This meant that even in a blue state with broadly progressive politics, the federalized nature of US health and immigration policies enabled medical legal violence to expand the regime of immigrant exclusion and surveillance in an unlikely place. While the blue state was by no means immune to the long-standing racist legal violence that has become more explicit (again) across the country in recent years, community clinics in the county I observed had created bureaucratic routines that maximized the inclusion of Latinx immigrants in the local safety net system. However, despite—and sometimes *because of*—local and state policies that promoted immigrant integration and resisted immigrant criminalization to greater degrees than other states (especially the red and purple states I describe in other chapters), federal control over immigration enforcement and subsidized health care programs like Medicaid created a surveillance hazard that made patients wary of engaging with agencies that are (or are perceived to be) aligned with government agencies. My encounters in the blue state clinics revealed how the immigration system may enlist health care institutions as sites of surveillance and punishment—*even and especially* in a relatively progressive, immigrant-inclusive locale.

Before the 2016 election, clinic workers felt confident in navigating Latinx noncitizen patients through the many federal exclusions to health care and other public benefits by optimizing such patients' eligibility for local, state, and federal benefits without risking immigration enforcement penalties. In the absence of more inclusionary federal reforms, they had created strong networks among community organizations and government agencies that maximized resource availability for liminally legal and undocumented immigrants and mixed-status families. After the election, however, these once-crucial relationships made clinic workers and patients wary of how clinics might become an inadvertent site of immigrant surveillance and immigration enforcement. More overtly racist anti-immigrant rhetoric and general policy chaos in the early years of the Trump administration enhanced these fears and anxieties and complicated care for noncitizen patients, mixed-status families, and clinic workers alike. Even though immigration enforcement agents never physically entered clinics I observed, everyday clinic routines became suspect as participants perceived them to be potential spaces for expanding medical legal violence. Somewhat paradoxically, this was especially true *because* the state was so vocally opposed to anti-immigrant measures at the federal level, meaning that their progressive policies drew unwanted attention to immigrant-inclusive institutions such as the safety net clinic I observed. These tensions led clinic workers to seek legal guidance to reconsider how they might resist federal policy priorities without compromising the security of their patients.

Disillusionment and Dreams Deferred

The blue state clinic where I began my research in 2015 was located in a county with relatively progressive politics but limited public health care resources compared to more populous areas of the state. While the US Department of Agriculture considers the county "metropolitan" because of its proximity to a large urban area (US Department of Agriculture 2020), the county itself only has a population of about 260,000 and did not have a public hospital at the time I conducted my research (US Census Bureau 2021). Additionally, nearly half of the roughly 45,000 county residents who identify as Hispanic/Latino/a/x in the county were born in Latin America—almost none of whom have naturalized as US citizens (US Census Bureau 2021)—thus making them particularly susceptible to medical legal violence. Unlike major nearby cities that had comprehensive academic medical centers and universal health care safety nets for low-income residents irrespective of legal status, undocumented and liminally legal residents of the county I studied primarily had to rely on charity care and Emergency Medicaid at private hospitals or travel to other counties for more intensive, high-level care than was available to them locally. And while the county did not have explicit sanctuary status when I first began research, its "proactively inclusive" immigrant incorporation context (Young and Wallace 2019) made it a unique place to explore how health care federalism might play out in an environment with a relatively less criminalized yet medically underserved immigrant population.

On a bright and balmy day in July 2016, I returned to the neighborhood where I had observed Isabel at the health fair nearly a year before. It was a commercial area near the low-income neighborhoods where most of the area's Latinx community (including the clinic's patients) lived. I had scheduled meetings with two community organization workers whose offices were a couple of blocks from one another, both nestled amidst auto shops, storage units, and businesses with a variety of Latin American flags over their doors. One of these organizations provided services specifically for immigrant families, while the other coordinated wraparound services for the local Spanish-speaking immigrant community that included everything from emergency housing support to immigration law expertise, education, and job training programs. Both organizations also worked in tandem with the nearby community clinic network I had been shadowing.

Through my network, I had connected with Sofía, a community worker originally from South America who had legal training in her country of origin and now worked to facilitate legal and social services for members of the local Latinx community. Sofía described how her organization provided legal assistance to patients whose legal status complicated their health care opportunities. While they had only two staff attorneys and one paralegal in house and were the only organization in the community providing immigration legal services, they also collaborated with larger national organizations like the Catholic Legal Immigration Network, the Immigrant Legal Resource Center, and the American Immigration Lawyers Association to help direct clients to the resources they needed.

While I waited for Sofía to call me into her office for our scheduled interview, I sat in the lobby with clients who were chatting with one another and watching Spanish-language election news. It was July 12, 2016, exactly one week before Republican National Convention delegates would formally nominate Donald Trump to represent the party in the 2016 election. Hardline immigration policies had been at the heart of the convention, and many Republicans were celebrating the Supreme Court's recent decision (on June 23, 2016) to let stand a Texas court's ruling to block President Obama's DAPA program. The racist, anti-immigrant rhetoric of many Republican campaigns alongside the dismantling of what were already piecemeal immigration reforms had raised alarm among immigrant rights advocates, but it still seemed too soon to tell which path the nation would choose in the coming months.

Given the salience of these issues, it was not long after I began speaking with Sofía that our conversation turned to the recent DAPA decision and the upcoming presidential elections. Sofía described the previous month's Supreme Court decision as "very disappointing." She told me that the organization's clients—many of whom were hoping to benefit from DAPA—were surprisingly disengaged from the Supreme Court debate. Sofía supposed that this was because once Texas blocked the program, clients believed that the outcome was a foregone conclusion. And even though Sofía also believed that things would turn out this way, as a legal services coordinator she had to at least try to persuade people to get their paperwork ready in case the decision went in their favor. Such paperwork would have involved providing numerous documents to federal agencies, which would of course alert the government to her clients' currently unauthorized presence in the country, in hopes that this risk would be worthwhile by securing them a deferred action status.

Sofía described this as an uphill battle. "People were just very—they were just not that confident that they were gonna get the ability to get some document, work permit," she remarked to me in English. "It's basically a work permit," Sofía added acerbically. "They're not even gonna [get] a path to citizenship, it's just a work document. . . . They don't trust the current political environment. They don't trust Congress. They don't trust political, you know, Washington. So they feel that there's absolutely no reason why they will get a work permit. And they just feel like they lost this a long time ago." Sofía tried to stay positive and keep raising awareness in case things turned around, but she found the community's response discouraging. "You can see from their faces that [they] just don't seem that confident that something positive is going to happen when it comes to immigration."

Sofía understood this cynicism well because, as a highly educated immigrant who was unable to practice her profession in the United States, she also felt excluded. "But it's different," she said. "I'm in a much [more] privileged position myself." I asked Sofía how long she had felt this sort of exclusionary rhetoric or sentiment that she was describing in the American political system. "I think everyone's got a lot worse right now," Sofía replied. "It's a lot worse, and I think the people come in here, and they voice it." "What are they saying?" I asked. "Well," she replied, "they talk about Donald Trump. It's like, 'Oh my God, *imagínese si gane este señor*. What if this guy wins?' But the fact is, they almost think that it could happen, which is kind of funny. Well, no, not funny, it's actually kind of tragic. But they do think that—they feel that things are not gonna change, or that they're gonna get worse. And imagine if this person wins . . . ?" The national conversation perplexed Sofía because she felt that at the local and county level, immigrant integration policies were heading in a positive direction. She explained that the county had made great strides in recent years toward greater tolerance and inclusion of immigrants, undocumented and documented alike. Even though immigrant clients were wary of the federal government, she said she believed that local and county leaders were committed to helping the immigrant community, "particularly in health."

I asked Sofía what she thought had brought about this turn toward inclusion. "I would like to say that it's because maybe there's more political, maybe there's more community engagement," she began.

Maybe people realize that we are not the enemy? I don't know, maybe the county is becoming much more diversified. . . . Political will is changing. We're in a very liberal county. The thing is, it's liberal, but I think when it comes to immigration there's a little bit of a . . . I don't know, it's kind of a weird . . . I see more tolerance than not, from local authorities. Now the national conversation is very different, but the local authorities . . . I think [they're] actually much more willing to engage undocumented [immigrants] in part of the conversation. Particularly from health care.

Sofía's ambivalence over the state of the national debate tempered her reflections on the local situation. Like others, she expressed a sense that there was some political will to back "liberal" policies—albeit slowly and haltingly—and most of all in the sphere of health care.

Sofía explained that the county community clinics served a lot of the undocumented immigrants in the area, as did her organization, so there were many services available for immigrant individuals and families at the local level. Even though Sofía expressed frustration over local organizations' and agencies' inability to address barriers to legal status in the comprehensive way that national immigration reform might do—"that we cannot change," she said—she and her colleagues did their best to maximize local political will and resource support for the communities they served. "That's our message," Sofía asserted, "because we think that whether they're undocumented or not, we can help them with other tools and resources so that they can have access to a better quality of life." Short of structural change, Sofía's organization focused on how to help the acute and ongoing needs of clients who were working multiple low-wage jobs to survive. "There's just institutional issues that have to do with inequality, all sorts of problems that we don't have control over," she added, "that makes for clients being in a very vulnerable position."

In this context, Sofía expressed that it made sense that clients were distrustful of the political system. She told me that clients were not surprised by Trump's ascension but felt disheartened that things might go from bad to worse. "They're already pretty bad," Sofía explained, "because . . . there's not immigration reform. . . . After eight years [under President Obama], there's still no immigration reform." Community-centered organizations like the clinic and Sofía's organization worked closely with one another and with local government agencies to maximize political will to benefit their clients, but they acknowledged those clients' wariness to trust the broader political context itself. Many of the workers were themselves part of the community, Latinx immigrants and/or members of immigrant families who had to have enough faith in the process to mobilize resources while also remaining cognizant of the well-founded lack of trust many clients had beyond the clinic or community organization's walls.

Graciela, a Latina immigrant from South America who worked at the family services organization just blocks from Sofía, also spoke about the disillusionment that came about after the DAPA ruling and the grow-ing sense of anxiety that campaign rhetoric had lately triggered. She ex-plained to me that she had been a *promotora* getting out the word about DACA and DAPA and helping people enroll, but the Supreme Court's decision discouraged everyone:

> Those dreams that the community [had], in this moment, now that there are so many political changes, and they said, "No, we're back . . . at zero. What's going to happen?" That dream, or that window, has closed for now. Right now, specifically the desire to continue advocating, like there's a disappointment right now that there isn't that spirit of, "We have to continue and fight for a reform."

When I met Graciela in the summer of 2016, she believed that whether they were able to rekindle any momentum toward reform de-pended largely on who won the presidency—something that was not up to undocumented immigrants to decide. Graciela had become a US citizen through marriage, and she was able to vote, but she remembered well the frustration she felt when she could not. Speaking of herself and the Latinx community in the collective first person (in Spanish), she said, "The fact that we can't vote, we feel like we don't have a voice, and it's more difficult."

Graciela continued to reflect how the devolving national situation affected both collective and individual anxieties and contributed to a growing sense of insecurity: "Yes, we chat, or yes, it feels like if this per-son [Trump] will be president, definitively we will not have opportuni-ties. And because of all the racist commentaries that have happened. The community does feel like there could be something, even something really big, but we don't know what it is. Many people say, '*Híjole*, maybe now I'm going to have to go back to my country, or I don't know what will happen.'" This sense of uncertainty had led Graciela's organization to launch a nonpartisan get-out-the-vote campaign in the local Latinx community, where she and her colleagues helped register eligible voters and told them, "Our voice counts." She expressed hope that she could make a difference at the local level, which she felt was relatively more welcoming than the reactionary anti-immigrant rhetoric she observed on national news: "What I like is that for all that aggression, or for all that's happening and the attacks against whichever immigrant community [in other parts of the country], in this area there's more support, and it's a more liberal area."

Graciela's comment highlighted the complex interplay of immigration federalism, structural racism, and political ambivalence that she observed as both a member of an antagonized community and a leader within that community who perceived opportunities for resisting rising medical legal violence. As a naturalized US citizen advocating on behalf of an immigrant community that ran the gamut of legal statuses, she clearly conveyed that the degree to which someone could trust government and government-adjacent institutions (like the clinic) largely depended on their perception of federal immigration priorities. While she understood the looming sense of unease that national anti-immigrant politics portended, Graciela also looked to local politics and broader political engagement to buffer those risks. As the years passed, however, those locally progressive politics also became a lightning rod for federal retaliation and potential surveillance that extended medical legal violence into unlikely spaces.

Countering Fears and Optimizing Inclusion

Graciela's community organizing experience, which preceded her recent involvement in the voter awareness campaign, shaped her optimistic perspective on local immigrant incorporation prior to the 2016 election. In addition to her *promotora* work around DACA and DAPA, she also worked closely with clinics to coordinate health care coverage for her community. She described how representatives from community and government agencies around the county—including Medicaid—met once a month to share information and updates and gather small emergency funds for community members. Graciela emphasized that the community organizations almost always took the lead in these encounters. Through these meetings, Graciela was able to get to know Medicaid eligibility workers in person and get their direct contact information. Graciela stressed that having those personal connections gave her and her colleagues the confidence to reach out personally to resolve clients' issues.

Graciela found these connections especially helpful when it came to Medicaid because clients often came to her in distress after receiving emergency room or hospital bills that they were unable to pay. She frequently stepped in to help clients enroll in or renew Medicaid coverage, whether Emergency or state-funded full scope, by helping them communicate with government agencies and explain and complete all the necessary paperwork. Her organization played a key role in getting undocumented children enrolled in Medicaid when the state made it available to them, and she also helped eligible parents and other adults enroll in Emergency Medicaid.

When I asked Graciela to describe her experience enrolling undocumented adults in Medicaid, her response echoed Elizabeth's conversation with Maribel that I recounted in the book's introduction. Her primary concern had been that connecting noncitizens with government services might expose them to unwanted surveillance and punishment. "In the beginning I was worried because I wasn't sure about whether it was something that might harm someone, because it had to be reviewed [by a government agency] and all that," she recalled. "I recommend that they go and talk to their lawyer because I don't want it to later harm them in their application for services." Over time, Graciela had observed that patients benefited from Medicaid without suffering negative immigration consequences, and she felt more confident about the relationships community organizations like hers had cultivated with local government agencies.

Other workers I spoke with similarly highlighted the benefits of these county coalitions and described how the information they shared helped alleviate the anxieties of prospective enrollees who feared that receiving medical benefits might draw unwanted attention from immigration enforcement agents. One strategy that clinic workers used to counter patients' anxieties was to present documents that explicitly defined protections on medical information under US law and demarcated the boundaries between health care and immigration enforcement. "When [federal agencies] make a decision, it always comes in writing," clinic worker Olivia told me in November 2015. Olivia, a Latina immigrant originally from South America, emphasized that it was important for patients to see these explicit reassurances firsthand. In addition to information about HIPAA, Olivia also showed hesitant patients a printout of a 2013 memo from ICE stating that seeking health care would not make patients targets of immigration enforcement. She handed me the memo so I could see for myself. Scanning the document, I read the following lines: "ICE does not use information about such individuals or members of their household that is obtained for purposes of determining eligibility for such coverage as the basis for pursuing a civil immigration enforcement action against such individuals or members of their household."

These kinds of documents helped counteract patients' fears while also clarifying some of the confusion that clinic workers experienced based on mixed messaging at the county level. Beatriz, a community organization leader I spoke with in November 2015, described a meeting she attended with county representatives that tried to correct this messaging, particularly around state-funded Medicaid eligibility for undocumented immigrants. Some of the meeting attendees did not even know that state-funded Medicaid was an option for undocumented or recently arrived immigrants, and someone asked whether they had to send the paperwork to immigration agencies. Beatriz recounted one of the agency representative's responses, saying, "They said to us that they *keep* the information *in case* the Department of Immigration contacts the county. They're regulated to do that, but that they themselves don't send out the [undocumented immigrants'] applications to the Department of Immigration on an ongoing basis. They only keep record of it, unless the Department of Immigration wants to know, then they have the information."

Olivia apparently received a similar message. She explained that when undocumented and liminally legal patients applied for Medicaid, there was some mechanism in place for verifying a patient's immigration status through a shared database, but that it would be used only for administrative processing rather than immigration enforcement. Knowing this helped allay her own fears of triggering immigrant surveillance and punishment through patients' health care utilization. "We know exactly what they're doing," she explained to me in an interview in November 2015. "They're just checking your immigration status against the database they have access to," she added, "and I don't know if it's the immigration's database, I don't know exactly what it is, but they're just checking that against it and if it doesn't match, they will let you know it doesn't match." County Medicaid eligibility workers had told Olivia that patients' administrative records stayed on a shelf in their office, and once they had made an eligibility determination, the files stayed put.[1] Olivia therefore trusted that undocumented and liminally legal immigrant patients at her clinic would not be at risk of immigration consequences for seeking health care through Medicaid.

Beatriz was more guarded. Even though county administrators had communicated a similar message—that patients' records were not actively sent to immigration agencies but kept on file for administrative purposes—not everyone seemed to be on the same page with the messaging. She heard through the grapevine that some eligibility workers were warning clients that they had to report their applications to immigration agencies, which caused a cascade of confusion and distrust:

> Then, that becomes a fear factor . . . if you hear from a trusted community member that this is available for you, that these are the possibilities of getting care, and at that time, knowing that this is how your application is kept. Then, you're hearing from an eligibility worker that your information may be reported to Immigration. Then, the fear factor sets in. Then, they choose to opt out, or they go back to the community advocate or community liaison to figure out, "I don't want to do this. I don't know." Then, there's an uncertainty. I think with all of this misinformation in the community, it causes a lot of stress.

Like Beatriz, Sofía described "a lot of myths and misinformation around immigration, tons" that had been circulating in the county for many years. She tried to counteract such rumors by focusing on making those who were eligible for benefits aware of their eligibility and providing written guidelines that patients could review to make their own decision. "I actually have to kind of convince them to get these benefits, because they don't want to get it," she explained. "They are afraid that if they get our benefits, they will lose immigration status. It's like, that does not affect your status, don't worry, if you qualify for it, you qualify for it. But they are afraid."

Sofía added that, with the "public charge" rule (as it existed in 2016), there was some truth to the rumors, but the rule did not apply to most of their clients who were undocumented or had some kind of liminal legal status, like a U visa or TPS. As described earlier, "public charge" refers to criteria meant to determine whether an immigrant should be deemed "inadmissible" to the United States based on their supposed likelihood of becoming overly reliant on public benefits. While I spoke with Sofía in 2016, two years before the Trump administration would officially propose expanding the forms of public assistance that would count toward the public charge inadmissibility criteria (including certain health care, housing, or nutrition assistance benefits), the existing rule already generated substantial anxieties among clients.[2] To counter these anxieties, especially when it came to enrolling eligible clients in state-funded Medicaid, Sofía and other community workers throughout the county focused on guiding eligible clients to reliable information and the administrative support they needed should they choose to enroll.

While I revisit the theme of misinformation in more detail in chapter 5, it is worth noting here that even in a progressive state prior to the 2016 election, noncitizen patients expressed enough concern over government surveillance in health care settings that clinic and community workers had to rely on written policies and legal guidance from experts to reassure patients of their security. Clinic and community workers had to balance on a bureaucratic tightrope when navigating patients through the medical legal violence of federal structures that especially constrained undocumented, liminally legal, and recently arrived lawful residents' health chances while engaging more inclusive state-level policies to meet their needs. This delicate balancing act underscores how immigration federalism had become increasingly institutionalized in local safety net health care systems in recent years, and the looming sense of surveillance presaged the possibility of retaliatory medical legal violence under the Trump administration.

Citizenship Exclusions and the Long Road to Care

As my conversations with clinic workers before the 2016 election suggested, exclusionary noncitizen health and welfare policies had created entrenched barriers that local safety net institutions struggled against with varying degrees of success well before the Trump administration began. Despite the rising explicitness of anti-immigrant sentiment, these workers were often able to persuade patients to apply for government services when the health risk seemed to outweigh the potential for immigrant surveillance and punishment. Clinic attendee Alicia shed light on this process from a patient's perspective, describing the multiyear health saga that had first brought her to the clinic. Alicia had started coming to the community clinic a few years before we met for an interview in April 2017. She had been dealing with heavy, ongoing vaginal bleeding, and her friends told her to go to the clinic for help. "Look," Alicia remembered the doctor telling her after her first exam, "you've got tumors in your uterus, and you need it out, and you need to have a health plan [insurance] to do so." But Alicia did not have insurance, and as a low-income, undocumented immigrant without an emergency medical condition, she did not see how she could qualify for any. "I didn't have any insurance," she continued. "Here in [this county] it's difficult. Here there's nothing, no insurance, no nonprofit [health care organizations]. Here there's nothing. I don't know of anything."

After four years of dealing with bleeding so severe that she was hospitalized for two days and needed a blood transfusion, she was able to get a charity care appointment to see a gynecological surgeon in another county. The specialist agreed that Alicia needed surgery, but her situation was too complicated to manage within the limited parameters of the charity care program. For one thing, Alicia had lupus, so she was a high-risk patient who would need to be admitted for a potentially costly hospitalization as she recovered. For another, there was a chance that Alicia had cancer: "I think it took such a long time because [another doctor she had seen] said, 'Alicia, I'm thinking you also have cancer.' Because I had so, so many problems, you know?"

If Alicia did have cancer, she would require not only a gynecological surgeon but a surgical oncologist to participate in her surgery, and possibly expensive adjuvant treatments like radiation and/or chemotherapy after that. "I came back again," Alicia recalled, "without getting my uterus out. And the doctor [at the clinic] just kept giving me medicines, but I continued to get worse and worse, so much pain." Alicia even considered paying out of pocket for the treatments she needed, but she realized that her limited housekeeper's income would never come close to covering those costs. She had to manage her pain with whatever limited support the clinic could offer, all the while wondering whether she had cancer and how she would pay. "And I spent some four years without leaving the clinic," she said of this stalemate. "I think it's time, a lot of lost time."

Eventually Olivia, the clinic worker who showed me the 2013 ICE memo, reached out to Alicia and told her that she was going to try to help her "enter an immigration process" to qualify her for medical coverage and find someone to do her surgery. Alicia did not seem to know the details of this "immigration process," but she trusted Olivia and the clinic and was willing to do whatever they suggested to improve her health. They told Alicia that a doctor at a private hospital in the county was willing to do the surgery, but she would have to have some kind of medical coverage to take advantage of it. "The doctor said she would only do [the surgery] if it was with insurance, but I had no way [to get it]," she explained. "After two months had passed, Olivia called me and said, 'Alicia, bring your documents and we'll figure it out.' Then, Olivia got that emergency [state-funded Medicaid] insurance together with Immigration, and I was able to do it. But it was so difficult. It was like a process of four or five years just trying. . . . Yeah, since 2010 when I started. . . . And I was only able to do that surgery last year [in 2016]." Alicia was relieved to get the surgery and discover that she did not have cancer after all. She was also grateful to have the state-funded Medicaid that Olivia helped facilitate because she ended up back at the hospital twice during recovery for postoperative complications.

Notwithstanding her gratitude for clinic workers' support in eventually getting the treatment she needed, Alicia expressed deep frustration over the ways that her legal status constrained her options and those of the clinic workers who were trying to help her. She was willing to provide extensive immigration documentation because she trusted Olivia and saw no other way to get care, but she deeply resented having to do so. "There's no plan, no project to have insurance," she asserted bleakly. "If you go to [the Medicaid office], and you don't have papers, there's no way you can get anything. There's no way, if you're not a citizen, there's no way. And everyone who is not a citizen [and] who has all these problems doesn't have a way. There's a place for you when you're a citizen. You can go, or [Medicaid] pays, or the government pays for you, but for [undocumented] people—like a bunch of people—it doesn't work."

Even though Alicia eventually did find a way, through Olivia facilitating her enrollment in state-funded Medicaid, it was by no means a comprehensive solution. Alicia acknowledged that when it was a life-or-death situation, the hospitals had to help everyone, but sometimes it took too long. Before getting her treatment, Alicia described frequently going to the emergency room and getting a one-off treatment for pain without addressing the underlying issue and being sent back to the community clinics: "The [ER] doctor says, 'Look, go to the clinic doctor.' But the [clinic] doctor doesn't know what to do either. If you need a longer-term treatment, a more serious treatment, there's no way. . . . It's difficult. I think even [the doctors] don't know what to do. They don't have a direction to follow. . . . Even if the doctors put their effort into it, even though they are hardworking. They want to help you, they want to do it, but I think they all have a limit."

As Graciela, Beatriz, and Olivia described, frontline workers at the community clinic and affiliated community organizations worked closely with government agencies to overcome these limits and provide direction for patients and providers who were trying to negotiate narrow spaces of noncitizen eligibility. They worked in tandem with regional clinics and legal advisors to train frontline county Medicaid workers to understand noncitizens' statewide benefits eligibility. In cases like Alicia's, they often uncovered pathways to care that were unfamiliar to immigrant patients, their doctors, and Medicaid workers alike. By working closely with legal experts and regional clinic administrators, frontline workers optimized existing laws to circumvent the medical legal violence that excluded noncitizen patients from care. In doing so, they maximized the inclusivity of state-level policies despite the increasingly punitive turn in federal immigration policies and in resistance to growing anti-immigrant rhetoric on the national stage.

The workers I spoke with knew that they had to strike a delicate balance between taking advantage of state-level inclusions and remaining beholden to federal immigration and health policies. Olivia, emphasizing that this balance was highly contingent, said, "As we know, policy changes all the time. Right now, we know that if we help you fill out [comprehensive Medicaid applications] . . . we know that nothing bad is going is going to happen." "But," she added, eerily foreshadowing the direction the nation would take in the years ahead, "we don't know what could happen five years from now." As anti-immigrant rhetoric accelerated during the 2016 presidential campaigns, and as Graciela's and Sofía's reflections from the summer of 2016 attested to, community workers increasingly began to share patients' concerns that seeking health care might put noncitizen patients in harm's way by making clinics potential sites of the very violence they sought to deflect. There was a vague yet growing sense that something bad might indeed happen, and the disciplining force of this perception—of a threat that loomed but had not yet materialized—cast a powerful panoptic effect over the clinic.[3]

"What will I do to survive?"

Like patient Alicia, fifty-eight-year-old Rodrigo was counting on the clinic to see him through the many challenges he faced as a noncitizen patient awaiting intensive medical care—in this case, a liver transplant. Rodrigo had migrated to the United States from Central America when he was forty-two years old, and he had been coming to the same community clinic during all those years for primary care and to manage a thyroid condition. Clinic worker Elizabeth had put me in touch with Rodrigo in June 2017, and he had been working closely with her to manage his recent health complications. He described himself as a previously active person who enjoyed playing soccer and who worked hard at a variety of jobs—including as an agricultural machinist in his country of origin and a carpenter, sanitation worker, and gardener in the United States. Complications following a gallbladder surgery left Rodrigo with serious liver damage, however, and he was clearly distressed by this turn of events. When I met him at the clinic, he was biding his time and receiving primary care and social support care while awaiting a liver transplant at a large academic medical center in a nearby county.

Rodrigo explained that when he first came to the United States, he focused on finding work, which he said was difficult because the 9/11 attacks happened around the same time that he arrived in the country. He did not have a photo ID at the time, which complicated his ability to drive, work, and enroll in health care coverage, but his wife managed to enroll him in Emergency Medicaid all the same. Rodrigo's lack of documents was not an insurmountable challenge at first, but he explained that security and documentation requirements became more stringent in the years following 9/11. Indeed, Rodrigo drew a direct line between the rise of the post-9/11 surveillance state and more rigorous local documentation requirements.

During our conversation, Rodrigo casually mentioned a traffic stop wherein the police took his car and told him he would have to go to court. (This apparently happened during the early days of his arrival in the United States, when he still did not have a driver's license or ID.) Without mentioning any notion of arrest or deportation (unlike people I spoke with in the red and purple states), he described a low-security, low-key experience at the municipal courthouse where he went to resolve the traffic issue. Those were bygone days, however, and he connected more recent universal security measures—having to take off one's shoes, belt, rings, and other objects, and pass through a metal detector—with clinic recordkeeping. "It's because of that [9/11] that in the clinics, in the hospitals, they also ask for your photo identification," he asserted, referring directly to the toppling of the World Trade Center. The world was changing as national security interests justified an expanded surveillance state, and Rodrigo's observations emphasized how its dragnet zeroed in on Latinx immigrants.

Rodrigo explained that he was fortunate to have gotten Emergency Medicaid without these documents during the early window before government agencies required them. He also had a driver's license now, although it was unclear whether that was because he adjusted his legal status or because he was able to benefit from a recent state law that enabled undocumented immigrants to get a driver's license without proof of legal residence. Without asking him to disclose his legal status, I assumed the latter, because he explained that his rapidly declining health had made him eligible for full-scope, state-funded Medicaid. (If he were legally present, given his long tenure in the United States, he would have been eligible for Medicaid regardless of his health status.) In contrast to the situations of other gravely ill immigrants whose cases I describe in other chapters, the fact that Rodrigo resided in a blue state with expansive immigrant health coverage meant he could access the comprehensive medical treatments he needed to survive.

Even so, like others I spoke with across the three sites, Rodrigo worried about the risk of government surveillance and that he would have to pay back whatever support he received from government agencies. Clinic workers had helped coordinate Rodrigo's medical care across institutions, and they also informed him that he could qualify for disability income because he was unable to work as he once had. (If Rodrigo were indeed undocumented at the time of the interview, he could have still qualified for state disability benefits.) Elizabeth told him he could get $340 a month in supplemental income, but even though he was struggling financially, he decided against it. "No," Rodrigo told Elizabeth, "because I might have problems later, and they'll be charging me that money." I asked whether Elizabeth had actually said this might happen, or if it was something he suspected. "I suspect it," Rodrigo replied.

Rodrigo added that he was also reluctant to ask more of a nation that had already given him so much. "For me, I thank God because ultimately this country has helped me a lot," he explained. For years, Rodrigo had been able to work hard, support himself and his family in the United States, and send money back to his family in his country of origin. He added that—unlike some immigrants from his region—he came with the "right mindset" that allowed him to make the most of opportunities here, and he wanted to express his gratitude for those chances rather than be perceived as cheating the system. Like others I spoke with, especially other men, his sense of value was wrapped up in his economic productivity and ability to support his family without help and without being perceived as a burden in his new home country. As it had for others whose stories I tell in other chapters, Rodrigo's physical illness created additional existential and mental health challenges: "One time [a therapist] asked me questions, like if I ever thought about taking my own life, or [if I was] depressed, stressed. I told her yes, because there are times when you say, 'It'd be better for God to take me.' Because it's so much illness and you can't work anymore, you don't have the same agility as always, and the willingness to work. Because I didn't use to be like this."

These anxieties extended to the space where health care and immigration politics met, a topic that was front-and-center when we spoke in June 2017, a few months into the Trump administration. Rodrigo's primary concern was that he believed that the president wanted to cancel Medicaid and make immigrants pay back the services they had received. Indeed, most Republican candidates during the 2016 election campaigned on promises of repealing the Affordable Care Act and implementing hardline immigration enforcement. This worried Rodrigo because he desperately needed the care he received through full-scope Medicaid—even as he rejected other forms of assistance for which he was eligible. On the other hand, Rodrigo approved of the president's promise to deport criminal immigrants, who he felt were putting people like him at risk of losing benefits. He elaborated on his position using the dichotomizing rhetoric of "good" immigrants who came "to work to maintain our families" versus "criminal" immigrants "who are doing bad things." It was a refrain I heard often in conversations with immigrant patients, and Rodrigo stated his position firmly: "I think it's good that they deport them, but that they deport the people who are doing bad things, not because of someone who is doing bad things that someone else gets deported and you leave families destroyed. . . . Imagine that I had kids who were born here, and they deport me just because I'm not born here—what about my kids? Who's going to take care of them? That's a serious problem, that there are homes without fathers, without a mother."

When I asked whether Rodrigo was referring specifically to the county where he lived, he said no. He heard about such situations primarily in another part of the state. Despite this, he felt that it was a rarer situation in the blue state than in other places, and he felt confident that this state would not allow the president to carry out his most punitive health and immigration policies without a fight. "[This state] will not let itself be dominated," Rodrigo asserted. "The president wants to take control of everything, but [our blue state] won't let him, and other states are joining up with [our blue state]." I asked Rodrigo what this might mean for Medicaid, and that confidence seemed to waver. "For my part, there must be a lot of people who are like I am now, who need [Medicaid]. Hopefully it continues." He added that he had expressed this concern to clinic worker Elizabeth and recently asked her, "And if [because of these politics] they cut off my [Medicaid], what will I do to survive?" I asked how Elizabeth responded to these questions. "She says, 'I don't know,'" Rodrigo replied. "'There's nothing I can tell you.'"

Rodrigo's experience highlights several salient issues around the historical contingency of US health and immigration policy, long-looming criminalization and surveillance concerns, and newly emerging anxieties during the Trump administration. His account emphasizes the tensions underlying federalism in multiple spheres of law and how these can intersect as undocumented immigrants go about their daily life. Like others I spoke with in the red and purple states, Rodrigo explained how 9/11 created a surveillance state that complicated undocumented immigrants' ability to engage in everyday spaces of employment, transportation, and health care. Yet, unlike the experiences of undocumented immigrants in other states, Rodrigo's experience suggested a buffering effect as the blue state increasingly expanded noncitizen eligibility for driver's licenses and state-funded health and public benefits access.

Furthermore, while he engaged in many of the same rhetorical strategies that other participants used to convey their relative deservingness—namely, emphasizing his value as a formerly productive economic agent and "good" immigrant, Rodrigo's experience demonstrated some of the benefits of living in a state that resisted teaming up with federal forces to exacerbate his exclusion. Yet even despite the relatively broad inclusions that Rodrigo was eligible for at the state level, he nevertheless avoided some (like disability support) over fears of hidden costs and felt anxiety over others (like Medicaid) that were subject to federal politics that were heading in a decidedly anti-immigrant direction. Rodrigo's case represents a complex, two-decades-deep palimpsest of accelerating legal violence in the post-9/11 era, overlaid by the tempering of increasingly inclusive state-level policies, and later blurred by Trump-era immigration policy and health policy priorities. By the time I spoke with him, about five months into the Trump administration, it seemed unclear—both to Rodrigo and to the clinic workers trying to support him—how those federalism tensions would play out and what it would mean for his life-and-death situation.

Looming Surveillance and Clinic Resistance

The previous examples suggested that a disruption of everyday routines in the supposedly "safe" space of the clinic stoked fear and anxiety at the blue state sites I observed. While this kind of disturbance can create the conditions for collective resistance against actual and perceived threats (Snow et al. 1998; Zepeda-Millán 2017), such resistance may also draw unwanted attention. In the case of the blue state, outspoken state- and local-level resistance to the overt legal violence of the Trump administration drew threats of retaliation from federal agencies. This put immigrant-serving clinics in a difficult position as they balanced immigrant-inclusive practices against the perception that federal agencies—which opposed such practices—were paying greater attention to their work than ever.

In October 2017 I attended a conference where regional clinic leaders met with immigration law experts, advocates, and elected officials to discuss how health care organizations could protect the noncitizen patients and mixed-status families they served as the Trump administration increasingly dismantled health and immigration policies that previously benefited (or at least less actively harmed) them. The sense of urgency was palpable, and the speakers pulled no punches in describing the challenges before them. As various speakers took the stage, one elected state representative greeted the crowd by declaring, "We are at the center of the resistance." Immigration law experts provided updates and explanations of everything from HIPAA, the Fourth Amendment, and sensitive locations memos to the Muslim travel ban, DACA recision, ACA defunding, and the rumored change in the public charge rule.[4] Breakout workshops emphasized that while HIPAA remained the top federal law governing health information, health care workers should regard ICE as a "rogue agency" that would transgress the letter of the law if given the chance. Several emphasized that ICE must have a judicial warrant, not merely an administrative warrant, to seize an individual and/or their health information. This warrant must be signed by an appropriate judge, not simply an immigration official, and health care providers needed to confirm this by referring such warrants to the health institution's lawyers before acquiescing to them.

Because the Trump administration had vowed to increase immigration raids in places with sanctuary policies, which included most of the blue state at the time, much of the day's information focused on how health care centers could be "safer"—if not truly safe—spaces for immigrant clients. Many clinics had already been working with national immigrant advocacy organizations and the state's primary care association to develop standardized practices to protect noncitizen patients without getting clinics into legal trouble. This included designating waiting rooms as "private," where only patients and their immediate family were able to enter, thereby engaging Fourth Amendment warrant criteria, coordinating "Know Your Rights" trainings, developing an online toolkit with resources for providers and administrators, enacting sanctuary policies, and designating clinic personnel as immigration enforcement liaisons. Immigration lawyers also warned providers not to put anything in a patient's medical chart that might implicate them in the "inadmissible" or "deportable" categories of the Immigration and Nationality Act—just in case those records ever did come before a judge or immigration enforcement official. There was a real sense that the federal government would be scrutinizing local immigrant-serving clinics and punishing them—and, more importantly, their patients—for enacting inclusive clinical practices that adhered to state laws and policies.

The daylong, information-packed conference concluded with more calls to action by immigration experts and elected officials. "Despite all the attacks at the federal level," one immigrant rights advocate asserted, "there can be success at the state and local level and at your health care centers. This is such an important time in our country." The following speaker, a local mayor, acknowledged that what was happening now was just the latest moment in a long history of anti-immigrant sentiment and policies in the United States. He knew that vocal resistance to the Trump administration's immigration agenda would attract additional surveillance that could put the state and many of its municipalities in danger of heightened federal immigration enforcement, so it was imperative that they prepare now. The final speaker of the day, a US congressperson, declared, "This is a defining moment in history." "Stay woke," the congressperson urged the audience with a self-deprecating smile, "but also know that what you're doing . . . is the right thing to do. So stay strong, and stay woke."

As I took in the events of the day, I reflected on how the clinic network I had been observing was ahead of the curve in terms of preparing for the federal immigration retaliation that many thought was coming. The preceding months had been tense, and I had noticed—as many did in those days—a definitive change in energy despite an ongoing commitment to promoting the health and well-being of immigrant communities. The days and months immediately following President Trump's inauguration were marked by confusion and concern in the blue state broadly, and this made clinic workers unsure of how to counsel frightened patients. Later experiences in the red and purple states would make me realize how uniquely acute these anxieties were in the blue state, where the threat of surveillance and penalty was both relatively new and more politically explicit. The politics of immigrant incorporation had become a proxy for a larger ideological game of chess happening between the federal government and the blue state, and several participants in other states observed critically that blue state immigrants seemed to have become pawns in this game. While such observations appeared paradoxical at the time—one might expect *less* intensive surveillance, not more, in the blue state—federalist jockeying over immigration and welfare policies turned that dynamic on its head as the Trump administration's agenda came into force of law.

I spoke with Margaret, an oncology social worker whose hospital received referrals from the clinic I was observing, a few weeks after the election. She explained that the moment Trump was elected, undocumented immigrant patients receiving cancer treatment through state-funded Medicaid began calling her to ask whether they were on the government's radar now. Margaret did not know how to respond. "Don't worry until after January 21st [the inauguration]," she told them. "Then worry." Through tears, Margaret explained that no one at her hospital really believed that Trump could win the election, so their care plans assumed ongoing implementation of the ACA and deferred immigration action proposals. They were not prepared for the possibility of dramatic backlash from the federal government, which shook the carefully cultivated mutual trust and confidence in local health care institutions and federal agencies.

In June 2017 Elena, a Latina immigrant from South America and certified enrollment counselor at the clinic, expressed this sense of growing uncertainty as federal immigration priorities changed under the Trump administration. She had become concerned that her enrollment work, guided though it was by caution and robust medical legal partnerships, might now put patients at risk of immigration enforcement: "I would feel terribly bad if some day they start reviewing all these [state-funded Medicaid applications] and then people end up being deported. . . . Social services says that they don't send those documents to Immigration, but honestly, I don't know because I don't work [at Medicaid]. I don't know how things could change and somebody could be purging on those documents and some consequence would come to the patient. That's the part that I don't want to happen to immigrants. That's my concern." Following the election, it became more difficult for clinic workers to know what to tell patients and how to best balance their health and security needs. Even though they implicitly understood that, as Olivia had said, "Policy changes all the time," the sudden threat to two fundamental pillars of their work—health care access and immigrant well-being—was disorienting.

Mateo, a front desk supervisor who had worked at the clinic for about nine years, elaborated on some of this disorientation during an interview in April 2017. He explained that there were a lot of rumors circulating about immigration enforcement in the community, and he and his colleagues tried to reassure the patients that the clinic was a safe place. "Any patient that comes here," Mateo remarked, "we have informed them that they can't detain no one in our clinic unless they have a warrant, I believe. So I try to educate our patients not to stress about situations that they shouldn't be stressing about." He added that the clinic hosted an information session with a lawyer a couple of months after the election to address patients' and providers' questions and offer the most up-to-date and accurate information available. From Mateo's perspective, things were stable but uncertain: "Yeah. I could say yes, there is some uncertainty. They feel like they're living day by day unfortunately. They don't know if they can be taken, they can be detained, they're scared for the kids. I actually had a patient come here requesting what would happen if she ever got detained and she wanted someone else to be [the] responsible party for her kid. Parents are worried that if they do get detained, they'll get separated from their kids. Families don't want to get separated."

Mateo added that the clinic was proactively working to reassure patients that it was prepared to protect them and their health. "We're not here to throw anybody to ICE," Mateo asserted. "We want to let people know this is a safety zone here. . . . We have plans what we will do." When I asked Mateo to describe these plans and when they began, he replied that they started a safety protocol shortly after President Trump's inauguration. "When Trump became president and all those bans, . . . all the regulations he's been putting out there," he explained, referring to the Muslim travel ban and immigration enforcement announcements, "we started protocol here just in case it gets out of control out there. We will bring the patients to the back." He described an area with locking doors, which I assumed would have met the Fourth Amendment criteria of a "private" space but, upon further reflection, could have also subjected the clinic to charges of alien harboring.

Mateo also described how, even though he did not want patients to stress, it was hard for his team to stay on top of changing laws as well as how they were being communicated in the media. "It's both [the laws and media]. It's both," he began. "You respond to what media says. You don't know if it's true or not. It's everything. You get influenced by both. The Trump ban situations, he puts 'em out there but they don't get passed. It's nothing to worry about, but he's trying to make something happen, so we'll see what happens." Mateo expressed hope that, even as the president promised to punish immigrant-inclusive jurisdictions by withholding federal funds and increasing raids in those areas, state and local politics might temper these efforts. As a US-born Latino who was raised by an immigrant, Mateo felt confident that his state would resist the chaos. "[Our blue state] is awesome. We're very liberal," he affirmed. "It's very different compared to other states. I watch the media, how it compared to the Midwest and how things are out there. I'm very fortunate to be out here. Everybody else is very fortunate to be out here."

As time passed, clinic workers and patients adjusted to the tense and often contradictory circumstances of existing in opposition to federal priorities within a federalist health and immigration system. The state had been at the vanguard of immigrant inclusion and health care access expansion in recent decades, which made it—for better or worse—a center of gravity in the resistance to accelerating legal violence under the Trump administration. This put FQHCs like the clinic I was observing in a difficult position, a fact Dr. Carrera, the clinic's chief medical officer and member of the local Latinx community, made clear to me in an interview in June 2018. "We receive funding from the federal government," he explained, "so we need to comply with them. But there's also privacy issues that we have to comply with and HIPAA issues we have to comply with." He emphasized the importance of medical legal partnerships in the community and how this had enabled staff training around HIPAA patient privacy guidelines alongside "what we need to do to comply to be in good standing with the feds in terms of ICE agents showing up to a clinic." Like the speakers at the conference I attended in October 2017, Dr. Carrera described the warrant standards necessary for ICE agents to detain a patient in the clinic and how clinics could employ private spaces without becoming accomplices to immigration and/or criminal infractions.

Dr. Carrera contextualized the present situation historically and geographically. He recalled waxing and waning immigration enforcement intensity in the state and local area over the past several presidential administrations and asserted that "history repeats itself." Unfortunately, the history that was repeating itself in the summer of 2018, when family separations at the border were registering public outcry across the nation and the world, was a traumatic one:

> Openly, there's another level of acceptance or tolerance for speaking badly of other individuals that don't look like you, which is more than it's been in a long time. During the previous [Obama] administration, you know, it was a little bit more subdued in terms of how people addressed one another and how people accept differences. And now it's open, it's open on the media for folks to come out and picket and, you know, wear KKK kind of outfits and talk about racism just openly, and it's a little bit different than it's been in the past. It hasn't changed, it's always been underlying, but now it's okay to say bad things about different people whether they're gay or Black or Brown or Asian or white. . . . You know, so folks are a little bit more concerned, I think, about their well-being and their safety just generally.

This concern translated into people avoiding services the clinic might have persuaded them to accept in the past unless it was an immediate life-and-death situation. Dr. Carrera cited the rumored change in the public charge rule (which the Trump administration would formally announce a few months later) as well as the family separations drama as factors that were impeding patients from seeking care, and clinic workers from being able to provide that care. Unless it were an immediately "life-threatening situation," he explained, it seemed to him like patients now saw services like preventive care or vaccinations as not worth the risk.

As a physician, Dr. Carrera said that this kind of situation made it hard to sleep at night. "'Cause we're lifeguards," he remarked, "and we're supposed to help somebody get to some place where they can get treated. And so when people don't wanna fill out [state Medicaid] paperwork, and they'd rather either go back to their country or just ignore it, that's, you know, pretty difficult for folks." Dr. Carrera also emphasized that community health centers "are made up of folks who live in the community"—including employees with DACA status and members of noncitizen and mixed-status families. With DACA in legal limbo and the spectacle of family separation at the border, anxiety permeated the clinic, even while they tried to maintain a sense of safety and stability.

Given how media attention around the family separations drama had apparently made its way into local communities with a relatively chilling effect on immigrants seeking health care, Dr. Carrera asked me to suspend patient interviews. While he could not yet make any statements about patient attendance numbers, fear and mistrust suffused the atmosphere in an almost palpable way. Dr. Carrera expressed concern that having any outsiders in the clinic might undermine the trust they were trying to maintain despite the chaos at the border and the Trump administration's promises of immigration raids in a state that had become "the center of the resistance." I turned my attention instead to clinic workers' perspectives and the fieldwork and interviews I was doing elsewhere.

I met with Olivia again in June 2018, almost three years after our initial interview, to talk about these changes in more detail. We met at a restaurant near the clinic, and while we had spoken mostly in English during our first interview, Olivia was wary of being overheard this time and chose to use her native language instead. Rumors of public charge rule changes collided with the family separations spectacle to undercut their own confidence and that of their patients because it was so hard to know what might happen:

> We keep trying, but it's more difficult now because we aren't confident. We don't have a—our message is not clear. . . . Because [before] we had a clear message, and we were *confident*, and we knew exactly what could and could not happen with a patient. Even so comfortable that we would say, like, "If anything happens, call us because we're behind you and we'll go"—we were real advocates. And now it's not that we aren't, but we don't know. . . . But with all that work that we do in community clinics, people come to us—why? Because they have a *trust*, we already have a *relationship* that we built, there's already that trust that was there. Now it's not that they don't trust us, but since we're not confident, like, we're—it's difficult.[5]

Olivia's halting reflections emphasized that the lack of information the clinics could rely on was now combined with the generalized sense of uncertainty facing immigrant communities as the Trump administration cemented many of its policy positions.

Back in 2015, Olivia had told me that the clinics worked so closely with lawyers and government benefits agencies that they trusted that immigration information would be used only for benefits eligibility determinations and not for enforcement activities. She reiterated this point in 2018, adding that these records were "view only" and were used only to cross-check the applicant's immigration status with the benefits eligibility categories in the application forms. Knowing this had given her team the confidence to inform patients that their paperwork would be reviewed only at the county office and would stay on a shelf. "The risk was practically zero," she emphasized, "because we knew exactly where the application went." Unfortunately, while the workflow had not changed in recent months, the possibilities of who might review the files may have altered:

> Today we know where [the application] goes, it goes to the same place, but these days we don't know because anyone could show up there and ask to see those [state Medicaid] forms and ask to see the information. It can change their workflow and make them send that to the state, make them send it to—I don't know. Anything could happen. Before, we could say, "Look, we've already helped lots of people; nothing's ever happened to anyone. We know where the forms go, we know the forms don't go anywhere." So when we gave that certainty, added with the trust that people already had in working with us, we didn't have—it was really easy. Now when we speak, we say that we don't know, that we can't guarantee anything. That is the message: we can't guarantee anything at the moment.

Olivia's comments revealed how US health and immigration federalism could work for or against community clinics like hers that were committed to safeguarding the health and safety of the patients who trusted them with their care. She expressed extreme frustration that many of the meetings they had at the county now were about immigration enforcement rather than health care per se because the generalized panic made it hard for them to do their jobs and allay the anxiety in the communities they served. On top of all the stress they normally had as essential safety net workers trying to address patients' health, nutrition, housing, and financial crises, they now had to contend with the media spectacle of immigration chaos and the fear it generated among patients and clinic workers alike.

Olivia described spending valuable time they could have used to discuss concrete health administration updates to review clinic safety plans in case ICE showed up on site. "That created so much anxiety in everyone," she recalled, as they collectively envisioned how medical assistants and dental assistants would have to call everyone back into exam rooms quickly and empty the waiting room with ICE hovering over them. "But then, everyone had questions," Olivia continued. "What if they want to see, if they ask to see medical records?" they asked. "And our own staff, too?"—referring to the many immigrants employed at the clinics. "We spent a whole meeting talking about immigration things," Olivia remarked heatedly, "and it created that anxiety in everyone. I was really angry that day, you know?" Olivia and her colleagues had a million things to do, and now the possibility of immigration enforcement on site was taking up all this energy and time Olivia felt they could better use focusing on direct patient care.

In the community, meanwhile, people had been dealing with such threats on and off for years, but the Trump administration had rekindled that anxiety in new ways. Alicia, the patient who had eventually received a hysterectomy through state-funded Medicaid, told me that even though immigration raids had been a perpetual threat in the community, people were afraid now in new ways. "Now we've lost hope with that president [Trump]," she explained. "He doesn't like immigrants. He already said so. Well, at least he's frank about it." Alicia emphasized that immigrants' health would certainly not be a priority now. "Here, I don't think there will be anything good in terms of health for immigrants, no," she remarked seriously. "I don't think so, no." Now, between the news they saw on TV and immigration attorneys telling everyone not to open the door if ICE came knocking, Alicia explained that everyone was stressed out and could not believe that their health would be a priority anymore.

Just as Olivia and Dr. Carrera worried about the effects of the escalating immigration chaos on clinic patients, patients like Alicia expressed concern about immigration enforcement in the community. As news spread that then attorney general Jeff Sessions had begun ordering the reopening of administratively closed immigration cases, clinic pediatrician Dr. Green told me in July 2018 that several of her patients who "really thought their immigration stuff was behind them" were now panicking at the very real prospect of immediate family separation. It was hard for Dr. Green to assess how much of this "sense of desperation" was just because of "people absorbing the overall kind of feelings around immigration, or whether their experience is really different." And the anxiety and uncertainty surrounding immigration issues were not limited to the patients, but—as Dr. Green explained—were also hard to manage for the clinic workers. "It's disorienting and overwhelming, the amount of stuff that's being reversed by this administration," she remarked, considering the changing dynamics, "things that we've taken for granted and protections we've taken for granted."

Conclusion

US health care and immigration federalism enabled progressive states to carry out expansive, immigrant-inclusive social programs in the first decades of the twenty-first century in ways that tempered increasingly anti-immigrant trends at the federal level over preceding and concurrent decades. The blue state where I conducted research had taken advantage of ACA resources, paired with relatively robust state funding and sanctuary movements, to blunt some of the legal violence that targeted immigrants and hampered their health chances. Yet that same inclusiveness created a hazard for noncitizen patients and immigrant-serving institutions as federal policy priorities sharpened their punitive turn under the Trump administration. This resulted in medical legal violence as clinics became a potential site for immigration surveillance and enforcement. Even though no one I spoke with actually experienced the physical presence of immigration agents within the health care space—unlike the red and purple states I describe in other chapters—the mere threat of it had a disciplining effect on patients and clinic workers alike.

While federal law already excluded many undocumented, liminally legal, and recently arrived immigrants from health and other social benefits in ways that progressive jurisdictions often struggled to overcome, the Trump administration's health and immigration policies significantly exacerbated these challenges. Prior to the 2016 election, community organizations and government agencies worked closely and established mutual trust that clinic workers could transfer to patients to allay some of their concerns. They could also counter myths and misinformation that might discourage patients from seeking the care they needed. As the Trump administration touted a more militant immigration enforcement regime, however—and as the spectacle of this regime played out discursively and visually in news and social media—it became harder for people to separate fact from fearful fiction. It shook the faith clinics had in themselves and their ability to convert that faith into confident, care-centered messaging for their immigrant patients, thereby expanding medical legal violence into spaces that once firmly resisted it.

What makes medical legal violence so insidious is that ICE agents never had to physically enter clinics to shake this confidence or convey that their everyday routines might become biopolitical surveillance tools for an increasingly panoptic administration. The Trump administration managed to extend the same legal violence that has increasingly criminalized Latinx noncitizens and mixed-status families in other everyday spaces for decades into the clinic while also targeting the people who provide their care and enrolling them in the biopolitical surveillance regime. This medical legal violence harms Latinx noncitizens' health chances while threatening the efforts of those who aim to counter that violence in their community-centered work. The Trump administration did not create all these laws, but it succeeded at reinterpreting many existing laws to maximize the impact of their legal violence and subject clinics and their noncitizen patients to a coordinated strategy of biopolitical control. The resulting anxiety and confusion effectively eroded some of the trust that had previously enabled more inclusive practices to flourish and raised questions about how clinics should best resist this violence and restore faith in their capacity to shield those they served from its danger. In the following chapter, I pick up this story in a purple state that shares some characteristics with both the blue- and red state sites while still emerging as a relatively new immigrant destination in the US South. This nuanced lens underscores the widespread nature of medical legal violence in the contemporary United States while highlighting its dangers for noncitizen patients, clinic workers, and clinical institutions.

4

"No Safe Zones"

Criminalizing Patients and Providers in the Nuevo South

Rain clouds gathered as I drove down the empty highway at dawn on a bleary Saturday in January 2020. I was running late as I turned off the highway and followed a two-lane road onto the main drag of a rural southern town I knew little of, and I resented that the battered pickup truck ahead of me was driving well below the posted speed limit. As my own speed slowed, I took in the archetypal sights of small towns across the United States: several fast-food chain restaurants, a Walmart, and an unassuming courthouse where I was told prominent white supremacists had rallied twenty years before. This last fact might have been remarkable were it not for the rising frequency of such events across the United States at the time of my fieldwork. I suddenly recalled the immense Confederate flags I had seen along the highway driving through this part of the state a few months before and wondered how those who raised the flags were responding to the fifteen-fold increase in Latinx residents of the area over the past three decades. I also wondered who was driving the car ahead of me and whether they might have a good reason—or several—to drive cautiously through this town.

As I left the main street for smaller residential roads on my way to the free clinic I would be observing, I caught sight of the Spanish signage on businesses in the squat buildings that lined the street. Here was a *carnicería*, there an *iglesia pentecostal*. Buildings that had lately been ranch-style homes now housed all manner of small businesses catering to the local Latinx community. Weaving through the final blocks to the modest clinic, which was nestled in the basement of an unassuming brick building, I thought about how different this fieldwork felt from the work I had done in the red and blue states. It had taken me a long time to get to the point where I could actually conduct research at a clinic in the purple state, and as I took stock of where I was and tried to situate myself in time and space, so much felt at once contradictory and familiar. Another election year loomed, and on my way to the clinic I had driven through self-styled progressive cities where residents displayed Black Lives Matter and multilingual "All Are Welcome" yard signs. As the buildings became fewer and farther between, I felt a shift in the overt political climate—not from state to state as I had experienced during the early years of my research, but from county to county.

I had lived in the South briefly as a child and adolescent, but returning as a researcher in 2019 made me see the region with new eyes. I began to realize that, as different as the blue and red state contexts seemed politically, they might have more in common than either did with the purple state. The red and blue states' histories were inseparable from the history of the Latin American countries many of their residents came from and the legacy of migrating borders and people. Their contemporary politics were very much a product of the force of and reaction to Latinx, Chicanx, and immigrant social movements that have existed there for centuries—the blue state arcing toward greater inclusion as the red state enacted more aggressive, racially motivated profiling of Latinx residents.[1] But that was then, and even as I write this book, in the wake of the 2020 elections, such distinctions seem less tenable in the face of formidable grassroots Latinx organizing in formerly red and purple states, forcing the country to reckon with the collective power of their coalition building (see, e.g., Campbell and Vercellone 2020; and Han and McKenna 2021).

As the red and blue state responded variously to the demographic force of Latinx communities, the purple state was still evolving into its role as what some scholars refer to as el Nuevo South (Fink 2003; Mohl 2003; Furuseth and Smith 2006; Marrow 2011; Stuesse and Helton 2013; Deeb-Sossa 2016; Jones 2019). Unlike the blue and red border states where I did fieldwork, the purple state has fewer and relatively more recent historical ties with Mexico and other Latin American countries. Latinx communities in these states have been smaller than in some other regions of the United States (such as border states or the Northeast) but have grown substantially in relation to changing immigration and labor dynamics. In the state where I conducted fieldwork, this demographic shift was due in large part to the influx of Latin American migrants working in agricultural, factory food production (especially poultry and pork processing), and textile industries.

In my efforts to learn more about this distinct statewide immigration context, I attended an immigrant rights talk in the fall of 2019 at one of the state's chief law schools. The two speakers, from the university's law faculty, spoke about immigration as a civil rights issue and emphasized that immigration enforcement did not happen only at the US border. "The border has come to us," one of them said, and she explained that the immigration courts in the state—like those in much of the rest of the US South—had increasingly become "asylum-free" zones. These courts were eagerly emulating (and sometimes surpassing) DHS's hardline stance against asylum applications, and they were also disregarding immigrant protections under the Violence Against Women Act. She added that when the governor and mayors of some cities in the state publicly rejected ICE partnerships in response to increasingly anti-immigrant policies early in the Trump administration, ICE retaliated with immigration raids in February 2019, during which hundreds of people were arrested.

At the same time, as I mentioned in the book's introduction, the state had declined to expand Medicaid under the Affordable Care Act, meaning that it was much more difficult for low-income residents of the state to enroll in health care than in the red and blue states I visited. This also meant that safety net clinics across the state had to make do with fewer resources to serve US citizens and noncitizens alike. The tension between state-level resistance to the accelerating criminalization of immigrants and city- and county-level collaboration with federal immigration enforcement agencies exacerbated this stratified health landscape by politicizing the provision of health care to noncitizens and mixed-status families.

In this chapter, I argue that these tensions resulted in medical legal violence that harmed both noncitizen patients and the clinic workers who provided their health care in ways that uniquely institutionalized that violence in the local safety net. Overlapping political and bureaucratic factors complicated the health chances of rural noncitizens by excluding them from public health benefits and legitimate employment and documentation opportunities. In contrast to the Latinx populations in the blue and red states, the Latinx population in this purple state was relatively small and recently arrived.[2] While this worked against Latinx noncitizen patients—especially those who were ineligible for Medicaid due to their legal status—in that they lacked the co-ethnic political representation that existed in the blue and red state, clinic workers nevertheless found ways to get the relatively small share of such patients the care they needed through public and private financial assistance programs. The acceleration of anti-immigrant policies at the federal, state, and local level complicated this work, however, by forcing biopolitical surveillance into health care spaces and increasing confusion and fear.

Ultimately, despite a remarkable capacity for care in a resource-strapped setting and the will among many clinic workers to provide it, the extent of this criminalizing potential for both patients and providers in the purple state was greater than I had seen in my earlier observations elsewhere. Whereas in the previous two chapters I documented patients' and clinic workers' *fears* that increasingly aggressive immigration enforcement policies might result in their respective criminalization by way of the clinic, it was only in the purple state that I became aware that people had actually been investigated or deported on this basis. Importantly, these direct consequences of medical legal violence happened well before I ever set foot in the state, and yet the chilling effects continued to reverberate through communities for decades. Echoes of this prior violence shaped both the willingness of people to speak with me in the purple state and the limitations of noncitizens' health chances under the continuing presence of anti-immigrant politics.

This chapter thus focuses on two primary axes of medical legal violence, both of which epitomize its criminalizing potential for clinic patients and workers alike in ways that surpassed what I observed in either the red or blue state. The first is how the everyday life of migrants in this region of the country is criminalized in ways that make it hard for them to seek care. The second is how the same legal mechanisms that exclude and penalize immigrants can also criminalize health care workers and force biopolitical surveillance into clinical spaces. Latinx immigrants living in the rural South have faced what Young and Wallace (2019) categorize as an "enhanced deportability" situation, in which these immigrants have been minimally integrated into society through social rights and benefits eligibility but highly criminalized through surveillance and immigration enforcement practices. The red and blue states I described in previous chapters were spaces of high immigrant *integration*, even as they diverged in their relative degrees of immigrant *criminalization* (high in the red state, low in the blue). The purple state, on the other hand, represented the worst of both worlds: low integration and high criminalization. As emerging low-wage industries transformed many rural areas into relatively new migrant destinations in the South, many of the immigrant workers who would become essential to this regional economic development faced the intertwining burdens of economic exploitation and racialized criminalization without the benefit of long-standing co-ethnic support.

As in the other states I visited, most of the patients I spoke with in this part of the country were undocumented, and most had been living in the area for several years, if not decades. When economic opportunities in the agricultural and textile sectors first drew them to the region, employers seemed fairly lax about investigating the validity of people's work authorization. Back then, the state also offered driver's licenses to people without a social security number—a practice that ended through state legislation passed in 2006. This was around the same time that DHS began offering a website called E-Verify, one of many post-9/11 bureaucratic technologies that deepened criminalization in the everyday spaces of undocumented immigrants' lives—in this case by enabling companies to determine whether their employees were eligible to work in the United States. While such apparently race-neutral administrative efforts purported to protect US security interests, in effect they bolstered the ongoing legal violence that disproportionately penalizes Brown and Black non-US citizens.

In the purple state, these policies made it harder for Latinx immigrants to establish a legitimate presence in a space that increasingly greeted them with suspicion and interpersonal and institutionalized discrimination on the basis of their racialized legal status (Asad and Clair 2017; Menjívar 2021). Eliminating undocumented immigrants' ability to legitimately document their identity at work and in the activities of everyday life—such as driving (an essential activity in rural areas) or seeking health care—rendered the (il)legal status of these relative newcomers even more visible than it had been already.[3] Yet, as is true for much of the legal violence enacted on immigrant communities of color, the function of these identification laws was not to remove all unauthorized migrants from the United States. Rather, it was to instill fear and pro-mote the docility and uncontested economic exploitation of the region's newest residents. When this disciplining extended into the clinic and implicated health care workers, it underscored how anti-immigrant laws can become institutionalized in clinical settings and manifest as medi-cal legal violence that harms patients, while forcing providers to choose between being agents or collateral targets of that harm.

Precarity of Undocumented Labor in el Nuevo South

Many scholars have drawn attention to the relationship between agribusiness—particularly meat and poultry processing—and (im)migrant labor in the US South (e.g., Fink 2003; Striffler 2005; Cuadros 2009; Ribas 2015; Stuesse 2016; Gill 2018). While I had been aware of this economic context through the scholarly literature before visiting the region, the importance of the poultry plant in the local Latinx com-munity became starkly apparent the first time I conducted ethnographic observations at the free clinic. It was a rainy Saturday in November 2019, and I had arrived before 8:00 a.m., just as the clinic was opening for the day. The staff kept remarking with dismay about how few patients showed up for their once-monthly clinic and wondered whether patients had mistaken the date. When I asked whether the rain might be a fac-tor, they replied that bad weather would not keep patients away who had been waiting weeks or even months for care. Finally, a clinic vol-unteer named Natalia contacted one of the clinic's regular patients, who informed her that a new *pollera* (poultry plant) was hiring, so everyone was there—early on a Saturday morning—trying to get work.

When I asked Natalia about this during an interview in January 2020, she told me that the revival of the poultry industry in town was com-plicating the clinic's efforts to maintain patients' care. She had noticed more discontinuity in care and a decline in patient attendance at the monthly Saturday clinic:

> We see that something is happening now because we're having a smaller number than we were having, which was about sixty, fifty patients a day. And we've discovered that it's because of *la pollera*. . . . Apparently, a lot of people in need of work have gone to work [at the poultry plant], and

they work on Saturdays, too. Obviously, they don't have permission to leave work to have their health care. Basically, that's really the worry, that they're not taking their medicines, but that's what we've realized. . . . That's what happens. Apparently by not giving them permission [to go to the clinic], obviously people [choose] work. But the worry that we have is this, that the majority of the patients we have, they're patients with high blood pressure, diabetes . . . they need follow-up. And they're patients who come regularly and who we haven't seen in several months.

As I have been recounting throughout this book, undocumented workers often face exploitative and precarious labor conditions that increase their risk of acute injury and chronic illness. While US citizens are also subject to such exploitation, undocumented and liminally legal immigrants have fewer opportunities to seek medical legal protections. Their constructed illegality (De Genova 2002) makes them especially vulnerable to abuse in the workplace and less able to seek support through legal advocacy and health care institutions.[4] In her 2010 book about Latinx migration to North Carolina, Hannah Gill explains that migrant labor has been a boon for pork and poultry industries in the South because they can count on less unionized labor than in the Midwest and Northeast, alongside the willingness of recently arrived immigrants to do fast-paced, low-wage work under conditions that few US-born workers would accept. Gill emphasizes that new immigrants are often willing to do this work and unable to advocate for safer conditions given anti-union laws in these states. Additionally, anthropologists Vanesa Ribas and Angela Stuesse have detailed the experiences of such workers in North Carolina and Mississippi, respectively. Their work contextualizes these labor relations within the specific histories of the US South while vividly revealing the social and bodily harms of these enduring legacies of racialized economic exploitation.

The availability of foreign nationals to work for low wages in dangerous and dehumanizing conditions has been one of the driving forces of Latinx population growth throughout the region, particularly in rural areas. Clinic patient Jorge described these conditions to me during an interview in January 2020. When Jorge, whose story I told in chapter 1, came to the purple state from Central America in 1999, he immediately began working at *la pollera*. He vividly recalled his time on the factory floor under dangerous conditions that he supposed US citizens would never accept. "*La pollera* has a lot of people working there, and more Hispanics are coming because it's the rare American or Black person who would work there," he told me.[5] "Because *la pollera* is one of the hardest jobs that there is, and most people won't [do it]." Jorge disliked working at the poultry plant and described the dangers inherent to working under pressure with sharp instruments. "It's always with knife and scissors," he continued. "Your hands get hurt. But since there's no work, you have to do it. . . . There are a lot of knife injuries." Even though it was not until Jorge left the *pollera* to work as a furniture mover that he suffered a debilitating on-the-job injury, he told me he preferred that literally backbreaking labor to the conditions inside the *pollera*. He explained that working at the poultry plant was heavy, dangerous work in its own way, and that it left him with no transferable skills to seek better employment. "When you learn to do work that's different than the work at *la pollera*, you can go look for another job, . . . they'll pay you better," he said. But if someone only ever worked at *la pollera*, Jorge added, it was difficult to get the skills that employers wanted for better-paying jobs.

In addition to the human cost, overreliance on a single industry in these small towns can have serious consequences for economic stability, such as when companies relocate outside the United States or close, as many businesses did in the wake of the Great Recession. Many of the patients I spoke with had come to the state to work in agriculture and poultry processing but had lost their jobs shortly after those industries evaporated following the 2008 recession. Like Jorge, Alejandra and her husband left their home country of Mexico for the purple state because of the work opportunities at the *pollera*. Alejandra's husband and son both worked there, and Alejandra earned money by providing child-care for some of the factory workers. She recalled that when the poultry plants closed, times got hard for the Latinx community. Much of the local economy was dependent on that industry, so when they closed, Alejandra said that everything collapsed:

Back then there were three *polleras*. There were a lot of Hispanics working [there]. On one occasion they closed those *polleras*, and that's when everyone, not just me, was out of work. The little that we had, we had to sell. We were without work, both the parents and the children, like us. When that *pollera* closed . . . everything closed down for us. Many people went to Mexico, many people went other places. It was chaos for us Hispanics, because closing that plant where there were so many Hispanics working—closing those three plants was when it got really difficult for us. After about two or three years . . . people found their jobs in other places, many people left here, from [this town], and they started to offer work and all that, but now outside [this town].

Alejandra and her husband made ends meet by selling food and looking for work in outlying towns and cities, and they relied heavily on her son-in-law (who did not work at the poultry plant) to pay rent for their trailer and the utilities.[6] When I asked whether they considered leaving when the jobs were gone, Alejandra explained that because they already had their trailer in this town, they were literally "stuck" there.

The undocumented status of many of the workers in town reinforced the precarious economic situation that Natalia, Jorge, and Alejandra described. The poultry industry benefited from the surge of prospective laborers from Latin America, and within a relatively short time, entire families had made lives and homes nearby. Workers' productivity did not translate into enhanced social inclusion more broadly, however. The people I met painted a contradictory picture of rural life in a new migrant destination. Many praised the relative tranquility of life in the countryside and generosity of their new neighbors while at the same time describing experiences of discrimination and legal violence that made them feel not only unwelcome, but insecure. In particular, statewide driver's license laws and local anti-immigrant politics created barriers to equitable social integration that undermined the well-being of noncitizens and mixed-status families, while impeding clinic workers' efforts to provide an equitable standard of care to everyone in the community.

Driving While Brown

After the first poultry plants closed, Alejandra's husband and son eventually found work in other cities, which meant they had to commute—despite not having a driver's license. Perhaps Alejandra's family would have preferred to work closer to home once the new poultry plants opened, but by the time we spoke, they were gone. In the intervening years, Alejandra's son had been deported, and her husband had returned to Mexico to be with him. She explained that her son had been arrested during a traffic stop, during which the police said that his blood alcohol level was "a little high." He got a lawyer, went to court, and was sentenced to community service. When he went to sign his sentencing paperwork, however, immigration enforcement agents were waiting for him. Alejandra said that the court clerk had called the agents to turn over her son and several others who were in court at the time, and they took them all. "Right there, the same person who they go to to sign, they say it was him who called Immigration," she explained, "on various people, there when they went to sign, that's where they'd turn them in. They turned people in."

While Alejandra was the only patient I spoke with who had close experience with the traffic-stop-to-deportation pipeline (Stuesse and Coleman 2014; Armenta 2012, 2017; Smith and Besserer Rayas 2020), several others I met described how the inability to get or renew a driver's license complicated their life. As Provine and Varsanyi (2020, 97) argue, the driver's license "is a state government's most powerful tool in expressing its views about migrants"—a tool that shapes interactions well beyond the road by encompassing myriad civic and commercial spaces where anyone from a retail worker to a bank teller might demand photographic identification. Other scholars (e.g., Rhodes et al. 2015; Hagan, Leal, and Rodríguez 2015; and Philbin et al. 2018) have also drawn connections between restrictive statewide driver's license laws and negative health and well-being consequences for immigrant individuals and communities.

Raquel, a fashionable middle-aged woman who brought up some of these issues when I met her in February 2020, had come to the purple state from Mexico in 1995. She was visiting the clinic to get dental care, and while she waited, she spoke at length about how challenging it was not to have access to a driver's license. She explained that there used to be a lot of checkpoints, every eight days like clockwork, during which the police would target Hispanic drivers. I asked her what would happen if someone tried to go through a checkpoint without a license. "When you go through a checkpoint without a license, they give you a ticket and they don't let you drive anymore, they take you out [of the car] there, or some people have even been arrested." Raquel said that sometimes people got lucky, and that if the cop was a good person, they might let someone with a license come pick up the car on their behalf.

Raquel had been in the purple state long enough to have a driver's license, which she told me she was able to obtain and renew during the Clinton and Bush administrations, respectively. (Even though driver's license eligibility is largely governed at the state level, she anchored the chronology in presidential administrations.) As we spoke, she took out her driver's license from her wallet and showed me that it had expired in 2008, two years after the state began requiring registered drivers to have a social security number. I asked why she still kept the expired license with her, and she explained that she needed it in case she got pulled over by the police. She had been pulled over only once at a checkpoint, and they saw the expired license and gave her a ticket. The fine was $200, Raquel explained, but she ended up paying $500 because she also had to hire a lawyer to avoid going to court herself to pay the ticket. "You better pay the court costs," a friend had warned her. "Pay the lawyer so you don't go to court, where you'll risk them deporting you." Raquel heeded this advice and maintained that, despite the costs, she was glad to have the expired license at all. "When I've presented my license, [the police] just say that I need to go renew it. They give me the ticket, but [say] I need to renew it. If I renew it, I don't have to pay the ticket," she continued, "but since I can't renew it anymore here, it's like . . ." Raquel's thought trailed off, unfinished—a rhetorical shrug at the catch-22 in which she found herself.

María, a middle-aged mother of four originally from Mexico whose cleaning chemical exposure crisis I recounted in chapter 1, described a similar logic behind keeping her expired license. Like Raquel, María also described frequent traffic stops where the police would stop someone "for the tiniest reason" and ask for a license. "Sometimes it's just a checkpoint or something, and they take advantage," she explained. "'There's your ticket.' And so I say—that's why it's good to have a license." Again echoing Raquel's experience, María enumerated the compounding financial costs of such a stop. It was $250 for the expired license but more for having no license at all. Then there were the additional charges for a broken taillight or anything else they could find. "They take advantage of that," Raquel continued. "The sneaky thing is that it ends up costing you almost $500, because if you get a lawyer, it comes out to $400 and change."

Carina, a thirty-four-year-old woman from Mexico who had lived in the United States since she was twelve, was tired of this vicious cycle of surveillance and penalty. I met Carina at the free clinic early on a January morning in 2020. She and three of her young children squeezed into a small exam room that had been converted into temporary storage space so that she could chat with me in semi-privacy. With her daughter falling asleep on her lap as we spoke, Carina told me that she had been coming to the free clinic for about ten months, where she received care for diabetes and thyroid issues. She had recently suffered a frightening—and costly—miscarriage in the county where she lived (adjacent to the one where the free clinic was located), but she made the monthly trip to the free clinic because it did not charge her for care and treated her better than the staff at her local clinics and hospitals.

Carina expressed frustration with several intersecting experiences of being an undocumented, uninsured young Latina struggling to manage chronic illness. She explained that her life would be easier if the state would grant driver's licenses to undocumented residents. "It's the way you live here," she began. "It's a really peaceful place, but at the same time there's a lot of racism, at least in the town where I live. There are a lot of people that are from the countryside and give you bad looks. I understand the situation that because of a few, we all pay, but it would be really good if they could give licenses. . . . Not that they give us any other kind of help, but with a license you can do a lot of things, so many things."

Carina carefully tempered her reflections, suggesting that she did not want a handout and knew that some people in her situation might be abusing the system. The statement "because of a few, we all pay" was a rhetorical negotiation I had heard frequently in some version across all three states among people who were or had been undocumented. It was an explicit acknowledgment that honest, hardworking immigrants were painted with the same brush of criminality as dishonest, delinquent ones. In a testament to the insidious rhetorical power of this symbolic violence, many participants expressed this unambiguous dichotomy between "good" and "bad" immigrants even while describing the many gray areas between them. It meant that even though this dichotomy was anchored in a problematic, racist premise and out of proportion with reality, Carina and others felt this symbolic violence acutely and actively tried to differentiate themselves from the dominant narrative of criminalization.

Carina emphasized how the simple fact of a driver's license could ease her own burdens and keep her from further criminalization:

> Unfortunately, they've given me a ticket four times, and I got a letter from License Services, the DMV, that if they catch me again, they're go- ing to put me in jail. I haven't had a license since 2009. It's been ten years already, that if I've had to take my kids to the doctor, I have to go so carefully, so that I don't crash, so that nothing happens, that the kids are always in their car seats, with the seatbelts, everything to avoid arrest. You're always between a rock and a hard place, what with all you have to do for the kids, taking them to school, to some appointment, or some- thing, but you also go with that fear.

When I asked Carina about the circumstances of her tickets, she re- plied that they were always at a checkpoint. "Not because I've crashed or anything," she explained. "All four have been at a checkpoint." She described what it was like to have police stop her at checkpoints, which she said were all over the state, not just in the area where we met. "They make a checkpoint in an area where they know a lot of Hispanic people go by," Carina elaborated, "or where there's a lot of traffic." She explained that at these checkpoints, which would be in place for one to two hours at a time, the police usually provided some flimsy pretext for pulling over drivers. "They say they're looking for someone, but you know what they're looking for is people without a license, that there's a lot of us." Re- flecting on the exorbitant costs of the tickets and towing, and the threat of arrest, Carina said, "Yes, it's serious. There's no way you can keep doing this all the time. . . . Now we know precisely that they're looking for us. . . . There are no safe zones."

The longer I spoke with Carina, the more apparent the precarious- ness of her position became, balanced as she was on a tightrope with "no safe zones" around her. Like other undocumented patients I spoke with in the area, she tried to stay out of trouble but could not alto- gether avoid interacting with government agencies. She had to drive, and sometimes that meant driving through checkpoints. She had to rely on presumptive Medicaid for the birth of her US-born children, and she regularly provided endless documentation (including her own consular ID card) to keep them enrolled in full-scope Medicaid. Like many of the women I spoke with, Carina shouldered the family care-giving responsibilities that put her constantly in contact with agents of the state; her situation highlighted how so many families exist in the tense, in-between space where conditionally engaging with the punitive and benevolent arms of government agencies becomes a matter of everyday life. Low-income US citizens, especially those who are Black and Brown, are subject to similarly insidious surveillance, but Carina was also undocumented. The stakes for her to negotiate this space were even higher, and she knew well that the consequences of a misstep could be more severe.

Carina had not always been undocumented. She had been living in the United States for twenty-two years—almost two-thirds of her life—and had arrived here with a visa that expired in 2010. I asked Carina whether, since she had come as a child and been living here so long, she had thought about applying for DACA.

Look, I did the process, but without support from a lawyer. I provided so much proof, so many documents. In fact, I had some boxes made with a notary, from people who are residents and who've known me since I arrived here, and they never approved [my application]. All they told me is that they needed proof that I had been here in school, that I had been enrolled in school. I sent them that proof and never heard anything after that. Since I was pregnant with [my daughter], I put my fingerprints in the IRS [Internal Revenue Service], and they've never told me anything. And for economic reasons I also never inquired. Now I'm, like, lost in the system. I'd need to talk with a lawyer to figure out everything about the process from my whole case.

"The government has your documents, but . . . ," I began. "They've got me stuck there," Carina said, concluding the sentence I had started. To get unstuck, she would need a lot of money. "It's really expensive, it'll cost me around four thousand dollars," she explained. "It's so much money. For our economic situation, it's so much money."

Later in our conversation I asked whether Carina thought she might still qualify for DACA, which was in legal limbo between the Trump administration's efforts to end the program and litigation over the legality of its suspension. Carina had asked a lawyer the same question—was she still eligible?—and was told that she would have to begin the application process all over again from the beginning. Given the political climate at the time, that seemed like a risky move: "It's really hard. Right now, as a matter of fact, it's been what? Five months since I spoke with, made an appointment with a lawyer, and they told me that right now it's not recommended for anyone to move my case along because it could be irreversible. I want to do it right now, but it makes me scared. . . . Let's hope there's a change in the president or that some new law comes about or something that I can avail myself of to not leave the country."

No Safe Status

This shifting political climate not only affected undocumented immigrants like Carina but also tempered liminally legal and legally present immigrants' perception of federal agencies. I met Magdalena, a perpetually smiling middle-aged woman with graying hair, at the free clinic in January 2020. She told me that she had been coming to the clinic for the past five months to get medications to manage her diabetes and hypertension. Magdalena had moved to the state from Mexico six years ago with her daughters to reunite with her husband, who was already working there in a sawmill. He had gotten his legal permanent residence and was able to petition for Magdalena and their daughters to join him, meaning that, unlike most others I spoke with in the state, Magdalena's family always had permission to live, work, and drive in the United States.

In the past, Magdalena's husband had received health care through Medicaid, and she would have been eligible for it as well after her first five years as a legal permanent resident. A couple of years ago, however, they heard on the news that using Medicaid would compromise her husband's ability to become a citizen and her ability to maintain her own status or return from Mexico if she went for a visit. Even though Magdalena supposed that this was probably something the president said just to scare people, her family did not want to chance it: "All of a sudden, they started saying [on the news] that those of us with Medicaid were going to have problems later, so [my husband] dropped it. I think it's been about three years now that he dropped it. . . . My husband wants to become a citizen, and I—who knows? To renew my residence later, it's better to drop it."

When I asked Magdalena why she thought it would harm their legal status to use Medicaid, she replied, "Supposedly because we're a burden for the government." I asked Magdalena whether she continued to hear similar warnings on the news now, and she said no. "No, I think that's not happening anymore," she replied. "It's that they suddenly say [these things], and I think it's to scare people." When I asked her to clarify who was saying these things, she answered, "More than anything the president. But I tell my husband, 'How can we be a [public] charge?' You go shopping, and they're charging taxes. As I've said, every time they take me to the doctor, it means paying [out of pocket]. . . . I ask you, how are we going to be a burden if when we buy [things] we're paying their taxes?" Magdalena did not limit her commentary to only those who had legal status, like her family, but considered the broader exclusionary rhetoric of such statements: "They say that those who don't have papers, even those who are working, get money taken out at work by the state. I don't know all the things they say. But we can't be—because they do take [our money]." As it had for Carina, whose attempts to exist within the narrow bounds of legality made her status unstable as laws changed around her, the political uncertainty around the public charge rule made Magdalena's family withdraw from benefits opportunities.

Alejandra, whose son was deported and whose husband "self-deported" to join him in Mexico, also heard that any immigrant using public benefits would be at risk of deportation, regardless of their legal status. When she required emergency surgery to remove her gallbladder, she was able to qualify for the hospital's financial assistance program but never considered Emergency Medicaid. "No, we don't have Medicaid, nothing like that, miss. Not us," she said emphatically. When I asked why not, Alejandra replied, "No, because being undocumented, the fear—we know that coming here illegally, there are none of those services for us. We don't even mention it, to be honest." When I asked Alejandra to elaborate about the political situation that she was obliquely referencing, she demurred: "I couldn't say much about that because I don't really get into the news. It's just that sometimes people talk, like now with this president [Trump]. What they told me is that he wants to take citizenship away from the Hispanics who already have it—from the moms whose kids are already grown and who could get them their residence. That they're not going to give it to them because if they got [food] stamps, if they got cash assistance, I don't know what else. That's the only thing I've heard . . . just what the ladies chat about."

Legal violence—the sense of pervasive surveillance and exclusionary policies that prevented many purple state patients from obtaining valid identity documents and receiving vital health services—also affected people who found work by using false identity documents. I met Lorena, an undocumented immigrant from Mexico who was probably in her forties, in the lobby of the free clinic on a mild but wet Saturday morning in January 2020. She and her husband were among the first to arrive, and by 8:00 a.m. there were already a dozen people lined up outside the clinic waiting for an appointment with the medical and dental volunteers from a nearby university medical center. Lorena and her husband joined me on mismatched chairs in the small medical exam room where I conducted interviews to share her experience seeking health care while she awaited her appointment.

Lorena explained that this was her first time coming to the free clinic, and she had come hoping to see a specialist about diabetes complications. Diabetes had damaged her retinas so much that she was nearly blind, and she took fifteen pills a day in addition to insulin to manage the diabetes itself as well as diabetes-related kidney disease and hypertension. Lorena had been going to a nearby FQHC for years and had seen eye specialists through charity care at the state university medical center, but the eligibility requirements had changed recently, and she no longer qualified for financial assistance. Now her husband was paying for all her medications and treatments out of pocket, which was a monumental task considering he earned only eleven dollars an hour.

Lorena urgently needed care but had been unsure where to turn for help until she heard about the free clinic. Part of her wariness stemmed from her previous experience getting into trouble while seeking care as an undocumented immigrant. When Lorena first arrived in the United States, she had trouble finding a job without a work permit. Back then, people told her she would not find work unless she "bought some papers" (false identity documents). But Lorena had to work, so she felt compelled to do so under someone else's identity:

> Now, it's not at all easy to find work without documents. We keep working in this way, without our own documents. They are other people's documents. That's the way we work, and that's the way they [the employers] offer us [health] insurance. Yes, they offer some insurance, but out of fear you don't go, because they'll ask you for identification. They're not official identifications. They're identifications purchased by other people. Now what they do is they put those in the computer to verify that they are the correct ones, that they are official. They're not official, so you say, "I'm not going to go because they're going to review the ID and they're going to realize that it's not official. It's better if I don't go." And that's what happens, that people don't go [to get medical care] because they're afraid they'll review their identification.

Although she conflated them sometimes as she spoke, Lorena later distinguished between two kinds of documents—the false papers people once used before E-Verify and the real identity documents that belonged to other people that they had to use after employers started checking records electronically. Lorena had purchased "official" identity documents that would enable her to work even in the E-Verify era, and she found work first at a poultry plant and later at an electronics factory. She had no plans to tempt fate by seeking medical care in someone else's name, but unfortunately, she soon began experiencing diabetes symptoms. She went to a clinic and asked to pay out of pocket so that no bills would be generated, but unbeknownst to her, the laboratory sent a bill to the person whose documents she had been using.

The woman, who lived in Puerto Rico, got Lorena's information from the clinic and phoned her to say she knew that Lorena was using her documents, warning her that she could go to jail for this. Lorena told the woman that she was just using them so she could do honest work and feed her kids, and the woman seemed persuaded not to press the matter. Lorena felt "safer" after that because the person whose documents she was using knew about it now, and she returned to the clinic with a clear conscience. Unfortunately, the lab again sent a bill to the woman in Puerto Rico. The next time Lorena tried to check in at the clinic, a Spanish-speaking woman working at the front desk caught Lorena before she went to the check-in window. She asked Lorena whether she was using someone else's name, and Lorena admitted that she was. Without drawing the attention of her colleagues, the worker warned Lorena that they were about to call the police and that she should leave right away and never come back to the clinic. In Lorena's mind, it was a "miracle" that the woman spoke Spanish and subtly warned Lorena before the police came.

After that, Lorena had to find a new clinic and a new way to pay for her diabetes care without any kind of insurance. She saved up for a diabetes-related surgery so she could pay as much as possible up front and the rest in installments, but she lost her job before being able to complete the payments. She also had medical bills for her kids—who were born in Mexico and ineligible for Medicaid—that she was still paying off. "If I could get some kind of medical assistance with what I earn and with my work, I wouldn't have debts with anyone," she said. As it was, she despaired of ever paying off her family's medical debts.

When Lorena expressed this fear to someone at the state university medical center where her son was undergoing a series of surgeries, she was informed of the hospital's charity care (financial assistance) program and enrolled him in it to cover the costs of his care. It also sounded like she was able to get one diabetic eye surgery through charity care before the hospital's visa-related requirements changed and she became ineligible. This was a huge blow to her because the eye surgery had not worked. She was now blind in the eye that had been operated on and was going blind in the other eye, and her only hope was that the free clinic might help her save her eyesight before she lost her vision completely.

When I asked her why she no longer qualified for financial assistance, Lorena explained that the university medical center had recently changed its residence requirements to disallow people on a visa from receiving charity care. She had come to the United States in 1997 with a visa that did not include work permission, and which had long since expired—thus making her undocumented. According to the charity care program worker who assisted Lorena, however, entering with a visa made Lorena a tourist, not a resident. As Lorena understood the issue, it was this distinction that disqualified her from financial assistance, a fact she found rather unfair: "To me it seemed somewhat illogical because normally if someone wants to do something correctly, for me that would have been entering this country correctly with residency or with a visa. And I did it correctly, I entered with a visa. Yes, I stayed, I committed the error of staying, yes, but I did it correctly. I didn't break the rules. . . . I said, 'I think that if I tell the truth and I do things correctly, it's more likely that they'll help me, because I'm not lying, I'm telling the truth.'"

The news from the charity care worker deeply disappointed Lorena. When she asked how she might become eligible for financial assistance, hospital workers told her that the only thing she could do was fix her immigration status. Lorena thought that telling the truth about her visa had been her downfall, and now she had not been able to access health care for some time because she could not afford it. The last specialist she had seen had told her she might have better luck returning to Mexico and getting her eye treatments there. The doctor did not grasp that being undocumented meant that Lorena could not return to Mexico. Frustrated by the suggestion, Lorena left his office and never returned. "The only thing that keeps me from having good medical care is my immigration status," she said bluntly. "That's what most impedes me."

Lorena's succinct analysis of her situation was accurate. If she had legal status, she likely would have had access to health care at the moments she needed it most. She would not have had to work under someone else's name, nor flee from the clinic when that someone found out that Lorena was using her documents. Hospital workers would not have told her that she was ineligible for charity care. Even though Lorena believed that she had come "the right way"—with a visa—everything went wrong after that. In the dichotomy of "good" versus "bad" immigrants, Lorena positioned herself as someone who tried to follow the rules but sometimes was compelled by circumstances to transgress immigration and labor laws. What Lorena did not mention, but what is clear from the literature, is that when immigration agents raid workplaces to root out undocumented workers, the employers seldom face sanctions—even as the workers are detained and deported (Bacon and Hing 2010). Lorena filled a gap in the low-wage economy and might have continued to do so had her health not deteriorated. Her illness made her visible to law enforcement agencies, however, and her undocumented status made it nearly impossible for her to get care in the United States or travel to

Mexico to seek it there. Now she was effectively blind, no longer able to work, and unsure what steps to take next.

The accounts of Carina, Magdalena, Alejandra, and Lorena illustrate how much of the legal violence enacted on Latinx immigrant communities results in people forgoing benefits for which they may be legally eligible or paying into welfare schemes from which they may never benefit. Just as prior scholarship has highlighted how the *perceived* threat of immigration enforcement can have material health impacts—for example, in worse birth outcomes among immigrants (see Novak, Geronimus, and Martinez-Cardoso 2017; and Torche and Sirois 2018), these women's perception that they were subject to constant surveillance and scrutiny resulted in conditional engagement with government agencies. The patients I spoke with described interacting with medical and law enforcement agencies when it seemed unavoidable, such as during a medical emergency, traffic stops, or to ensure care for their children. These inescapable interactions served to further criminalize noncitizens going about their everyday life—even those like Magdalena and her family, who were legally authorized to live in the United States and entitled to government benefits yet nevertheless experienced the racialized spillover effects of constructed illegality (Asad and Clair 2017; Menjívar 2021). In the purple state, the threat of deportation loomed behind this sense of pervasive surveillance, but more often punishment took the form of ongoing economic exploitation through insecure labor conditions, costly traffic stops, and racialized benefits disenfranchisement that wore away at noncitizens' physical and financial well-being without physically removing them from the workforce. This cycle of exploitative economic inclusion and social exclusion extended to the clinic, and—especially in the purple state—its punitive consequences sometimes spilled over onto clinic workers.

Enrolling Clinics in Biopolitical Surveillance

In my attempts to get to know the purple state immigrant health context, I spoke with physicians and clinic administrators in several safety net health care systems in the area. Due to increasingly stringent requirements of local institutional ethics boards—which would have required a letter of support from each institution where I conducted a patient *or* provider interview, as well as the social security number of each participant (including undocumented immigrants)—very few people were willing to do an interview with me at the outset of my fieldwork in the area.[7] As I worked to clear these bureaucratic hurdles, the CEO of a large FQHC network I had reached out to apologized sincerely for his wariness to speak with me on the record. He agreed to share some contextual information from his perspective, as long as I kept the source anonymous, and he emphasized that the recent state political context threatened the clinic's financial stability at the same time that it made Latinx families drop out of coverage. He stressed that there was a growing perception in certain political spaces that their clinics, which originally emerged to serve low-income, primarily African American residents, now chiefly served Latinx immigrants.

Natalia Deeb-Sossa (2016) has written about racialized conflict over public resources like health care in new immigrant destinations in the American South, and how racialized constructions of citizenship and belonging play out through tense clinic interactions. To stay afloat, resource-strapped clinics in the purple state needed to signal that they served deserving citizens, not just immigrants. The Republican legislature, which was already committed to blocking ACA implementation at every turn and defunding Medicaid as much as possible—with serious consequences for poor Black and Brown citizens, who were disproportionately uninsured—would not be generous to clinics it perceived as putting immigrants first. The clinic CEO told me that he did not want to be a "coward" on the issue of immigrant health, but he said that he "lived in fear" of losing state funding when their resources were already so tightly marshaled. His statement suggested that the constructed illegality of many immigrants in the community spilled over onto health care institutions and made safety net clinic leaders wary of falling into anti-immigrant lawmakers' bad graces.

In a separate meeting, the CEO's colleague, the medical director of the FQHC, shed some light on why this fear ran so deep. She informed me that several years ago, the state had investigated two providers in an adjacent county for their role in providing health care to undocumented immigrants. At the time, the county was trying to force the health department to turn over health records to the sheriff. This sent shock waves through similarly positioned safety net clinics in the state and, as the medical director told me, made providers extremely cautious about putting anything related to immigration status or history in a patient's medical chart. Even though this investigation had happened many years before my conversations with the FQHC administrators, the collective memory of it persisted in area safety net clinics. As ongoing anti-immigrant politics at the state level intersected with new bureaucratic strategies to target perceived benefits fraud among immigrants in safety net clinics, clinic workers became implicated in the expanding biopolitical surveillance of the Latinx noncitizens in their care.

By chance, the day after my conversation with the FQHC's medical director, I met with a physician who, unprompted, mentioned the same state investigation of immigrant-serving providers as soon as we began speaking. She worked at the health department in the county where I would eventually do my fieldwork, and she explained how those events continued to reverberate throughout nearby safety net health care centers. She offered to introduce me to the providers who were investigated, and eventually I was able to connect with each of them. Justine was a bilingual nurse who agreed to speak with me on the condition that I did not record our conversation, use her name, or publish the location or name of the institution where she had worked. She seemed traumatized by the experience but was willing to share her general impressions of what had happened. In contrast, her supervisor, Dr. Beckett—a physician who had been the medical director of the health department at the time—was more unguarded and open about her experience of being investigated by the state.

It all started in the summer of 2008. On the national scale, Barack Obama and John McCain were heading into the home stretch of their presidential campaigns. The Tea Party movement was gaining momentum and influence across the country, particularly in the South, and the Great Recession fueled racist anti-immigrant sentiment as US unemployment skyrocketed (Portes and Rumbaut 2014).[8] This sentiment was already brewing in the purple state, however, playing out in policies such as the state legislation passed in 2006 that made it necessary to have a social security number or a valid unexpired visa to get a driver's license. In addition to making driving a far riskier endeavor, it limited the ability of undocumented residents to have up-to-date photo identification beyond a consular ID card. Functionally, this increased their visibility as "illegal" in law enforcement, employment, and other bureaucratic spaces—including health care centers (see also Jimenez 2021).

Furthermore, as Lorena's story illustrated, the purple state where I conducted this research was one of six states that have laws requiring the use of E-Verify for nearly all employers (Feere 2012). (This was also true in the red state I observed.) Alejandra, the free clinic patient whose family lost their jobs during the poultry plant closures and whose son was deported, recalled how challenging things became when E-Verify went into effect: "Since E-Verify came about, we couldn't work anymore. I don't really remember when that came about, but before they didn't [have] it. You worked sometimes cutting strawberries, you'd go, and they'd let you work. Then when this [E-Verify] came about in the factories, almost in the majority of places of work, many of us couldn't work anymore. That's what ruined us, too [in addition to the poultry plant closures], because not having what E-Verify [needed], that they'd be checking papers and all that, well, then a lot of us couldn't work anymore."

Most of these state laws went into effect during the 2008–2012 period, around the same time that many poultry plants were closing in the area. As many undocumented immigrants, like Lorena, resorted to using identity documents that belonged to someone else for employment purposes, medical legal violence increasingly extended into health care spaces and implicated providers as well as patients. Situations like those Alejandra and Lorena described sometimes led to patients using one name at work (an alias) while using their real name at health care institutions. Dr. Beckett, one of the providers investigated by the state in relation to providing health care to undocumented immigrants, explained that in order for the clinical staff to write a medical note excusing a patient from work, they would need to indicate the name the patient used at work—which might not match the name in their charting system. Justine, the nurse who worked under Dr. Beckett at the health department, realized that this might become an issue when women who had just given birth asked for work letters in another name. She asked Dr. Beckett how to manage these discrepancies, and Dr. Beckett told her that this must be an institutional decision.

Unfortunately, there was some turnover with health directors during this time, and no firm policy ever materialized. In the absence of a systematic policy, Dr. Beckett suggested that Justine should write the letters with the name the patient used at work, but in the medical chart, she should document both names to ensure that there would be no conflicts. At the same time, some maternity nurses who "had not been part of the broader conversation" of documentation protocols noticed that there were records being made with multiple names, and they reported this to the nursing director. Soon after, Dr. Beckett received a phone call telling her to report to the nursing director and county attorney the next morning. She was told to bring her badge, keys, and anything else she would need to turn in to the health department. Bewildered, she showed up the next morning to find "quite the show of force" awaiting her. Not only was the nursing director there, but so were the health department director, a human resources representative, and the county sheriff.

At the time, a member of the board of health was campaigning locally for elected office, and he was running on an anti-immigrant platform that aligned well with the sheriff department's priorities and ramp-up of a local 287(g) agreement. The county had also recently built a jail to federal standards in order to benefit from federal funding and become a regional detention center under the Criminal Alien Program (CAP).[9] In Dr. Beckett's words, the board of health member and sheriff seemed to see this clinic's bureaucratic issue as a "rallying cry" for their political base, and what should have been an internal matter became front-page news in the local paper. The health department suspended Dr. Beckett and Justine while the State Board of Investigation (SBI) investigated them, and they were critically scrutinized in the local press.

Notes from a county board of supervisors meeting after the events described the allegations in detail, stating that "at the request of some patients, the health department provided work notes and prescriptions in alias names." The investigation sought to determine whether providing such services "would assist illegal aliens in maintaining assumed or stolen identities which may be a violation of state or federal law pertaining to identity theft and fraud." The report also reveals that authorities identified five "illegal aliens" during the course of the investigation and processed at least one for deportation by the time of the board meeting. Importantly, however, the investigation also determined that "none of the five individuals received Medicaid benefits in violation of any law."

In the time between when the allegations were made and when the SBI ultimately cleared Dr. Beckett and Justine of any wrongdoing, they were blindsided by the investigation and the political attention and felt completely unsupported by the health department. They had no idea what was going on, and they often learned of the charges being leveled against them in the newspaper. Justine found this all very distressing, isolating, and confusing. She explained that they kept changing the charges against them, and no one provided any guidance or support. Justine recalled that by the time all was said and done, she had been variously charged with aiding and abetting, HIPAA violations, and Medicaid fraud, and she had to hire a different kind of lawyer for each charge. She feared not only losing her job, but also losing her license and going to jail.

Justine described the whole thing as an "ethically really tough" situation. She was doing the best she could to follow the health department's limited guidance while also providing the care her patients needed. Some of her patients legitimately did not know their date of birth, and she told me that even the SBI detectives acknowledged to her that it was not her job to figure out someone's immigration status. Her job was to prevent patients from harm, especially new mothers who might hemorrhage or get an infection if they went back to work too soon after giving birth. Justine needed to provide work notes to do her job and meet the standard of care, but no one at the health department seemed to know how to do that when patients used multiple names.

As Dr. Beckett reflected on the investigation, her impression was that the whole thing was blown way out of proportion. While she seemed less concerned about her job, reputation, and liberty than Justine had been, the way the investigation unfolded bothered her on a political and legal level. Dr. Beckett explained that things got especially "sticky" in terms of the medical records investigation. The board of health member who was running for political office and coordinating the SBI and sheriff's investigations seemed hell-bent on outing undocumented patients and making an example of Dr. Beckett and Justine. Dr. Beckett recalled him saying, "I want those names. I want to look at those charts. I want to see what you wrote and see what you did." He could not get the records himself because he was not a physician at the health department, and Justine explained that HIPAA protected those patients' confidential medical records. To be sure of this, Dr. Beckett and Justine consulted a lawyer with expertise in the state's public health laws for guidance. Dr. Beckett remembered the whole situation as extremely complicated because HIPAA prevented the board of health member from accessing medical records for individual review. However, if the matter was a "systems" issue rather than a question about an individual patient, then the investigative teams could access the medical records. The board of health member made the case that this was likely a systemic problem, not just a matter of one or two patients, and thus was able to pull every patient chart in the health department to look for evidence of wrongdoing.

Finding no evidence of chart falsification, the board of health member then asked for the SBI to investigate possible Medicaid fraud. The investigations ultimately cleared both providers of any wrongdoing, but Dr. Beckett got the impression that the board of health member was angry that the legal analysis did not support his view that their actions were morally reprehensible and deserving of demotion or termination. Dr. Beckett, meanwhile, suspected that it was the board of health member who had transgressed legal boundaries. "You know," she remarked, "I'm not at all convinced that they legally got those records."

When I asked how the health department ultimately resolved the charting issue, both Justine and Dr. Beckett told me that moving forward they had developed a written policy to document each of a patient's names in the chart, as well as for any medical letters they wrote to a patient's employer. Dr. Beckett said that the charting aspect of this was very similar to what they had been doing, although it was not explicitly written out anywhere until after the investigation. While this protected the health department from future accusations of wrongdoing, functionally Dr. Beckett thought that writing a medical letter in multiple names was "untenable in terms of that patient continuing to work" after being exposed for using an alias. This tension underscores how the overcriminalization of immigration and bureaucratic technologies can intersect to increase safety net clinics' responsibility for surveilling immigration "fraud" well beyond the workplace and immigration enforcement operations.

Eventually everyone went back to work, and the routines of daily care resumed, but my conversations with administrators and providers at other safety net clinics several years later suggested that substantial fallout remained. Some months after my conversations with Justine and Dr. Beckett, I spoke with Caitlyn, an administrative assistant who had been employed for nearly thirty years at a health department that neighbored the one where the two investigated providers had worked. Caitlyn oversaw registration, reception, medical records, and data entry and ensured that staff were following the health department guidelines and state policies. She told me that the state audited their health department every two years, so she really had to stay on top of these documentation rules, even when they were contradictory or not in the patient's best interest. As an example, she described a policy that had come out four or five years ago requiring pregnant people seeking presumptive Medicaid to answer questions about whether they were a resident of the state. Caitlyn and her colleagues asked the state for guidance on the definition of "resident" and why they had to ask it—especially since low-income pregnant people were eligible for pregnancy-related and birth-related Medicaid regardless of their legal status. "If we don't care about immigration status, legal status and so forth," Caitlyn asked, "why do we need to be asking that?"

Caitlyn explained that this policy tied her colleagues' hands and ended up alienating patients. "We're just the filter," she lamented. "It's just filtering through us. We don't get to make the decisions; we just have to follow the guidance given." She expressed feeling conflicted between wanting to maintain trust with patients and making sure that she and her team accurately registered patients' use of health care services—for the patients' sake and the health department's. She brought up the issue central to the state's investigation of Justine and Dr. Beckett: how to manage patients' use of multiple identities when seeking care. Caitlyn explained that while she wanted to establish trust with patients, not knowing their identity also compromised the health department's ability to keep track of patients' medication allergies and manage public health issues like tuberculosis. Because many patients did not have photo IDs—a fact exacerbated by the state's driver's license laws—the clinical staff could not be sure who they were treating at any given moment. "We tried to explain to them how this was life-threatening," Caitlyn remarked.

Emphasizing the degree to which this biopolitical surveillance was becoming institutionalized, Caitlyn also made it clear that she knew from experience and advice that her team received from the county attorney that the state was monitoring them closely and would investigate any suspected instance of insurance fraud. Eventually, the health department bought what Caitlyn referred to as "an expensive photo ID machine" to begin taking photographs for their own records. From her perspective, the photo machine was a great advantage because they could now visually verify whether they had the right patient and the right medical chart. She explained that over time patients seemed resigned to the fact that they would have to submit to photographic recordkeeping to get care through the health department. "I think people have probably said, 'No, it's okay. Just tell them [your real name],'" she mused. "I think maybe that's because of the community," she continued, suggesting that patients had sufficient confidence in the community now to feel more comfortable sharing their true identities and submitting to having their photograph taken for their medical record.

Whether this was objectively true, I could not say. Caitlyn did not mention a perceptible decline in patient attendance after the photograph program began, and her sense that patients accepted the change with equanimity may be an accurate assessment of the situation. On the other hand, it is possible that patients submitted to these terms because the only alternative was to forgo health care entirely. Without speaking with such patients in Caitlyn's clinic network myself (which became impossible after the COVID-19 pandemic struck), I can't know how current and prospective patients felt about this new layer of biometric recordkeeping and whether it shaped their health care decision making. Even so, given how easily an erstwhile political candidate with ties to a nearby health department was able to access patient files and get patients and clinic workers into trouble—and how such surveillance led to the need for a photo ID machine in the first place—this technological "solution" highlighted the burgeoning overlap between medical and legal bureaucracies in the health care safety net.

A few months after my conversation with Caitlyn, I spoke with an oncology nurse and an oncology clinic administrator at the state's primary safety net hospital. They echoed Caitlyn's and Lorena's comments about changing documentation requirements for safety net care and emphasized how confusing such bureaucratic hurdles could be for patients and clinic workers alike. To protect against international "tourists" abusing the charity care/financial assistance programs, the hospital—the same hospital that turned Lorena away for diabetic eye surgery because of her

visa status—instituted more onerous proof of residence criteria. Applicants had to submit multiple items from a long list of qualifying criteria, including income proof, residency proof, a photo ID (valid, but not
necessarily from the United States), tax records or a letter from the IRS
confirming that the applicant did not pay taxes, and bank account statements and/or a letter of support from the applicant's sponsor/family/
friends if they had no bank account. The photo ID requirement created
confusion because applicants using international photo IDs were often
classified as "international" patients, even if they had been living in the
United States for years. To resolve this, the hospital had instituted the
criteria requiring two proofs of state residence. This meant that, in es-
sence, the hospital required proof that someone with a non-US ID was
undocumented and not simply coming to the hospital as a "tourist" to
avail themselves of discounted medical care.

Another member of the hospital's oncology staff, social worker Nadine, explained that there had been a lot of institutional back-and-forth
over how to balance noncitizen patients' health needs against the bureaucratic demands of justifying discounted health care at a safety net
institution that was directly accountable to state and federal government agencies. Nadine described some of these institutional policies as
"frustrating" and "discriminatory" because they often encouraged misinformation about patients' eligibility for care. Nadine heard colleagues
say, "Well, they are illegal, they can't get [care] here, can they? They
can't get this program, can they?" Nadine bristled at hearing patients
described as "illegal" and realized that they were being dismissed from
care. "It makes you wonder, well, how many times did someone get
turned away? . . . Like what if somebody just said, 'You're not eligible,
sorry. You don't have a driver's license.'" Nadine explained that she and
others within the institution were working hard to push back against
this miseducation, and she was optimistic that things were slowly
changing for the better, but my conversations with her colleagues and
Lorena suggested that substantial confusion remained. As recordkeeping strategies became more totalizing and technocratic to account for
a politically charged state health care regime that actively excluded
noncitizens, clinic workers increasingly bore the burden of arbitrating
identities and rationing care.

Conclusion

The examples discussed in this chapter illustrate how the insidious legal violence of anti-immigrant politics made its way into clinical spaces to become medical legal violence that undermined noncitizen patients' health chances and undercut clinic workers' ability to facilitate their care. The economic and political context of this rural southern locale made Latinx noncitizens and their families especially vulnerable to exploitation and exclusion from social services. This included overreliance on low-wage, high-risk labor in the poultry industry and the criminalization of noncitizens through state-level policies regarding driver's license and work eligibility verification. Additionally, the minoritized racial status of Latinx immigrants in this new immigrant destination made the people I spoke with targets of employment exploitation and law enforcement surveillance, and it made getting consistent health care that much more difficult. This, in turn, created challenges for clinic workers who struggled to provide care to patients who oftentimes felt uneasy making themselves visible to any institution, particularly those associated with government agencies. Some providers responded to these challenges by playing down the extent of their support of undocumented immigrants, while others got caught in the political cross fire of trying to balance medical ethics against anti-immigrant governance.

In the red state and blue state clinics I observed, clinic workers had described anxieties over anti-immigrant politics making their way into the clinic and negatively affecting patients, and to some degree they had taken steps against such incursions. In the red state, the people I spoke with recounted instances of anti-immigrant intimidation in the health care context and strived to maintain patients' security and trust through their enduring, unwavering presence. In the blue state, this was something of a hypothetical that loomed alongside the uncertainty of the ascent of the Trump administration. In the purple state, on the other hand, the providers and clinic staff I spoke with both directly and obliquely expressed their collective concern over providers and administrators getting caught up in the medical legal violence of those anti-immigrant politics in a relatively newer immigrant destination. The constructed illegality of undocumented immigrants became a legal liability for clinical institutions and raised ethical tensions about how to care for those the government increasingly deemed criminal.

The reflections of the patients and providers I spoke with also reveal that in the United States, where health care systems are predicated on employer insurance for workers and publicly subsidized care for unemployed or underemployed US citizens, there is little space in the safety net for someone who holds neither legitimate employment nor valid US documents. Even when state investigations concluded that providers had engaged in no wrongdoing and patients had not received benefits for which they were ineligible, the chilling effect persisted. Undocumented immigrant patients often continued to work in the shadows, and the state frequently managed to narrow the scope of their legitimate participation in social life to the economic sphere. These dynamics can also place safety net health care institutions in an ethically challenging position that local politics may either exacerbate (as in the red and purple states) or mitigate (as in the blue state). In the following chapter, I examine how non-medical clinic workers across the three fieldsites developed a kind of *medical legal consciousness* that enabled them to resist this increasingly institutionalized medical legal violence for themselves and on behalf of their communities.

5

Medical Legal Consciousness in the "Crimmigration" Age

Throughout this book, I have highlighted situations where medical care and the law collide, creating tensions for noncitizen patients seeking care and for the clinic workers who provide that care. This collision often leads to medical legal violence as US health and immigration laws increasingly construct many noncitizen patients as fraudsters who do not deserve the kind of material support that befits citizens and long-term lawful permanent residents. In this chapter, I describe how these dynamics also contribute to a specific kind of *medical legal consciousness*—an awareness of the law in health care negotiations and a feeling of being alternately "with" or "against" the law—for those who experience medical legal violence as health care facilitators.[1] While previous chapters explored the experiences of patients and health care providers in more detail, here I focus on the perspectives of *non-medical* clinic workers across all three fieldsites to understand how recent policy changes have shaped their medical legal consciousness and mobilized them in particular ways to advocate for their patients and communities.

If the phrase "legal consciousness" captures how people understand themselves in relation to the laws of the society in which they live, "*medical* legal consciousness" highlights the facets of that subjectivity that specifically relate to medicine and health care as socially embedded practices and institutions. Much of the time, people who seek or facilitate health care do not have to think about the law at all. If they do, it is usually because of laws that directly relate to patient care, such as those ensuring patient privacy, ethical consenting procedures, and HIPAA protections. When laws align in ways that prioritize health, medical legal consciousness is taken for granted. It is only when health and the law diverge that medical legal consciousness becomes readily apparent—for example, when putting information about an undocumented immigrant patient's legal status might put their health, livelihood, or security in jeopardy.

As health and welfare policies have increasingly merged with criminalizing immigration laws in recent years, tensions underlying clinic workers' medical legal consciousness are more apparent than ever. This is no accident. Rather, it is the direct result of criminalizing rhetoric embedded in health and welfare governance that reproduces notions of illegality and undeservingness while sustaining the existing balance of power. For more than a century, the United States has denied lawful admission and/or residence to noncitizens who seem likely to become reliant on public benefits in the United States. Welfare reforms have amplified such exclusions, increasingly framing immigrants as both potentially threatening to national security and particularly likely to defraud American taxpayers through government-funded services like Medicaid, cash assistance, and housing support. Indeed, when US Citizenship and Immigration Services (USCIS) director Ken Cuccinelli announced in August 2019 a rule changing the "public charge" penalty for immigrants seeking a visa or green card, he declared that the rule was necessary to reinforce "the ideals of self-sufficiency and personal responsibility, ensuring that immigrants are able to support themselves and become successful here in America" (Cuccinelli 2019b). When asked whether such policies aligned with Emma Lazarus's poem enshrined on the Statue of Liberty, which offers hope to "your tired, your poor, your huddled masses yearning to breathe free," Cuccinelli responded with an alternative reading: "Give me your tired and your poor who can stand on their own two feet and who will not become a public charge" (Ingber and Martin 2019).

Cuccinelli's exhortation underscores many noncitizen immigrants' precarious position in a country increasingly pursuing "America-first" policies. Those seeking to provide health and well-being support to noncitizens during the years of my fieldwork had to contend with a dizzying array of new rules and regulations, such as the public charge rule change and sweeping changes to asylum and visa laws, that disproportionately subjected noncitizens' health care to government surveillance in ways that revealed an inherent suspicion of criminality.[2] This criminalization, which is fundamental to the racialized and gendered preoccupations of ongoing welfare reforms over the past three decades (Neubeck and Cazenave 2001; Morgen and Maskovsky 2003; Soss, Fording, and Schram 2011; Viladrich 2012; Eubanks 2018), significantly impacted the clinic workers I met. It also emphasized how disruptions to mundane routines and the transgression of previously secure spaces can serve to mobilize people, like the clinic workers I met, against oppressive policies (Snow et al. 1998; Zepeda-Millán 2017).

In this chapter, I describe how clinic workers have developed a kind of *medical legal consciousness* through negotiating immigrant health care access while also navigating government bureaucracies that alternately enlist them in surveillance systems or target them as members of the same communities they serve. Throughout this book, I have described how, through the dynamic assemblage of actors, policies, places, and time, medical legal violence extends immigration enforcement into clinical spaces that are meant to protect people from harm. Because of medical legal violence, patients are not protected, and clinic workers are disempowered from protecting them. Medical legal violence potentially exposes noncitizen patients and their families to enhanced criminalization and surveillance while alternately *deputizing* clinic workers to act as proxy agents of immigration enforcement or *criminalizing* them if they resist that deputation. Here I focus on the experiences of non-medical safety net clinic workers in states with varying combinations of immigrant integration and criminalization policies to illustrate what medical legal violence—and resistance to it—looks like in practice.[3] While clinic workers' roles and responsibilities varied by geography and across time, their mission never changed: to provide health care to those in the community who needed it most. To understand the tensions embedded in that work, I build upon scholarship that has examined the role of community clinic workers in bridging the health care gap for Latinx immigrants in the United States (e.g., Findley and Matos 2015; Deeb-Sossa 2016; Castañeda 2017; López-Sanders 2017a, 2017b). I especially illuminate the shared experiences of clinic workers across three states with varied immigrant health policies during a time of rapid change and uncertainty.

Policy Transformation, "Crimmigration," and Medical Legal Violence

In October 2017 I sat beside enrollment counselor Gabriela in her red state clinic office, a small but tidy earth-toned room that she had been decorating for Halloween. As we chatted, patient Yesenia entered seeking to renew Emergency Medicaid coverage for herself and Medicaid coverage for her US-citizen children.[4] Yesenia, who had applied for these services in the past, had come well prepared for the interview. She brought all the documents Gabriela might need to send to Medicaid—which I quickly realized was a vast register of her family's embeddedness in various US government bureaucracies (see also Asad 2020). As Gabriela began walking us through the Medicaid form's innumerable fields on her computer screen, she explained to me (in English, although we had all been speaking Spanish until that point) that Medicaid required tons of documentation, and she handed me a complete list. "It really depends on the person who's helping you apply," she continued in English, "whether they give you a hard time or not."

Yesenia seemed to have understood some of what Gabriela was saying, because she interjected in Spanish that she preferred to address her Medicaid issues at this clinic after unpleasant experiences at the county public benefits offices, where she had gone previously for Medicaid and food stamps. She remarked that the lines were long, the applicants were treated poorly, and the staff were inflexible. For example, Yesenia had begun selling tamales around her apartment complex to make ends meet when her husband lost work hours, but she had no proof of income to satisfy the Medicaid documentation requirements. Without paycheck stubs, she did not know how to convince government agency workers that she was not cheating the system but rather genuinely unable to document her work. Gabriela listened, unfazed, and pulled out a blank sheet of paper. She used this to show Yesenia how to make a handwritten income calendar estimating her earnings over a thirty-day period. Rather than suggesting outright that Yesenia or her husband was undocumented and that this might compromise their benefits application, she explained that they could use the handwritten calendar to determine Yesenia's income, even if—as she delicately put it—"not everyone in [her] household had a social security number or could file their own taxes."

Gabriela then asked Yesenia whether she was interested in applying for food stamps now, but Yesenia declined. Gabriela turned to me and remarked, this time in Spanish, that food assistance was becoming increasingly stigmatized now (several months after the Trump administration's public charge proposal leaked to the public) because "many people think it's a public charge, but that's a myth." Many other clinic workers I spoke with around this time described patients expressing similar fears, especially when they considered that the little that someone could get in food assistance did not outweigh the risk of becoming inadmissible or drawing the government's attention to their illicit presence. As another enrollment counselor explained to me, "They say, 'For forty dollars or fifty dollars . . . I'm risking more than what I'm going to get.'"

Yesenia seemed to be of this mind and told Gabriela that she did not believe that food assistance was safe for mixed-status families like hers. In response, Gabriela handed each of us a form from the county's public benefits agency that specified (in English and Spanish) what counted as a public charge and what did not.[5] Nevertheless, Yesenia declined food assistance, and Gabriela did not press the matter. The two moved on to the Medicaid application itself, and I watched Gabriela scan Yesenia's documents into the computer one by one. These included not only Yesenia's income estimations for her and her husband's work, but also her minor children's social security cards, school names, and anticipated graduation dates. Gabriela then asked whether anyone in Yesenia's household was currently or had recently been in jail, in prison, or detained. Yesenia said no. Once she had finished scanning in every last piece of information, Gabriela told Yesenia that it was a waiting game now, and Yesenia left the office.

Yesenia and Gabriela's conversation illustrates the kinds of medical legal consciousness that emerge when individuals consider whether and how to engage with the medical and legal systems that delimit health and well-being services in the United States. Yesenia's concerns highlighted her ambivalent engagement with recordkeeping institutions that demanded a staggering array of documents to access governmental aid for herself and her family. While such requirements also hold for other low-income people (especially people of color) whom government agencies regard as potential fraudsters by requiring intensive documentation and ongoing surveillance, Yesenia's immigration status also meant that she had to factor in her assumed criminality when determining which aid to seek and how. In the end, Yesenia drew a line between applying for Emergency Medicaid for herself and full-scope Medicaid for her children—which she likely could not avoid doing—and applying for food stamps, which she decided her family could forgo. While clinic workers like Gabriela attempted to counter this pervasive sense of latent criminality by leveraging their own medical legal knowledge to persuade clients like Yesenia to enroll in benefits for which they were eligible, medical legal violence insidiously kept Yesenia and her family under close surveillance while disenfranchising her and her US-citizen children.

In this chapter, I focus particularly on the non-medical clinic staff like Gabriela who serve as essential frontline workers by brokering health care access for community members like Yesenia amidst increasingly anti-immigrant policies. Regardless of the state or clinic type, non-medical clinic workers draw upon bureaucratic knowledge and personal experience to screen patients for health coverage eligibility, assess their general health care needs, and coordinate services in ways that prioritize a patient's health and well-being. For US citizens and lawful permanent residents living in the United States for more than five years, this typically involved determining whether a patient qualified for Medicaid or—since the passage of the ACA—a subsidized health exchange plan. For noncitizens and mixed-status families, the need for immigration documentation and lack of clarity around noncitizens' eligibility for particular services often complicated this process. Implementing the ACA involved standardizing electronic health record (EHR) systems and making governmental databases more interoperable, which regularized frontline staff's eligibility workflows, but it also limited their flexibility and discretion in evaluating noncitizens' health coverage options (López-Sanders 2017a).

Post–welfare reform scholarship has highlighted the dynamic nature of clinic workers' roles in the face of changing benefits policies and bureaucratic technologies, but contemporary health and immigration politics put clinic workers in an increasingly difficult position. Just as they had begun mastering the complex demands of the ACA in the years directly following its implementation, immigration policies that increasingly cast immigrants as potential criminals forced clinic staff to develop new expertise in immigration law and enforcement mechanisms. Through deliberate institutional practices and compassionate interactions with patients, these workers maintained a delicate balance between serving the health needs of antagonized communities and engaging with some of the very government agencies that antagonized them. They often drew on their experience as both professionals and individuals personally impacted by exclusionary health and immigration policies to facilitate rather than gatekeep health care access. Despite criminalizing rhetoric and policy confusion, frontline clinic workers paved pathways to care that undermined medical legal violence, leveraged their unique medical legal consciousness, and put their shared mission into practice.

Myths, Misinformation, and Medical Legal Partnerships

From the moment I began research in 2015 through early 2020, one of the most salient themes that emerged was the ongoing challenge to counter the *mitos* (myths/rumors) that circulated in immigrant communities around public benefits use. These so-called myths included the fear that immigrant applicants might be detected through "public charge" and be deported with their families or without their US-citizen children. Patients also expressed concerns that US-citizen children would have to pay back the costs of Supplemental Nutritional Assistance Program (SNAP, or "food stamps") or Medicaid benefits, be drafted into the US military, or (if the patient was a homeowner) have their house repossessed by the government to recoup medical costs.[6] Such myths helped create a climate of fear in which medical legal violence could take root.

When I began this study in the blue state in 2015, it was relatively easy for workers to guide noncitizen immigrant patients and families regarding what public benefits they might be eligible for, what situations might disqualify them from such benefits, and what the possible immigration consequences might be. At the time, the parameters for public charge inadmissibility were clear under federal guidelines set in 1999, and the Obama administration had articulated specific infractions as deportation priorities (US Department of Homeland Security 2014).[7] While workers always counseled patients to seek legal advice in the face of uncertainty, there was a fair amount of policy clarity that gave workers the confidence to treat *mitos* broadly as just that: unsubstantiated rumors. As I mentioned in earlier chapters, however, in the transition from the Obama to the Trump administration, these policies became less clear, and workers found it harder to confidently distinguish between myth and reality.

Early in my fieldwork, workers often relied on written eligibility parameters from government agencies to quell patients' fears while stop-
ping short of guaranteeing applicants' personal security. Blue state health
navigator Elizabeth, whom I met in the summer of 2016 (and whom I
mention in this book's introduction and chapter 3), collected any written
information she could get—such as documents, memos, and letters from
DHS, Medicaid, and the Department of Health and Human Services
(HHS)—and had them translated to Spanish as evidence supporting her
recommendations. Elizabeth found this fastidious approach necessary to
build trust and disprove many of the rumors that circulated in the community. She described SNAP as one key example: US-citizen children
were eligible for food stamps, but—as Yesenia's concerns suggest—many
of the noncitizen parents who came to the clinic feared that putting their
name on a food stamp application without being a citizen or resident
would trigger a cascade of penalties that might lead to deportation, family separation, and/or fines for their US-citizen children in adulthood.

Like Gabriela and many clinic workers I met, Elizabeth countered
these "myths" by showing patients all the documents she assembled and
referring them to a legal aid center that worked closely with the clinic.
Still, many patients—even those who were legally present—declined to
enroll out of fear that doing so might further criminalize them or draw
unwanted government attention. Elizabeth respected this fear of criminalization, and she emphasized how logical a response it was when access to certain benefits—such as Medicaid—remained restricted even in
the midst of the ACA and immigration reforms (like DACA and DAPA).
Elizabeth described immigration as a "black curtain" behind which
opaque government agencies acted with apparent randomness and ab-
solute authority. These agencies were, as she put it, "incredibly powerful,
like life-alteringly powerful, and whatever decisions they make, they can
just kind of make." In Elizabeth's experience working at the intersection of immigration law and social welfare benefits, this perceived capriciousness encouraged undocumented immigrants to minimize their
visibility to government agencies to avoid presumptive criminalization:
"People who don't have legal status, from what I've seen . . . would prefer
to step back and stay unseen until they have to step forward. If you're
being hospitalized, if you have a serious condition, if you've been just
diagnosed with cancer, you're going to have to step forward, and that's

when stuff gets to be really scary and challenging, and you get slammed with paperwork that you don't understand and you have to enroll in these programs." Even during the Obama administration, which proposed expansive immigration reforms but had the most aggressive deportation record of any administration to that point (US Department of Homeland Security 2019), gravely ill patients like Esteban (with liver failure) and Víctor (with colon cancer) struggled when considering their own presumptive criminality alongside their medical needs.

Elizabeth recalled multiple undocumented patients who became so overwhelmed when faced with a grave medical diagnosis alongside the daunting bureaucracies of the US immigration and health systems that they actually left the United States to return to their countries of origin. "What immigration [agencies] would call 'self-deporting,'" Elizabeth said grimly. "When you are really sick, when you really, really need medical care, things get complicated and you have to make decisions, and that's where it gets . . . the hardest." Despite such challenges, Elizabeth tried to encourage patients to prioritize their health while being transparent about the stakes of becoming visible to a federal agency. She asked patients who were considering applying for government benefits whether they had any felonies or multiple misdemeanors, were considered a threat to public security, or had given the government any motivation to deport them. "Basically," she concluded, "are you a deportation priority under . . . Obama's deportation priorities?"[8] Elizabeth's goal was to preempt the questions that county agency employees would ask patients, and she believed that clinic workers had a responsibility not to put patients at risk, "or if there is potential risk to really explain it in its entirety and let people make that decision for themselves and not make it for them." Like many clinic workers I observed, Elizabeth elevated patients' autonomy by providing them with as much information and interpretation as she could while letting patients decide what was in their best interest.

Respecting patients' autonomy sometimes meant accepting that fear would prove the deciding factor in health negotiations. Elizabeth's colleague Isabel stressed that merely hearing the word "immigration" during eligibility interviews could be sufficient for a patient to decline enrolling in any number of services, including ones for which they were eligible. Furthermore, Isabel said that many eligibility workers at government agencies exacerbated this problem by perpetuating those myths themselves. For example, patients often told Isabel that eligibility workers at government offices warned them that if they lied in their SNAP or Medicaid applications, "the law" was going to come for them and punish their children when they were old enough to pay.[9] Isabel believed that Medicaid supervisors did not discourage such misinformation because they wanted to limit noncitizens' ability to "abuse this benefit." Yet Isabel understood that the law mandated that clinic and Medicaid workers alike inform everyone of all their options, regardless of legal status. "If we take the law into our own hands, and we decide who we're giving information to and who we're not," Isabel argued, "we are violating a person's right to inform themselves of all the possibilities to access a medical service." Isabel's perspective, which I observed in action across the three states I studied, was one that interpreted health care not as a commodity to be strictly rationed among only the most deserving citizens, but as a basic human right that clinic workers were legally obligated to facilitate for all patients, US citizen or not. Her comments underscored a medical legal consciousness that maneuvered between being "with" and "against" immigration and welfare laws and revealed that, even as the federal government increasingly leveraged exclusionary laws to restrict noncitizens' benefits access, clinic workers also looked to the law as a source of protection for what they saw as patients' inalienable rights.

The distinction between the clinics' mission to facilitate health care as a right and government agencies' commitment to keeping fraudsters from accessing a scarce commodity reserved for deserving citizens created tension between community clinic staff and county benefits agency employees. Isabel was especially alarmed when immigrant patients with irregular statuses told her that they heard that if they applied for state-funded Medicaid (which was available to otherwise unqualified immigrants in the blue state I observed), immigration agents would be alerted to their presence and deport them. When Isabel investigated, she found that this "myth" seemed to be coming directly from county Medicaid workers. Isabel recalled a county Medicaid worker warning a gravely ill patient with TPS that she would send his case to immigration agencies, and if he had lied about anything on the application, he would be deported. "They don't care if you're sick," the Medicaid worker reportedly chided him. He returned to the clinic and told Isabel that he did not want to apply for any medical benefits, despite his urgent need and deferred action documentation.

When a similar situation unfolded with a patient who decided to discontinue chemotherapy for fear of immigration reprisals, Isabel and her colleagues confronted the Medicaid enrollment workers who had processed his application. According to Isabel, the government workers defended their position that the county Medicaid agency was authorized to share applicants' information with immigration agencies. Isabel said that this kind of intimidation happened so frequently that her clinic's administrators had to intervene and meet with county Medicaid agency leadership to train the Medicaid staff on eligibility criteria. They brought in legal experts and county health department representatives who confirmed that authorized and unauthorized immigrants alike were eligible for many services, including various kinds of Medicaid; Women, Infants, and Children (WIC) benefits; and food stamps. They also explained how the different agency databases worked and assured everyone that there was no connection between health benefits databases and immigration enforcement databases. Functionally, they claimed, there was no way for frontline Medicaid workers to flag cases for immigration enforcement.[10] Nevertheless, the threat itself was sufficient to discourage many people from enrolling.

Clinic workers across my fieldsites described frequent tensions between patients' need to engage with Medicaid—at least for their children—and reluctance to enroll in emergency or non-medical benefits for themselves and/or their families. While they could not avoid interacting with the health care system completely, many avoided this aspect of surveillance as much as possible because they were undocumented or were in the process of completing their legal residency or citizenship applications. Regardless of their personal reluctance, most would agree to apply for Medicaid on behalf of their children so that they could have health care and receive the immunizations required to attend school. Gabriela's colleague Delmy found this contradiction confusing. "I'm like, 'Well, your name is on your kid's application,'" she said, "'so it's going to be tied to it, but you have the option to [apply for Emergency Medicaid] and this would be the perfect time to do it' . . . but they'll still decline." Blue state enrollment counselor Joaquín echoed this sentiment, saying, "Their concerns are that by filling out that document now, Immigration is gonna know where they're living. They're gonna know where they work. They're going to know their information. So in that moment, that person will think about it and say, it just might not be worth it."

Delmy's and Joaquín's observations suggest that conditional involvement in governmental health care bureaucracies was part of a calculated risk-benefits assessment that depended highly on the degree to which clients that believed their presumed criminality was registered through public benefits surveillance. Clinic workers understood the logic behind these calculations even as they tried to reassure patients and advocate on their behalf. As anti-immigrant rhetoric became more pronounced and increasingly codified in regulation, however, and as high-profile immigration raids and deportations intensified the potential of such events to disrupt participants' lives, many immigrant and mixed-status families continued to discipline themselves out of vital services. In the face of such heightened criminalization, clinic workers had to search for new ways to persuade patients to prioritize their health and humanity over threats to their personal security and family integrity.

A Matter of Trust: Personal Experiences and Patient Interactions

Many of the clinic workers I spoke with understood firsthand the fear that came with presumptive criminalization, and their personal experiences imbued their patient interactions with particular empathy. The majority of those I met were from immigrant families or were immigrants themselves, and several had been undocumented. This made them especially attuned to the challenges their patients faced in trying to access health care while worrying about their personal and family security. It also made them deeply aware of the ways that the institutionalized rhetoric of fraud and criminality reverberated through communities to surveil immigrants while at the same time restricting their health care options. Because of this, clinic workers consistently articulated strategies to distinguish themselves and their clinics from government agencies and earn the trust of wary patients.

I met Liliana, an amiable and energetic community outreach worker, while I was shadowing some of her colleagues at one of the administrative offices of a red state FQHC network. When we spoke in October 2017, she described how her family's experiences with Medicaid and food stamps informed her approach to clinic work. Liliana's father-in-law used to work at the county Medicaid office, and she asked him frankly why so many of her clinic patients described such terrible experiences there. He replied that it was how they were trained: to believe that everyone who walked into their office was going to lie to them to get free services. Hearing this, Liliana decided to accompany her own parents when they applied for Medicaid and food stamps to witness the interview process for herself. Despite her education and professional health care connections, Liliana spent six hours at the public benefits office, "got nothing accomplished," and walked out in tears. "They completely lost my trust," she said. Liliana was ultimately able to reach out to her personal contacts in the county health care network and resolve her parents' benefits application, but she said it was unfair that she could do so only by relying on connections and institutional knowledge that most clinic patients did not have. "We [community clinics] need to make sure we do everything we can to not be those [county agency workers]," she asserted. "We need to be welcoming, we need to trust people, and we need to work with them to get them services that they need."

To contrast Liliana's experience at the county, she walked me through her team's approach to eligibility interviews—an approach I saw in practice among her trainees as well as in other community clinics I observed. When a patient came in to enroll in a service, she would ask what kind of service they were seeking and then describe the relevant requirements. Liliana stressed that *how* they communicated with patients—everything from tone of voice to the words they chose—was key to earning trust. She emphasized to her colleagues that it was not only a question of doing their jobs and entering data, but really listening to patients. "You may think you know what they need," she would say, "or you may actually know what they need, but they may not know that. So just listen."

Once she understood the patient's needs and concerns, Liliana would begin working on an application with the patient, and if the computerized system asked for a social security number, she would pause and explain that *the application* was asking for this specific information. Liliana warned colleagues that failing to create this space for patients to express their needs and fears would shut down that essential trust. "If you start,

'Give me your social security number, let me look you up in the system,' you already lost their trust." Instead, she would say calmly, "You do have the option to not answer this question, but do understand that if you don't answer this question, it's going to eliminate this possibility. How would you like to proceed?" This approach prevented the patient from having to say explicitly whether they were undocumented or had a temporary status that precluded certain health care options. Liliana's goal was to ensure that patients never felt judged or threatened, which would inevitably undermine the trust she needed to build.

Blue state enrollment counselor Isabel also told me how her personal experience shaped her role at the clinic. Before Isabel had become a certified enrollment counselor and key outreach worker at the clinic, she was an undocumented single mother trying to make ends meet with odd jobs around the county. Isabel emphasized that without a partner's income and without legal status, she could not rent an apartment in the spectacularly expensive region where she lived. Violence in her home country in Central America had destabilized her relatively privileged life there, and after she came to the United States, she found herself homeless and sleeping in parks for a time. Eventually an acquaintance allowed her to stay in her living room while she got back on her feet. During that time, she found work as a gardener and began adjusting her immigration status.

While Isabel was working as a gardener, she applied for Medicaid—an experience that gave her a personal window into negotiating public benefits at the county agency. Isabel told me that when she met with a Medicaid eligibility worker, the worker told her—in Spanish—that she knew for a fact that gardeners made good money but often lied about their income because they were paid in cash. "Remember that I'm keeping tabs," the worker warned Isabel. She then pointed to the many applicant files beside her and said that she was tired of people trying to fool her into getting public benefits. She warned Isabel that she was an educated woman and would not fall for Isabel's attempts to commit benefits fraud. At the time, Isabel—who had a university education—held her tongue and did not react with the anger and hurt she felt. She stoically continued with the application despite the worker's warnings, but she knew that many other patients would have been intimidated out of proceeding.

Later, as a clinic eligibility worker herself, Isabel frequently observed the same interaction play out with clinic patients who were frightened by county Medicaid workers and opted not to apply for public benefits of any kind. She explained that many noncitizen patients saw Medicaid workers as authority figures who represented the government, a government that they perceived as increasingly intent on removing people like them from the country. "What happens to our people [*nuestra gente*] who come from really remote places, and someone [at a Medicaid office] comes and tells them that [warning]?" she asked rhetorically. "They see [the worker] as an authority, and she is the authority, she's from the government." Patients expressed fear to Isabel that Medicaid workers could send them back to countries they had fled for a variety of compelling reasons, and that fear kept them from applying. Isabel understood this deeply on a personal and professional level, and she was angry that the county Medicaid office actively reproduced a narrative of fraud and criminality that kept eligible immigrants excluded from services.

To counter this frustration, Isabel pushed back against these intimidation tactics from multiple angles. At the individual level, she focused on creating space for humanity and empathy during enrollment encounters. "Sometimes we've got such limited time . . . to enroll people that we forget that it's a human situation that's being affected and the paperwork can wait," she explained. "First [we must] give that person space and then we can begin the application, but always while asking the questions with sensitivity." She acknowledged that this could be a difficult job, especially when people were sick and scared and did not have the bandwidth to tackle the medical legal bureaucracy they were confronting. "Sometimes we're so focused on the paperwork," she continued, "and on enrolling [people and] we don't humanize the situation." After all she had gone through, Isabel emphasized how important it was for her to proceed with empathy and humanity rather than bureaucratic efficiency and scare tactics.

At an institutional level, Isabel worked with her own clinic administrators and legal experts to train county Medicaid workers on eligibility criteria and reinforce existing boundaries between medical service enrollment and immigration enforcement. At the community level, she also helped create a health advisory group, which included the county's Medicaid director, that focused on insurance enrollment challenges and cultural sensitivity strategies on behalf of the Latinx immigrant communities in the area. Additionally, she tried to be active in local politics around affordable housing and education, although the discrimination she faced from white people in the community while doing so made her miserable. She sobbed with suppressed rage and humiliation as she recalled being told by fellow attendees of a board of supervisors meeting that she was abusing the system and that she should go back to her own country. She cried in her car after that, but she determined to double down on her work. "That's why I said that I want to work in the health system," she told me, "because working in the health system will help me be able to help other people who have suffered the same, or who continue suffering the same, and don't deserve anyone putting them down, for their accent, for how they look, for their [skin] color."

Like Isabel, Camila understood on a deeply personal level many patients' experiences of anti-immigrant resentment and reluctance to trust the government. When I met her in the red state in 2018, Camila was working the front desk of the free clinic site I was observing. She described how the uncertainty of changing US immigration laws affected her personally and professionally. When DACA was first announced, Camila jumped at the opportunity. Like patient Yesenia, who provided myriad documents to enroll her family in Medicaid, Camila repeatedly provided everything from medical and dental records to school, employment, and domicile documentation to the federal government. When the Trump administration suspended DACA in 2017, Camila feared losing the modicum of security that the program had provided. Even though Camila told me that DACA only granted her permission to work and did not endow her with meaningful legal status, she worried what would happen now that the Trump administration had all her information and apparently intended to, as she said, "get all of the immigrants out of the US." Like patients I spoke with who feared what would happen if the government found out about their medical benefits use, Camila worried about what the end of DACA would mean for her and her family. "I didn't think of that," she remarked. "I thought it was just going to be ongoing, basically. I didn't think of the program ending or anything like that until, actually, it happened."

Camila's work at a free clinic during this time also attuned her to the possibility that some of this increasingly institutionalized anti-immigrant sentiment arose from many US citizens' perceptions that immigrants were taking benefits that rightfully belonged to them. Sometimes people who had health insurance called the free clinic to request an appointment, and Camila had to explain that they only served people without any kind of insurance (even Medicaid). When such callers asked what kind of people had no medical insurance, Camila replied that non-US citizens seldom had medical insurance. In response, she said, "They're like, 'Well, they get benefits from you guys, but we don't?'" Camila was frustrated by this perception—increasingly reproduced at the highest level of government—that "immigrants get all the benefits because they're immigrants." She believed that people did not understand all the eligibility restrictions that kept noncitizens excluded from programs like Medicaid, exchange, private insurance, and food and housing assistance. Camila understood such distinctions because it was her job, but also because she had applied for Medicaid and food stamps for her US-citizen children. At the time, the public benefits agents told her that despite her low income, she could receive only a maximum of sixty dollars per month in food stamps because she was not a US citizen herself. "[US citizens] don't understand the process and the limitations that we have," she continued. "They think that just because we're immigrants, we're taking everything that they are supposed to be getting."

Unlike Camila and most of the clinic workers I spoke with, Natalia was not a paid employee but a volunteer at the purple state free clinic I observed. I first met her in November 2019, as she wound her narrow frame to and fro throughout the small clinic, greeting patients, gathering supplies, and liaising among medical volunteers and patients. She was dressed casually, in jeans, sneakers, and a scarf to keep out the cold of the basement clinic, and she was generous with her smiles. In January 2020 I took advantage of a lull at the end of the day to speak with her about what brought her to volunteer with the clinic. Natalia told me that she had come to the United States from Central America six years ago. She would have liked to remain in her country of origin, but her daughter—who was a US citizen—had a serious chronic illness that required ongoing care in the United States. To secure her daughter's care, Natalia gave up her career as an architect back home and now worked as a housecleaner and Spanish tutor to earn money. She explained that volunteering at the clinic helped her cope with the drastic change in her personal circumstances. "I think it's one of the reasons I'm so committed to doing this work, because it helps me a lot emotionally. I like it," she continued, "it helps me, and it takes me away a bit from thinking about what I'm not doing."

Like many of the free clinic's patients, Natalia was uninsured and had no way to access health care coverage beyond what she could find at "low-cost" clinics in the area. I say "low-cost" because, unlike the free clinic where she volunteered, Natalia had to pay three hundred dollars for a simple checkup and pap smear at the community clinic she attended. Like most of the clinic's patients, however, Natalia also had a somewhat precarious legal status, in that her permission to be in the United States was tied to her US-citizen daughter's health care. Natalia explained that she had never applied for any government benefit unless it was on her daughter's behalf, but she had to stay on top of renewing her temporary status. "I have to constantly renew my status, and obviously I try to absolutely follow the [federal] laws."

I remarked that the Trump administration had announced a few months prior that it was beginning to terminate the kinds of medical exceptions that allowed many immigrants and immigrant families to stay in the United States to receive lifesaving care, and I wondered how this might impact Natalia.[11] She was at a loss to explain: "Yes, I don't know what's happened. As I told you, in the case of [my daughter], she's a citizen. The one who doesn't have any rights is me. . . . What could change is that they tell me that I can't be here anymore, and obviously I'd have to leave. Because my permission is in relation to her illness." While the Trump administration ultimately walked back the medical exceptions visa changes in the face of public outcry, Natalia—like many members of her community—knew that the situation was volatile. In the midst of this chaos, she sought refuge in the mission of the clinic and kept herself busy helping to carry it out.

The reflections of Liliana, Isabel, Camila, and Natalia illustrate how clinic workers' personal experiences as members of the community kept them grounded in the ethos of the clinic while contributing to a medical legal consciousness that rejected the insinuation of criminality often embedded in government agencies. Circumstances had compelled each of them to interact with recordkeeping agencies in often humiliating ways, and they described feeling unsupported or even derided as they attempted to seek benefits—whether Medicaid, food stamps, or deferred action—for which they were in fact eligible. Fortunately for each of them, however, they had the institutional knowledge to persist despite intimidation and uncertainty. They also had the opportunity to mobilize their medical legal consciousness toward enacting a more humane and advocacy-oriented approach within the community clinics where they worked. This placed clinic workers in a difficult position as they balanced this advocacy against uncertain policy changes and the constant need to interact with the various assemblages that discredited their patients and compounded their criminality.

Living Clinic Values: Facilitating, Not Gatekeeping

Given the nuanced individual and collective medical legal consciousness the clinic workers I met expressed, it was not surprising how little gatekeeping happened at any of the clinics I observed. From the front desk staff to the eligibility workers, referrals coordinators, and health care providers, everyone was engaged in facilitating services rather than rationing or blocking them. This in itself was hardly surprising. These community clinics existed to promote the health of community members, and many of the workers were members of that same community themselves. They were explicitly less concerned about the potential for fraudulent service use than government agencies seemed to be, and many clinic workers articulated this sentiment directly. Across all the clinics I observed, many viewed health care as something categorically separate from economic goods that could be defrauded. As Diego, an energetic red state clinic outreach worker, explained,

> The reason why we don't want to act as gatekeepers to that is, they are receiving health care. . . . It's not like they're trying to open up a bogus bank account somewhere. It's health care. Let's put it into perspective: . . . at the end of the day, we trust our patients, and they're going to trust us in return. . . . That's our mandate as a community health center. Obviously, we're going to do our due diligence . . . , but at the end of the day, they're not going to scam to get a doctor's visit, you know what I mean? It doesn't work like that.

Like others I spoke with in the blue and purple states, Diego explicitly differentiated between the driving ethos of the clinic to facilitate essential health care and the ethos of government agencies to ration resources among deserving citizens through suspicion rather than support. This shared institutional value, which I observed in every clinic irrespective of geography, situated health as a right, not a commodity that could be stolen by undeserving criminals. Yet because the clinic workers still had to interact closely with government agencies to enable patients to enact that right, they tread cautiously along the tightrope between patients' fears and the government's watchful eye.

Pedro, the founder of a purple state free clinic I observed, echoed Diego's sentiments regarding his aversion to policing whether the people who came to the clinic "deserved" the care or not. He explained that he was not concerned about whether someone might be "cheating" them out of medical care, especially because you never knew what someone might be going through, whatever their clothes or car or phone might look like. While Pedro's free clinic received private funding that made it more autonomous and less directly accountable to any government agency, it frequently referred patients who required specialty or complex treatment to the state university medical center, where they often would have to become visible to government agencies to access that care. Clinics like Pedro's therefore did all they could within the primary care context to expand access to vital services and build networks with trusted partners wherever possible to limit patients' medical legal vulnerability.

Despite the commitment to their patients' right to health and the empathetic trust-building strategies that frontline clinic workers engaged in, however, red state worker Liliana told me that fear continued to dominate patients' health decisions. She recalled rumors circulating that anyone who helped an undocumented person, or who had an undocumented person living in their home, could be prosecuted and jailed. Undocumented parents also expressed fears that they would be deported if the government discovered that their children were receiving Medicaid. This misinformation, which was reproduced through the county agencies where immigrant families sometimes sought benefits, sparked widespread anxiety. "I'd have people coming to my office crying," Liliana explained, "because they thought that, because I helped them get on [Medicaid], they were [going] to get deported and their kids were going to get left with nothing." In such situations, Liliana anchored herself in the facts she had collected, like the information sheets Gabriela and Elizabeth had shown me. "We can encourage them, we can suggest it, we can give them the facts," she asserted, "but we can never force them." She emphasized that it was up to the patients to make the decision from there, and that she would not compel them to enroll in a service they truly feared accepting.

Much as Camila had described from her personal experience in DACA limbo, Liliana observed that patients' fear of getting caught in the dragnet of immigrant criminalization through Medicaid or other public benefits was analogous to the way that many DACA recipients were now frightened of being on the Trump administration's radar. She recounted that many patients came to the clinic seeking answers from clinic staff about whether they would be deported once their DACA status was stripped. "The government has my information," they would tell her, and they wanted someone in a position of authority to tell them what would happen now. Trying to honor that position of trust and authority, Liliana and her colleagues struggled to calm patients' panic when the Trump administration announced the program's suspension. With so little concrete information at the time, they often felt that there was nothing they could do but say, "I don't know" or "This is what we know now." It was better to say that, Liliana explained, than to provide wrong information. "That sort of stuff affects people's lives," Liliana stressed. "Saying one wrong thing to a person, or enrolling a person into the wrong program, could seriously have effects on them, and we don't want to be the one that put them into that situation."

Given this rational hesitancy to place patients in harm's way, one of the most common refrains I heard across sites was that eligibility workers—whether at the community clinics or federal benefits agencies—could only present options, but the ultimate decision for how to proceed lay with the patient. Yet whereas patients and clinic workers tended to describe interactions with government benefits agencies as one of intentional confusion and intimidation, clinic workers examined eligibility parameters closely to find every way they could to get patients the vital services they needed. I frequently heard from clinic workers that they were trained to present all the options they could, without being directive, to empower patients to make whatever decision they believed was best for themselves and their family. I observed that clinic workers were also transparent about what they did *not* know and collaborative and creative in their efforts to find out more. They made phone calls for and with patients, they attended benefits eligibility trainings to stay up to date with new policies, and they looked at cases from all angles—often in informal partnership with legal experts.

Blue state enrollment counselor Joaquín often met immigrant families who came to the clinic after having negative experiences like those of Yesenia, Liliana, and Isabel at the county benefits agencies, during which workers intimidated applicants. Whereas these agency workers frequently told noncitizen patients that they did not qualify for any benefits because of their legal status, thus closing the door on their health care options, Joaquín and his clinic team conducted their own interviews, considered each case from multiple angles, and explored "every possible way to help them." As an example, Joaquín recalled the case of a young woman who was raped and left for dead at the US-Mexico border. Medicaid workers had told her that she could not receive subsidized physical or mental health benefits because she was undocumented. When Joaquín met her family at the clinic, he explained that because she had interacted with border agents and had a case pending with USCIS, he could help her apply for Medicaid to begin addressing her physical and mental health needs. Joaquín lamented that other people in similar circumstances—undocumented people with health crises—might not find the assistance they needed because public agency workers were less apt to gather such details, examine all eligibility pathways, and respond with appropriate solutions.

When I asked why Joaquín thought there was such a discrepancy between the county's and the clinic's approach, he replied, "You know, that's a question we've been trying to answer. We do not understand." Joaquín suspected that county workers provided all the information that the government mandated them to provide but did not go out of their way to help people understand benefits applications or answer questions. Instead, when patients went to the county, they received incomplete or misguided information in the context of an agency already leery of applicants trying to scam the system. At the community clinics, on the other hand, workers listened to what patients needed and provided detailed information so that they could explore all their options in a supportive rather than antagonistic environment and make truly informed decisions.

As the Trump administration began to dismantle the health and immigration reforms of the Obama administration, however, it became harder for clinic workers to provide patients with clear-cut information. While they might have become understandably discouraged in the face of so many obstacles to patients' health in the 2015–2020 period, many workers expressed that they felt compelled to stay positive. In the blue state, Joaquín emphasized that the clinic must stay "strong for our community," with a message of hope alongside a pragmatic commitment to prepare for whatever may come in the future. "At this point, I feel that there's no room for us to feel bad or have our spirits down," Joaquín added. "I mean, these are the people that look up to people like us to help them. If we're dragging our feet and not having any hope, then . . . what are they going to look forward to? Who's going to be there to help them?"

The political uncertainty and attacks on immigrant families' well-being that escalated during the years of my fieldwork motivated Joaquín even more to get all the information he could and relay this to the community to dispel some of the fear, anxiety, and misinformation that stood between Latinx noncitizens and their health. Like Liliana, Isabel, and Camila, Joaquín knew from his own experience that many people in the community who were eligible for benefits were being driven away because of fear of detention and deportation. He said that people watched the news and saw others being deported, and they decided that it was better to stay under the radar and not ask for trouble by applying for Medicaid, food stamps, or marketplace health plans. "There's so much help out there that they're leaving on the table," Joaquín lamented, "because of the concerns and fears of what could happen if they come out."

Joaquín understood this mentality and acknowledged that his clinic could only do so much to ameliorate it. "Before, our message was, you fill this paperwork, you're okay. It's not a public charge," he explained to me in the summer of 2017, well before the public charge rule change was formally proposed in October 2018. "If you apply for [food stamps] right now, you don't have to worry about that. Now we can't say that." Joaquín said that clinic workers no longer had the capacity to say with certainty that such benefits would not penalize noncitizens in some way. In particular, Joaquín worried that the Trump administration might decide to collect data on everyone who applied for Medicaid and even go back ten years into the system to discover who sought benefits when. This suspicion especially circulated among people who had legal status—even naturalized citizenship—and who declined benefits enrollment because they believed that they might be penalized and stripped of their citizenship chances.

Joaquín said that this all went back to the same fear of immigration enforcement and "losing something," and that everyone would be on edge with the extreme unpredictability of the Trump administration. "I mean, he has DACA right now hanging on a thread," he explained, and drew a parallel between DACA and Medicaid surveillance, saying that both amounted to "having all my information in the system." Red state worker Delmy echoed this sentiment, adding that Trump's election deterred many patients from applying for medical benefits, especially for Medicaid services that had to be renewed on a regular basis. "They can be people that have had it for years in the past and they've applied every year on the day that it's going to be due so that they don't have an interruption of service," Delmy explained. "Then now it's like 'Nope, the president that we have right now, who knows what's going to happen? This is just another way for them to keep tabs on me, and they might just decide to throw us all out of here.'"

Regardless of the state context, clinic workers engaged in similar strategies to build trust with patients while adapting their medical legal consciousness to a changing political reality. When I spoke with purple state oncology worker Nadine in early 2020, she described working closely with attorneys from a state health justice center to grasp the complex nuances of benefits eligibility to maximize patient care without compromising their security. Nadine mobilized this knowledge toward assisting undocumented and liminally legal patients who came to her for help financing their cancer care, and many of them had been told by other institutions throughout the state that they were ineligible for any kind of health care because of their status. Nadine explained that sometimes people misrepresented their status to her because they feared that if they were honest, they would not get care. "And in some institutions, that's true. But not in ours. So I'm really fortunate, and it's one of the reasons why I work in the institution I do, because I can honestly say to people, 'It doesn't matter what your status is. If you live in [this state], you're gonna get the care you need.' . . . But if I worked for another institution that's private and not public, I would be saying something different potentially."

Persuading patients to trust her was becoming more difficult as the public charge rule change went into effect and amplified fears in immigrant communities. Nadine learned from the health justice center attorneys that this was really a "fear-based campaign" rather than a fundamental eligibility shift—especially for undocumented immigrant patients—and that most of the existing pathways to care she relied on for her patients remained in place. She emphasized that as this fear-based campaign accelerated, it was even more necessary for her to build patients' trust and remain a source of clear, well-informed guidance: "You really have to build people's trust, and you really have to help them understand that they're safe. You know, this is a medical institution, we're here to give you care. We're not here to get anybody else involved or to get you in trouble. And people are scared. And they're more scared now than they ever have been."

In an effort to bolster trust in the face of rising fear, many clinic workers emphasized to patients that their respective clinics were originally established to serve migrant workers, so their historical and ongoing commitments were first and foremost with immigrant communities. Along with highlighting the clinic's roots in migrant health, red state nurse Maya also emphasized her clinic's staying power in the community. She explained that while she could try to reassure patients by citing government brochures and privacy legislation, the strongest reason for patients to trust the clinic was its continued presence in the community despite everything that seemed to be working against their mission. Despite constant attacks on immigrant communities over the years, the clinic continued to provide support. "We've still been here," she explained. "Every time you come in, it doesn't change. Every time you come in, we don't ask for your social [security number]." Even though patients continued to express fears about clinics or their affiliated agencies sharing information with immigration agencies, the frontline workers I spoke with believed that the strongest proof was in their work itself.

Conclusion

As social welfare and immigration laws in recent decades accelerated medical legal violence by expanding the surveillance and potential criminality of low-income immigrants of color via public benefits receipt, the Trump administration doubled down on these exclusions through policies like the public charge rule change and threatening medical deferrals. In the face of such violence, community clinic workers drew upon their medical legal consciousness to prioritize Latinx immigrant patients' well-being. While government agencies wielded policy uncertainty to reinforce myths and misinformation that persuaded many noncitizen and mixed-status families to preemptively avoid services for which they were eligible, clinic workers pushed back against this disenfranchisement. Instead of leveraging their brokerage positions to become proxies for immigration enforcement, as some of their Medicaid counterparts seemed to do, they mobilized their liminal position between community and government to engage in informational campaigns directed at both the community and the very agencies that often intimidated their patients. They did all this, even while federal policy making complicated those efforts and sometimes even threatened them with the possibility of surveillance and penalty through that very work.

The medical legal consciousness exemplified by the clinic workers I met between 2015 and 2020 enabled them to advocate on behalf of their communities—communities that have been largely excluded from health care—while resisting and sometimes attempting to reform the government agencies they worked with closely to facilitate that care. Despite the difficult balancing act such negotiations involved, clinic workers demonstrated an unflagging commitment to maximizing their patients' health potential while taking seriously their concerns about possible immigration consequences. The examples in this chapter illustrate how clinic workers' personal experiences as criminalized, surveilled immigrants and/or members of immigrant families contributed to their medical legal consciousness and compelled them to approach their patients' situations with humanity and perseverance in the face of rising medical legal violence. They mobilized toward an ethos of health care as a universal human right rather than a narrow privilege of citizenship by enacting individual and institutional practices that treated patients with dignity and compassion rather than suspicion. Even as contemporary policies exacerbated the physical harms of legal violence and attempted to enroll health institutions in federal immigration surveillance, clinic workers strived to help patients balance their health needs against fears that seeking health care might put themselves or their families at risk.

Despite major policy changes happening at the federal level and lack of clarity about how those policies, like public charge, would impact the communities they served, each of the red, blue, and purple state clinic workers I observed persisted in their mission to enact health care as a right for people regardless of their legal status. Their medical legal consciousness emerged as much from personal experiences of being "against" the law as from professional knowledge of working "with" it on behalf of their patients, and this dual consciousness allowed them to respond to heightened medical legal violence with ingenuity and compassion. Even so, clinic workers continue to face an uphill battle. Despite their efforts, medical legal violence remains a powerful and widespread structural force that relies upon the disposability of immigrant labor and the political exclusion of millions of Latinx immigrants to reproduce existing economic and racial inequities. As the COVID-19 pandemic began to unfold and bring my research to an end, it became clear that clinic workers' dedicated efforts to push back against this violence would fall short of ensuring patients' health in the absence of real structural change.

Conclusion

What the Pandemic Has Laid Bare

The COVID-19 pandemic struck my purple state fieldsite in the early days of March 2020. Among many changes it brought in its wake, I could no longer conduct observations or interview patients, and so in many ways my research project ended there. I was able to continue connecting with clinic workers remotely, however, and some of them updated me on how the virus was impacting the communities they served. Near the end of March, I spoke with a physician, Dr. McMillan, who was working at the health department in the county where I conducted fieldwork. Being in such a rural county, she had thought they would have more time to prepare for a COVID-19 outbreak, but in fact they had one of the first confirmed cases in the state. Suddenly everyone was scrambling to get a system in place, and Dr. McMillan was worried what might happen if the virus hit the poultry plants. She recalled a man who was working at three different poultry factories several years ago who contracted rubella and exposed many other workers. Several of the women working along-side him who were pregnant had to terminate their pregnancies because their exposure imperiled the fetus. This episode made Dr. McMillan fully cognizant of the danger such a contagious respiratory infection posed.

When we began talking, Dr. McMillan remarked that she had just driven by one of the poultry plants and saw five hundred cars in the parking lot. Meanwhile, some of the more progressive counties nearby were under a stay-at-home order, even though no such mandate had come down from the state yet. Dr. McMillan was nervous. She explained that the county health department did not have the authority to close businesses, but she thought it likely that the state would shut down the poultry plants if anyone tested positive there. The problem was that the SARS-CoV-2 virus often spread through asymptomatic carriers, so she could not be sure that this would be an effective strategy. "There's just so many nightmare scenarios when you have so many people working so close together with an infectious disease," she warned. Dr. McMillan added that there was the potential for massive contagion at the poultry factories, and she knew that it would be hard to keep the virus out of the community once it hit there. In the first place, she explained, poultry factories worked with a "very narrow margin of profitability," and if workers did not show up to work, they would not get paid. There was no incentive for someone to stay home to protect themselves or others because there was no economic safety net.

Second, she knew it would be difficult for people who tested positive to self-isolate. One of the first COVID-19 cases in the county was a man who she said lived "in a very wealthy part of the county in a ten-bedroom home." This made it relatively easy for him to quarantine at home without putting family members at risk. "They could self-isolate perfectly," Dr. McMillan said, "but if you're in a mobile home with ten people, you just can't do it. I think it's going to hit the poorer communities really, really hard when it starts there. That's what I fear." She also emphasized that this would particularly impact immigrant Latinx families because that was who worked at the poultry plant. "We are on the brink of seeing how the system works for undocumented people here," she said with a mirthless laugh. She also expressed concern that an outbreak among Latinx workers might fuel anti-immigrant prejudice as everyone looked for someone to blame.

It was not long before some of Dr. McMillan's fears materialized, as coronavirus outbreaks slammed poultry plants across the state. In early May 2020, I emailed her to follow up on our conversation and ask how things were going at the county health department. She replied with an email message that felt very much like a telegram from a war zone:

> [Our] county has been hit hard by the virus. the poultry processing plant has 1700 employees living in at least 4 counties. despite the numerous positives in employees and their families, 147, by our count to date, and remains open. It is nuts. no way to stop a pandemic which will now hit rural communities.

My blood ran cold when I read it. She was not exaggerating, and once again her predictions would bear out within weeks. Across the country, the virus was running rampant in rural areas where immigrant workers from around the world worked in poultry- and meat-processing industries (Vásquez 2020; Dickerson and Jordan 2020; Taylor, Boulos, and Almond 2020). Through my networks, I heard claims that suggested that about 50 percent of the COVID-19 cases at the state university medical center hospital were poultry workers. While the changing nature of the pandemic and HIPAA protections over hospital records prevent me from substantiating such claims, they do align with what we now know about COVID-19. The virus has struck Black and Brown "essential workers" and their families and communities with particular vengeance because of where they are positioned in relation to structural violence and systemic neglect.[1]

Around this same time that the virus began spiraling through the state, I gave a virtual lecture where I met a medical student named Emma. She was studying at the state university medical center and had recently volunteered to carry out COVID testing in the community. I asked Emma to walk me through her experience participating in COVID testing at a large poultry plant and an elementary school in the same county where the free clinic I observed was located, and where Dr. McMillan had witnessed the start of the local outbreak. As a medical student, she felt that it was "bizarre" to be a part of "something more important or more official" than her standard medical coursework. She explained that the testing was a collaboration among the poultry plant hosting the testing on site, the National Guard, a university-affiliated clinic, and the county health department. Many of us have struggled to describe the ineffable strangeness of pandemic life, and words like "bizarre," "weird," and "surreal" abounded in Emma's description. "To go to a place where you knew that there were so many actual positive cases of COVID was a little surreal," Emma recalled. "It felt like you were actually on 'the front lines.' It was a little strange."

Emma also found it strange to be working so closely with the National Guard. Even though clinical staff and health department workers were in charge of registering patients and documenting symptoms, it was the National Guard members who actually conducted the COVID tests. "They had a lot of their trucks and equipment out," Emma remembered, "which is another weird thing that I hadn't entirely expected." I asked Emma to elaborate and paint me a picture of what the testing looked like:

When you got there, the testing site was all outdoors. It was set up in the parking lot of the poultry plant. It included a few different tents where they had it set up. It had a tent with the public health department where they were doing some stuff on their end with registration and giving people paperwork to fill out. Then our section of tents was the second place that you would drive up to since most of the testing was being done from people's cars and not actually people walking up. Most of that dealt with registering them in the EMR [electronic medical record] of the health system so that we could keep track of the patients and have a place to order the tests and things like that. Then after that was the tents that were set up by the health department to actually do the testing. . . . The first people they meet I think would be health department employees. The next people would be people from the clinic. Then the last people would be the National Guard for the actual testing.

Emma described a scene in which employees from the poultry plant and their families drove into the plant's parking lot, showed a photo ID to the health department and clinic employees to get registered in the EMR, and then passed through the parking lot toward the National Guard station where they would be tested. Emma said that representatives from the poultry plant were present but not very involved. She described this as one of the more "cooperative" poultry plants because, unlike many other plants in the area, its leadership actually agreed to work with local health officials and the National Guard to carry out testing on site.

When I asked what kind of identification the health department accepted to register people in the EMR, Emma replied that most people used their employee ID from the plant. She added that they "accepted anything as a photo ID" and recalled that "somebody had a driver's license that had expired over ten years ago, possibly twenty years ago." They were not preoccupied with whether someone had a valid government ID, but they did want to have a record of who was tested to determine (1) who might need follow-up after a positive test or evidence of exposure, and (2) who might pay for the test if the patient had insurance.

Emma explained that they used the whole length of the parking lot and had people snake through in their cars from one tent to another, with the final destination at the National Guard tents. I asked Emma what it looked like from her perspective once the workers and their families had provided their identification, gotten registered in the electronic record, and then headed toward the National Guard. She said that there were a lot of guardspeople gathered around their big National Guard trucks, but the atmosphere was fairly relaxed. They were wearing what she referred to as a "casual uniform" and seemed to keep to themselves for the most part. "It seems like they had shifts during the testing," she added. "There'd only be two of them doing the testing at one time. There were a lot of other people from the National Guard there, I just don't exactly know what their job was. The two people doing the testing would have hazmat suits, everybody else was just in the regular uniform with a mask."

One of the things that stood out most to me in my conversation with Emma was that, for the most part, people were required to come to the testing sites in their vehicles. (This was common at the poultry plant and required at the elementary school parking lot.) Emma remarked that some of the cars were "incredibly beaten up and clearly very old and probably would not pass inspection." She specifically recalled that the person who had the "extremely expired driver's license" also had an "incredibly broken-down" car. Someone else carried a gallon milk jug filled with some kind of engine fluid. Every time their car broke down while moving through the testing line, they had to get out of the car and pour fluid in the engine. "It was kind of a bizarre thing that happens," Emma concluded blandly.

Emma's observations brought up many of the questions that occupied my mind since I began research in the area, and that the pandemic underscored dramatically. I thought about how the 2008 health department investigation had precipitated new bureaucratic practices in health centers to monitor patients' identities in the name of patient safety and institutional accountability. I considered the expansion of interconnected EMR systems whose proliferation was important for continuity of care and contagion tracking, but also made patients more visible to government agencies that could exercise broad surveillance authority in the name of public health and safety. I also recalled the many times driver's license issues came up in my interviews, as I imagined workers lining up with expired licenses (or no licenses), in cars that likely would have gotten them pulled over on the road or stopped at a checkpoint, at the poultry plant in front of their employer and the US National Guard to find out whether they had been exposed to a deadly virus.

Of course, the connections between legal violence and the COVID-19 pandemic extend far beyond the purple state. The same exploitative labor relations, systemic racism, and medical legal violence that people in the red, blue, and purple states described well before the pandemic are the very forces that have made the virus so staggeringly destructive in low-income communities of color across the United States. As I write this now, the pandemic is still unfolding, and it will likely be some time yet before we can assess the precise human toll—let alone the state of the broken families and communities left in its wake. By early 2021 alone, the *New England Journal of Medicine* reported that in twenty of the forty-five US states that had COVID-19 data available by ethnic group, "The proportion of Covid-19 cases among Latinx people is at least double what would be expected on the basis of population, and in 11 of the 45 states, it is more than three times as high" (Page and Flores-Miller 2021, citing data from the COVID Tracking Project). And those data only include race and/or ethnicity (an already complex question among Latinx groups), not legal status, so it is difficult to know the magnitude of the pandemic among Latinx immigrants with varying citizenship status.

What we do know, and what should be abundantly clear at this point in the book, is that COVID-19 has flourished within *and because of* the state of exception that US health and immigration policies have created. The same inclusion/exclusion dynamic I discussed in chapter 1 is playing out in front of our eyes as millions of Latinx immigrant "essential workers" remain excluded from basic health and labor protections while facing the ongoing symbolic and material threats of anti-immigrant rhetoric and policies. If the compounded bodily harms of medical legal violence were not sufficiently clear in the previous chapters, the reader will find no better evidence of its consequences than in the current coronavirus pandemic. The pandemic's astounding racial and ethnic disparities are the direct result of an economic system that relies upon the disposability of low-wage workers within a society that privileges the well-being of white citizens of means. If there is any doubt about this statement, one must only look at the epidemiological statistics indicating a higher burden of disease and death for nonwhite groups (COVID

Tracking Project 2021), or the mismatch between exposure potential and eligibility criteria for COVID relief, to disabuse them of that notion.[2]

Looking Back

The coronavirus pandemic has revealed that while much has changed since I began writing this book, much has stayed the same. In trying to write this story, I have faced tension between a daily barrage of immigration news and a more measured sense that the present moment is not in fact a major departure from the existing dynamics of immigrant health opportunities in the United States. I have tried to render faithfully the widespread sense of upheaval that the Trump administration generated and the way uncertainty proliferated during those years, without overstating its uniqueness. I have asked myself whether the latest political transitions in the United States represent a departure from the past or an amplification of some of the nation's more troubling characteristics as we build our collective future. These questions remained ever present as I considered my conversations over the years and began assembling a small piece of the story they told.

Each of the preceding chapters illuminated the human stakes of changing immigration and health policies in the contemporary United States. I began by describing how accelerating legal violence has facilitated continued attempts to exclude many Latinx immigrants from full social belonging in the United States, focusing on the discursive and material "state of emergency" as a form of legal violence typifying the Trump administration's approach to immigration law. I argued that the symbolic violence of anti-immigrant rhetoric and increasing legal violence kept Latinx immigrants with varying legal status in a "state of exception" (Agamben 2005) that compounded their experiences of being indispensable yet disposable labor, with both immediate and compounded injury. I then examined these dynamics in three different states—a red, blue, and purple state—and compared the circumstances of their medical legal violence.

In the red state, an assemblage of bureaucratic obstacles, punitive immigration laws, and restrictive health policies subjected thousands of Latinx immigrants to medical legal violence. There, local and federal immigration policies coupled with exclusionary health policies to trigger serious health consequences for many noncitizens and their families. In the blue state, the 2016 election challenged clinical care in a progressive jurisdiction under enhanced immigration enforcement priorities at the federal level. Despite—and often *because of*—the state's uniquely expansive pathways to comprehensive care for noncitizens, the power of federal immigration surveillance and enforcement destabilized local clinics' ability to optimize the health care safety of those who needed it most. In the purple state, we saw the unique permutations of medical legal violence in a "new" immigrant destination in the US South, where in a relatively short time, the politics of criminalizing immigrants have become increasingly institutionalized in safety net health care institutions. In each site, clinic workers have leveraged their medical legal consciousness to resist this medical legal violence and reinforce their commitment to immigrants' health rights. Despite dramatic differences in the political context of each state, the surprisingly similar situations of patients and clinic workers I have described across the three fieldsites underscore the inescapable force of federal immigration and health laws to shape what is possible for noncitizens' health chances irrespective of local conditions.

The stories in this book capture a volatile moment of rising fear and uncertainty in immigrant communities and focus on how perception shapes health choices. By illuminating patients' and clinic workers' perspectives, these stories enable a more thorough consideration of the human consequences of legal violence—both in its structural and symbolic aspects—on noncitizens' bodies, as well as the details of how these harms are intensified by anti-immigrant practices and policies of surveillance and penalization. Further, by exploring some of the specific dynamics whereby medical legal violence has expanded in three distinct fieldsites, I have drawn attention to how micro-, meso-, and macro-level structures and processes reproduce and compound these different types of violence on its targets—both Latinx noncitizens and, in some cases, the clinic workers who facilitate their care. I locate the tension between embodied health risks and sociopolitical risks within the trajectory of both health and immigration policies in the contemporary United States, since both intersect to shape Latinx noncitizens' health decisions today. These stories provide new evidence for how this accelerating phenomenon materially affects Latinx immigrants facing health crises.

They also underscore how the legal violence that constructs Latinx immigrants as both criminals and essential workers puts many in harm's way while foreclosing opportunities for remedying the physical injury and/or illness resulting from that harm.

Moving Forward

I close here by suggesting several directions for future research and policy making in the field of immigrant health. My research found that even the *perception* of enhanced immigration surveillance had consequences for how Latinx noncitizens and clinic workers made health care decisions. Scholars and journalists had already begun identifying a chilling effect on immigrants and mixed-status families seeking health care in the wake of the Trump administration's promises of enhanced immigration surveillance and enforcement (K. Kennedy 2018; Bernstein et al. 2019; Haley et al. 2020; Guerrero, Dominguez-Villegas, and Vargas Bustamante 2021; Nwadiuko et al. 2021), and the stories I have described here align with this trend. More research is needed to determine whether such a decline in health service utilization has indeed occurred and, if so, at what rate and with what potential consequences. Quantitative and longitudinal studies are well suited to such an investigation, and their findings will be especially relevant to clinicians and policy makers concerned with noncitizens' and mixed-status families' well-being.

As the Biden administration pursues its immigration policy priorities in the months and years ahead, we must consider carefully the direct and indirect effects of contemporary health and immigration policies on Latinx noncitizens' and mixed-status families' health chances. On his first day in office, President Biden announced several immigration actions designed to symbolically and materially undo many of the harms of the Trump administration, including protecting DACA, rescinding the Muslim and African travel bans, revising civil immigration enforcement priorities and pausing removals for one hundred days, ending border wall construction, suspending new entrants into the Migrant Protection Protocols, and promoting legislative reform through the US Citizenship Act of 2021 (National Immigration Law Center 2021a). Additionally, after much litigation and a decision by a federal court to vacate the Trump-era public charge rule change, the Biden administration announced that it did not intend to pursue the Trump administration's appeal. Therefore, on March 15, 2021, USCIS issued a rule removing the 2019 public charge rule change from the Code of Federal Regulations and restoring public charge inadmissibility criteria to their previous terms.[3]

These changes and proposed reforms signal the possibility of a relatively less punitive immigration regime under the Biden administration. While it is too soon to gauge the potential scope of these new policies, they undoubtedly represent a more inclusive turn and create some space for positive change. So far, however, the real and proposed changes discussed by the Biden administration stop far short of proactively dismantling the exclusionary health and welfare policies that have become entrenched over the past few decades. Real, lasting change must take into account how heightened medical legal violence over the past few years may continue to reverberate in immigrant communities unless the underlying legal violence they face is addressed in material ways. As the National Immigration Law Center emphasized in its overview of the Biden administration's immigration program, "Current law denies many types of immigrants access to [health care and nutrition] programs, leading to harmful effects that have been profoundly exacerbated during the COVID-19 pandemic, in particular because of the high number of immigrants who are essential workers" (National Immigration Law Center 2021a). Such laws are not inevitable, and this moment of crisis and change is the time to reimagine what might be possible if the United States were to abandon some of its most discriminatory and least humane policies in the realms of immigration and health.

Regardless of one's political affiliation, there is nearly universal recognition that both the US immigration system and the health care system are broken. There is also growing acknowledgment, especially in the wake of COVID-19, of the role of white supremacy within a capitalist economic order in the creation and maintenance of those broken systems. Until we collectively reckon with these realities at a societal level and commit resources and energy toward dismantling them, they will continue to fuel health inequity and perpetuate the medical legal violence I have written about in this book. Truly comprehensive immigration and health reforms would require a serious realignment of economic and political priorities in the United States, one based on the fundamental humanity of those whose lives have long been constructed as disposable and criminal. What choices would federal and state policy makers make differently if they proceeded from the same ethos of care and medical legal consciousness that the clinic staff I met employ in their everyday work? What would it look like to elevate the notion of health care as a basic human right and build policies around that core value?

The tragedies of the coronavirus pandemic offer lessons for how we can and should transform health policy in the United States as it relates to citizens and noncitizens alike. At one point in April 2020, twenty-three million people in the United States were unemployed (US Bureau of Labor Statistics 2020). While this situation has stabilized over the course of the pandemic, such massive economic crises reveal the dangers of an insurance system primarily predicated on employment. The exogenous shock of this public health emergency also reveals the interconnectedness of individual and population-level health. If the nation's health care safety nets are to absorb the pandemic's long-term fallout, policy makers must prioritize strengthening programs and institutions that promote health irrespective of employment and legal status, ability to pay, or racial and ethnic background. Just as many states—like the blue state I observed—optimized ACA opportunities to expand their health care safety nets while cultivating more immigrant-inclusive policies than have existed at the federal level, pandemic recovery efforts represent a space for states to reevaluate their health and welfare programs in relation to those most impacted by COVID-19. Even when the federal government pursues exclusionary policies like the 2020 Coronavirus Aid, Relief, and Economic Security (CARES) Act that lock many immigrant and mixed-status families out of vital support, states can decide whether to remedy that exclusion—as California and New York did by making additional economic stimulus support available to undocumented immigrants and their families—or exacerbate it (Kaur 2020; Correal and Ferré-Sadurní 2021).

Health equity for Latinx noncitizens and their families living in the United States will require addressing the many barriers to social inclusion that I have discussed throughout this book. While these barriers are by no means novel in the broader arc of US history, the exclusionary anti-immigrant policies that have unfolded across distinct political administrations in recent years have cast the contours of exclusionary rhetoric, practices, and laws in a brighter light than ever before. In particular, during the time that I conducted research for this book, the explicitness of the Trump administration's politics meant that everything was illuminated without the polish of more deft political maneuvering. Even casual observers could witness and precisely name discrimination in real time. Previous federal administrations had obscured the harms of their immigration policies behind guises such as criminal law and welfare reform (Clinton), the War on Terror (G. W. Bush), or the supposed prioritization of criminal removal in favor of noncriminal aliens (Obama); in contrast, the Trump administration pursued policies that were boldly anti-immigrant in ways that more clearly revealed legal violence, and its concomitant biopolitical surveillance and social control, in the contemporary United States.

Throughout fieldwork and the writing of this book, I witnessed a kind of natural experiment in immigration and health policy from 2015 to 2020 in three distinct states. I found that anti-immigrant policy priorities made their way into medical bureaucracies to expand legal violence against Latinx immigrants of varying legal status throughout the United States, resulting in bodily harms while reproducing existing social inequalities rooted in the United States' long history of capitalism and white supremacy. The empirical evidence of these impacts suggests that they had material consequences for the health of Latinx noncitizens and mixed-status families as well as clinic workers, whose medical legal consciousness and commitment to health rights made them strive to facilitate care without exposing their patients or themselves to immigration surveillance or enforcement.

Ultimately, this book reflects a particularly challenging moment in history for Latinx immigrants negotiating health care in the United States, and I acknowledge that the story I have presented here is a fairly bleak one. At the same time, these situations could have been worse for the patients I encountered. That they were not is a testament to the incredible efforts of the clinic workers I observed. Time and again, the violence I have described in the preceding pages was met by the subtle, collective resistance of clinic workers, often in the most mundane ways. When the medical legal violence that Latinx immigrant patients faced led them into illness and injury, the workers at the clinics I observed fought valiantly to keep them whole. Much as communities of color, led especially by Black women, organized to get out the vote and overcome voter suppression during the 2020 elections to deliver Democratic victories in key states in ways that by now fundamentally challenge the "red, blue, purple" schema I have used in this book (see, e.g., Campbell and Vercellone 2020; Herndon 2020; and Han and McKenna 2021), clinic workers mobilized within their respective institutions to prioritize the health and security of the patients they served. While it is impossible to include everything in one book, I conclude here by highlighting their efforts and celebrating their many successes.

As I drafted the previous chapters, I frequently consulted fieldnotes I had written that were bursting with the everyday, repetitive clinic tasks that seldom make for compelling reading by outsiders. Yet, having been a case manager myself, I understood that there were many ways one could approach the bureaucratic hurdles between a patient and their potential health care coverage or service. Frontline workers have the opportunity to act as facilitators or gatekeepers for those who enter their queue, and every single worker I encountered chose the former. Beyond the fact that this was an explicit, essential characteristic of the institutional culture at each site I observed, clinic workers often expressed personal reasons for their humane approach to health provision. Some had been undocumented immigrants themselves or currently held DACA status. Others were the children of immigrants who witnessed, and often tried to resolve, their parents' struggles to get such services themselves.

The clinics I observed in the red, blue, and purple states serve as an example of resistance against the inclusion/exclusion dynamic that I describe in chapter 1, and in so doing they exemplify the possibility for positively exceptional spaces that push back against racialized oppression by enabling individuals and communities to thrive. Many of the clinics I observed began as migrant-serving institutions whose reason for being was to bring health care to Latinx agricultural workers, and many continue this effort as a key pillar of their work today. In this way, contemporary immigrant-serving clinics function as a space of positive, life-affirming exception within a state of negative, life-denying exclusion. Amidst the compounding chaos of immigration policy and health policy destabilization, these clinics have remained open and welcoming, and their own "essential" workers continue to provide vital services despite being increasingly constrained by the medical legal infrastructure that otherwise threatens to create conditions of bare life. It is a difficult act to balance, and they are not always aware of all the risks or possible unintended consequences, but they manage incredible feats in the face of federal priorities that make life unbearable for those who are often cast as illicit, undeserving, and disposable. For their tireless work, I express my profound admiration.

ACKNOWLEDGMENTS

That this book exists at all is due in large part to the steadfast support of my family, friends, and colleagues. This book is the collective product of everyone who has helped, challenged, and loved me over the past several years as I have learned and faltered in equal measure. I thought this process would be easier, but much has happened in this time that I never anticipated. Rather than recount these challenges here, I celebrate those who enabled me to weather them. To all of you, I am grateful.

Thank you to my family. To my parents, Joan and Tim, I will never find the words to express my appreciation for all the ways that you have been there for me through the years. You are still here for me today, and I am so grateful for the miracles that made this small fact possible. To my siblings: thank you for how you have inspired me over the years. Pete, your strength, intelligence, and willfulness are an example to us all, and I thank you for bringing Katie, Raylee, and Ryker into our family to brighten our lives incalculably. Canaway, I have yet to meet anyone who is at once so kind and yet so fierce as you. Your quiet power never ceases to amaze me. Amy, I have always admired your boldness, creativity, and generous spirit. You inspire me to live in the moment and hold fast to joy, and I thank you for that. Timog and Ian, you have taught me to be strong. The lessons we have learned as a family have sometimes been hard ones, but we have borne them together and will, I hope, become stronger because of them.

To my extended family and friends: I could not have made it this far without you. Pais and Phil, I appreciate your constant support more than I could ever express. I can never repay your kindness to me, but I will strive to live in your example. Thank you to my grandparents, especially Grandma "Nana," who blazed this trail for me in so many ways that I am only now beginning to know and appreciate. *A la familia Fuentes, gracias por todo lo que han hecho por mí y por mi familia. Siempre llevaré en mi corazón el ejemplo de su cariño, apoyo, y generosidad.* Meilyn Santana, *o livro que apresento aqui não existiria sem você, e agradeço a você e Jean por me apoiarem desde o início*. To Christina Araiza-Quiter and the Araiza family, I am especially grateful for your generous support as I got this project off the ground.

While I am grateful to so many friends whose encouragement has buoyed me through these tempestuous years, I'd like to specifically thank the following for their unflagging support: Crystal Loucel, not only did you enable the expansion of this project beyond where I ever envisioned it could go, but you lifted me up whenever I stumbled and helped me always see the light at the end. Celina Gonzalez, the depth of your wisdom, patience, and kindness is unmatched, and I am humbled by your example and grateful for your support. Amy Lithimane, thank you for your remarkable generosity, hospitality, and ability to summon adventure amidst chaos. RaeAnn Anderson, for more than a decade you have shown me what it means to be a true friend and a committed scholar, and I am grateful every day for both. Nessa Nemir, you taught me to find my confidence and to boldly become the person you knew I could be. Carmen Gutierrez, my pandemic quaran-twin, you held together a world that was falling apart at the seams and created magic when reality was too much to bear. I would have to write another book to truly capture what that meant to me. Zainab Altai, you have been both my biggest cheerleader and greatest source of inspiration. *Te agradezco por tu entusiasmo, alentamiento, y amistad.*

I also owe much to my erstwhile classmates and peer mentors at UCSF and beyond, including Chadwick Campbell, Taylor Cruz, Naina Khanna, Tessa Nápoles, Sara Rubin, Ariana Thompson-Lastad, and Lily Walkover. Special thanks go to Mel Jeske, Florencia Rojo, and Rosalie Winslow for their dedicated emotional and writing support—particularly as I neared the end of this project. Your remarkable patience and kindness have carried me forward more times than I can count. I am also grateful to my most recent colleagues, including Alessandra Bazo-Vienrich, Camila Álvarez, Stephanie Canizales, and Thomas Williams, for their brilliance and mutual support. Finally, I deeply appreciate my various writing accountability group members over the years, including Margaret Bostrom, Ami Schiess, Dalia Magaña, Aditi Chandra, Yiran Xu, and Irene Yen, for creating community and being "there" for one another despite never actually converging in the same place.

To my mentors, I deeply value your patient guidance and unwavering support. Rina Bliss, Howard Pinderhughes, and Janet Shim: I have learned much from each of you and appreciate how you have, in your own ways, helped me grow as a scholar and human being. Thank you for teaching me how to see the world as a sociologist, letting my mind run wild, and helping me rein it back in when needed (which was often the case). Cecilia Menjívar, I am grateful for your deep expertise and focused guidance as I have navigated research obstacles and ethical challenges throughout the course of this research. Nancy Burke, thank you for the many opportunities you have made possible for me throughout my doctoral education, postdoctoral journey, and early faculty career. I am also grateful to Tiffany Joseph and Nita Farahany for their expert guidance as I pursued this book project.

This research was inspired by my previous work at Operation Access and funded in part by UC MEXUS, the University of California San Francisco (UCSF) Department of Social and Behavioral Sciences' Harrington and Strauss Scholarships, the UCSF Graduate Division, and the UCSF School of Nursing Century Club. During the writing of this book, I also received funding from the Duke University Initiative for Science and Society and University of California Merced Center for the Humanities. Additionally, I received ample, insightful feedback from the anonymous readers who reviewed various iterations of the book manuscript, as well as an earlier article (published in *Social Science and Medicine*) where I first conceptualized some of the ideas that appear in this book. I truly appreciate their thoughtful feedback, and I am also grateful for the developmental editing support I received along the way.

To the participants and the extended community who made this research possible, *les doy mil gracias desde el fondo de mi corazón*. This research unfolded during an especially painful time for immigrant communities in the United States, and the patience and generosity of participants and community partners allowed me to be a witness to both the violence of this moment in history and the strength of human resistance against it. I hope that I have done your stories justice and that my work can contribute in some small way to that remarkable resistance.

APPENDIX 1

Additional Data and Methods Details

This book relies on ethnographic observations and interviews conducted with eighty participants in three states—red, blue, and purple—between 2015 and 2020. In the red state, I interviewed thirteen patients and nineteen clinic and/or community workers. In the blue state, I interviewed nine patients and eighteen clinic/community workers. In the purple state, I interviewed twelve patients and nine clinic/community workers. Of the thirty-four patients I interviewed across the sites, thirty-three were born in Latin America, and one was a US-born Latina in a mixed-status family. And although I did not ask about the ethno-racial background of the clinic and community workers I interviewed, the vast majority of frontline clinic staff referenced being from Latinx/Hispanic families and communities. Many were immigrants themselves, with current legal residence, naturalized citizenship, or DACA status. Only a few of the clinicians (e.g., nurses or physicians) spoke about being Latina/Latino, Hispanic, or Chicana/Chicano themselves (mostly in the red state), and two were immigrants from Latin America (both in the purple state).

The total number of interviews and the ratio of patients to clinic professionals and community affiliates were matters of timing and politics rather than any systematic sampling plan on my part. It was a sensitive topic in a sensitive place (the clinic) during a sensitive time in US immigration politics, and I made the best of whatever goodwill and trust brokering I could manage at each site over the years. I recruited patient participants from the clinics during ethnographic observations, and I recruited clinic and community workers through professional networks and snowball sampling, and during observations. I conducted almost all of the in-depth interviews with patients in the clinics I observed, most often in a conference room or empty exam room. I usually interviewed clinic and community workers in their place of work (clinic, hospital, or community organization), but I sometimes met with them in a public place, like a café or restaurant, or (very rarely) spoke with them by phone. I did the interviews in each participant's language of choice (English, Spanish, or Portuguese), audio-recorded the interviews, and analyzed the transcripts in their original language according to constructivist grounded theory principles (Charmaz 2014).

TABLE A.1.1. Research Site, Sample, Demographics, and Policy Context

Blue State	Red State	Purple State
n = 27 (9 patients, 18 clinic/ community workers)	n = 32 (13 patients, 19 clinic/ community workers)	n = 21 (12 patients, 9 clinic/community workers)
Widespread sanctuary city/ county jurisdictions	No sanctuary city/county jurisdictions	Few sanctuary city/county jurisdictions
No local history of §287(g) participation at or near study site	History of §287(g) participation at study site prior to study (not ongoing)	History of past and ongoing §287(g) participation near study site (not in-county, but adjacent)
Expanded Medicaid under the Affordable Care Act	Expanded Medicaid under the Affordable Care Act	Did not expand Medicaid under the Affordable Care Act
Provides Presumptive Medicaid to pregnant people	Does not provide Presumptive Medicaid to pregnant people	Provides Presumptive Medicaid to pregnant people
Provides state-funded Medicaid to certain undocumented children and adults	Does not provide state-funded Medicaid to any undocumented immigrants	Does not provide state-funded Medicaid to any undocumented immigrants
Provides Emergency Medicaid to income-eligible undocumented immigrants	Provides Emergency Medicaid to income-eligible undocumented immigrants	Provides Emergency Medicaid to income-eligible undocumented immigrants
Approximate % of Latinx residents in state = 40	Approximate % of Latinx residents in state = 32	Approximate % of Latinx residents in state = 10
Approximate % of Latinx residents in county of observation = 16	Approximate % of Latinx residents in county of observation = 31	Approximate % of Latinx residents in county of observation = 12
Approximate % of state population Latin American immigrants = 13.4	Approximate % of state population Latin American immigrants = 8	Approximate % of state population Latin American immigrants = 4

Sources (in vertical order): Immigrant Legal Resource Center (2019); Kaiser Family Foundation (2019, 2021); US Census Bureau (2021).

APPENDIX 2

Note on Using the Terms "Latinx" and "Hispanic" in This Book

There are many ways that people with Latin American backgrounds refer to themselves—as well as how others in the media, academia, state institutions, and so on categorize them (see, for example, Torres 2018). These categories are contested because of the complexity of language and the nuances of cultural, ethnic, racial, and gender identity, and I do not intend to arbitrate these debates in this book. Instead, I aim to be as inclusive as possible when speaking about the diverse groups of people with Latin American heritage living in the United States while at the same time reflecting with precision the ways participants referred to themselves. In Spanish and Portuguese, nouns and adjectives are gendered as masculine or feminine. This dichotomy does not include people with a nonbinary gender, and attempts to create more inclusive language have led to the emergence of modifiers like "Latinx" and "Latine" to encompass Latinos, Latinas, and nonbinary people with Latin American heritage. Even though the term "Latinx" is not as widely used as "Latino/a," and even though many people who self-identify as Latina/Latino oppose the term, I use it here to be as inclusive as possible. When referring to specific individuals, however, I use the gendered adjectives that correspond to how participants gendered themselves when speaking with me.

Beyond the gendered components, the terms "Latino/a/x" that I use in this book are also more geographically inclusive than "Hispanic" or "Chicano/a/x" because they include Brazilians, who speak Portuguese—a Latin-based, but not Hispanic, language. However, many Spanish- and English-speaking participants referred to themselves and their communities as "Hispanic" (and occasionally Chicano/a). This was especially true in the red and purple state and almost never the case in the blue state. I took my cue from participants and tried to be consistent about using the language that they used during our conversations. Therefore, the language throughout this book is somewhat inconsistent, but this inconsistency reflects the nuanced reality of Latin American heritage in the United States.

APPENDIX 3

Note on Anonymizing Fieldsites

When drafting early versions of these chapters, I decided to anony-mize not only the research participants, but the implicated sites and policies as well. When I began this research in 2015, I was not con-cerned about identifying the region and relevant policy context of my fieldsites, and I looked forward to carrying out an in-depth historical contextualization of bureaucratic documents and developments to bet-ter frame my own empirical findings. The 2016 presidential campaigns and election made me rethink this openness. I had always intended to anonymize my research participants, given (1) their precarious legal status (in many cases), and (2) the health information that they might share during interviews or observations, but the realization that clinics might face federal reprisals over assisting undocumented immigrants gave me pause.

In an effort to gauge how much of the specific policy context I could ethically reveal in my writing, I consulted with immigration law ex-perts, who told me in no uncertain terms that publishing on some of the specific policies and practices that emerged in my data could very well jeopardize noncitizens' health care access. I took this response seriously and elected to use pseudonyms for people, places, policies, and bureaucratic practices. While I was particularly concerned about reprisals against the "blue state" site given its widespread sanctuary policies, I decided to be consistent in my handling of specifics across all sites. Of course, this may make it difficult for readers to understand fully the nuances of each site in relation to immigrant health or grasp the relevance of my finding to other sites and research projects. I ac-knowledge this challenge and have strived to provide as much detail as I could to render these empirical stories accurately and situate their implications beyond the three sites at hand.

Note on Participants' Gender and Gendered Labor

In a project that focused on the utilization and provision of health and social well-being services, it is perhaps unsurprising that most of the people I spoke with were women (see table A.4.1). At the risk of emphasizing dichotomized notions of gender that are incorrect and highly problematic, I raise this point here not to justify such a binary, but to highlight the gendered construction of care work as "women's" labor. In each of the three states where I conducted research, and irrespective of social role (patient or clinic worker), more women participated in this study than men. There are several likely reasons for this. For patient participants, research has shown that women are more likely than men to interact with certain spaces within the health care system (especially primary and preventive care) for a variety of reasons—although this does not necessarily mean that their health needs are being more adequately addressed (Bertakis et al. 2000; Vaidya, Partha, and Karmakar 2012; Manuel 2018).

Even if they would rather have avoided certain spaces because of security concerns, the socio-medical demands of motherhood, as well as intergenerational caregiving responsibilities that have traditionally fallen to women, brought many of the noncitizen patients I met into unavoidable contact with health care institutions. Many of the women patients I spoke with interacted with the health care system primarily through pregnancy, childbirth, and caregiving for their children and/or parents. Thus, they were potentially more likely to experience medical legal violence related to the frequency with which they had to engage with government-adjacent agencies while carrying out these gendered roles. Like the other work I describe in this book, such work was also "essential" but irreducible to a specific economic value. It therefore represents a unique space within the "inclusion/exclusion" dialectic (De Genova 2002) that I detail in chapter 1.

For clinic workers, the fact that many of the frontline clinic workers and safety net health care providers I met were women also aligns with what we know about the gender distribution of such roles within the broader social services and health care workforce (see, e.g., Salsberg et al. 2017; and US Bureau of Labor Statistics 2021). Again, this is unsurprising, given the historical gendering of caregiving and social service provision as "women's work," especially in community health settings (as opposed to surgical and other specialty care, for example). Thus, overall, while I have fewer observations of men than women, this distribution is reflective of what have historically been considered "women's" roles within families and "helping" professions.

TABLE A.4.1. Interview Participants' Gender Distribution

Patient Gender	Blue State	Red State	Purple State	Total
Male	4	8	1	13
Female	5	5	11	21
Provider/Staff Gender	Blue State	Red State	Purple State	Total
Male	5	3	2	10
Female	13	16	7	36
Male (all interviews)				23
Female (all Interviews)				57
			TOTAL	80

Note: This assignment of gender is based on pronouns/adjectives that participants used to describe themselves and/or contextual information from interviews.

NOTES

INTRODUCTION

1 All names are pseudonyms.

2 "Credible fear" is the threshold that asylum seekers must meet to qualify for asylum and receive immigration and other benefits that this relatively protected status confers in the United States. The applicant must demonstrate to the interviewing immigration agent that their fear of returning to their country of origin meets specific criteria of potential harm based on the applicant's race, religion, nationality, membership in a particular social group, or political opinion (US Citizenship and Immigration Services 2015). This is a higher bar than the "reasonable fear" criterion, in which the applicant must "credibly establish that there is a 'reasonable possibility' [the applicant] would be persecuted in the future on account of [their] race, religion, nationality, membership in a particular social group, or political opinion" (US Citizenship and Immigration Services 2013). The reasonable fear criterion may be sufficient for granting deportation relief, but it does not confer the benefits of asylum status.

3 In the second half of the twentieth century, the US government supported many violent authoritarian right-wing regimes throughout Latin America. Combined with economic austerity policies, land reforms, privatization of previously public goods and services, and trade liberalization, this political economic destabilization created push factors that spurred emigration to the United States—particularly from Central America. As Central American migrants quickly became targets of racialized criminal justice and immigration enforcement agencies during the War on Drugs and anti-immigrant policy reforms, gangs like the Mara Salvatrucha and Barrio 18 that sprang up in the United States were exported to Central America through deportation (see, e.g., Menjívar and Rodríguez 2005; and Esparza, Huttenbach, and Feierstein 2010).

4 See appendix 2 for note on the use of terms such as "Latina/o/x" and "Hispanic" in this book.

5 See, for example, the Naturalization Act of 1790, which limited US citizenship to "free white persons . . . of good character"; the Chinese Exclusion Act of 1882, which prohibited entry to Chinese laborers into the United States; the Immigration and Nationality Act of 1924, which established national origin quotas for immigrants outside the Western Hemisphere; and the Immigration and Nationality Act of 1952, which upheld those quotas.

6 Under DAPA and expanded DACA programs, almost half of the nearly 11.5 million undocumented immigrants living in the country at that time might have qualified for deportation protections and access to certain health and welfare benefits (Krogstad 2016; US Citizenship and Immigration Services 2014).

7 The Trump administration announced the termination of the DACA program on September 5, 2017. Following litigation in support of DACA by various groups and individuals, district court orders kept some provisions of DACA in place while the legal fight escalated to the Supreme Court. On June 18, 2020, the Supreme Court determined in *Department of Homeland Security v. Regents of the University of California* that the "arbitrary and capricious" way DHS had terminated DACA was unlawful (see National Immigration Law Center 2021b for a detailed timeline and discussion). On January 20, 2021, President Biden issued a memo entitled "Preserving and Fortifying Deferred Action for Childhood Arrivals (DACA)" (86 Fed. Reg. 7053), which suggested plans to strengthen the legislation and bolster it against future attacks.

8 As with the term "Latinx," which I use here despite ongoing debates and imprecisions that I describe in appendix 2, I use the phrase "of color" to signify the racialization of individuals and groups relative to whiteness in the United States. This is a problematic standard, but I use the term to acknowledge the various ways Latinx individuals and groups may be racialized and/or self-identify within this historical racial stratification system.

9 Examples of such rhetoric abound among prominent right-wing and right-center political platforms, including within the US Republican Party and the United Kingdom's Conservative Party. This does not mean that such tropes are absent from more progressive political movements (they are not), but rather that they provide a central organizing logic and particular momentum behind more explicitly anti-immigrant politics.

10 Notably, Congress passed the IIRIRA in the same year it passed two other laws that would reshape immigration and social welfare laws as they relate to noncitizens. One was the Antiterrorism and Effective Death Penalty Act (AEDPA), which expanded the "aggravated felony" category to penalize noncitizens charged with a variety of low-level, nonviolent crimes and restrict them from certain immigration benefits on that basis. The other was the Personal Responsibility and Work Opportunity Act (PRWORA), which excluded many noncitizens from public benefits, and which I discuss in more detail elsewhere in this chapter.

11 The 287(g) programs operate through one of four models: (1) the jail enforcement model (in which correctional officers screen arrestees' immigration status and begin immigration enforcement proceedings for those charged with a crime); (2) the task force model (in which local law enforcement agents perform immigration enforcement activities out in communities); (3) the warrant service officer (WSO) model (in which ICE authorizes certain state and local law enforcement agents to execute ICE administrative warrants); and (4) the hybrid model (which involves some combination of 1–3) (American Immigration Council 2020). The

287(g) amendment garnered little attention until the September 11, 2001, terrorist attacks, when momentum behind the program grew exponentially under the guise of enhancing national security. However, the activities carried out under these agreements frequently led to civil rights violations and racial profiling, particularly among Latinx individuals who were targeted for traffic stops and checkpoints (see, e.g., US Department of Justice 2011, 2012a, 2012b). As legal opposition to these practices mounted, the US Department of Justice turned to a more technological solution: Secure Communities. This program, piloted by the George W. Bush administration in 2008, enabled the uploading of arrestees' fingerprints to FBI and DHS databases.

12 Under the Secure Communities program, even if a noncitizen arrestee did not have a criminal record, local law enforcement could determine whether that person had legal authorization to be in the country. If they did not, ICE could issue a detainer allowing the arrestee to be held for an additional forty-eight hours after their scheduled release to provide time for ICE agents to take them into federal custody (American Civil Liberties Union 2021). While Secure Communities began as a voluntary program, it became mandatory in 2011 and resulted in thousands of deportations, frequently through traffic stops of noncitizens without a criminal record (Stuesse and Coleman 2014).

13 In 2014 the Obama administration replaced Secure Communities with the more targeted Priority Enforcement Program (PEP), which aimed to focus on criminal noncitizens and provide more discretion to law enforcement agents over whether to pursue investigation and/or deportation proceedings; nevertheless, the biometric dragnet remained in force. Federal biometric surveillance capabilities never disappeared—in fact, they have proliferated as technology has advanced (Kalhan 2014; Hu 2017)—but, theoretically, PEP offered a modicum of discretion over whether and when to use them.

14 "Enhancing Public Safety in the Interior of the United States," executive order, 82 Fed. Reg. 8799 (January 25, 2017), www.federalregister.gov.

15 Interim ICE guidance from the Biden administration highlighted three priority enforcement categories: (1) national security threats, (2) border security threats, and (3) conviction of aggravated felony under §101(a)(43) of the Immigration and Nationality Act (Johnson 2021).

16 For a detailed discussion of Medicaid, federalism, and immigrant health, see Makhlouf (2020). In this comprehensive article, the author not only describes how federalism influences state policies on noncitizens' Medicaid eligibility, but also outlines the implications of these dynamics for national health policy writ large.

17 Sometimes the cost of uncompensated care for undocumented migrants goes beyond what Emergency Medicaid will cover, in which case hospitals may initiate medical repatriation. This refers to the practice of deporting individuals directly from hospitals to their country of origin, usually when they are gravely—and sometimes critically—ill. For more information on this practice, see Sontag 2008 and New York Lawyers for the Public Interest 2012.

18 In New York, for example, radiation and chemotherapy treatment for undocumented immigrants is covered under Emergency Medicaid services (Western New York Law Center 2021). In California, New York, and North Carolina, outpatient dialysis is also covered under Medicaid for undocumented immigrants (Gusmano 2012).

19 This shorthand has many limitations—principally the inability to reflect political heterogeneity within states, changes over time, and the systematic gerrymandering and voter suppression efforts that constrain democratic participation. One participant in the "red" state expressed dismay when I mentioned that I would be referring to his state in these terms. Others in the purple state told me that their state would be blue were it not for intensive voter suppression. Indeed, the 2020 election altered the red/blue map in significant ways. For example, political organizing "flipped" Arizona and Georgia—two states with recent histories of anti-immigrant policies—from red to blue in terms of the presidential (as well as some key congressional) elections (Han and McKenna 2021; Herndon 2020). The categories I use here reflect the 2016 landscape, but it is important to recognize that they do not represent a static condition.

20 As I describe in chapter 4, according to Young and Wallace's (2019) framework, the red and blue states had a relatively high degree of immigrant integration, whereas the purple state, as a newer Latinx immigrant destination, was a more exclusionary environment overall. However, the blue and red states diverged in terms of their criminalization of Latinx immigrants. In the blue state, there was a relatively low degree of criminalization, whereas it was high in the red and purple states.

21 The adjective "panoptic" refers to Foucault's description of how people come to discipline and govern themselves even in the absence of a disciplinary authority (e.g., a police or military officer) (Foucault 1977). Foucault drew upon Jeremy Bentham's carceral invention, the panopticon, which involved a tower overseeing prison cells arrayed within a 360-degree view of the inmates. A guard in the tower could see the prisoners at any hour of the day, but they could not see the guard, so there was no way to know when or whether they were being surveilled. The idea was to get inmates to behave as if they were always being watched. In other words, and importantly for the stories of medical legal violence I tell in this book, the mere *perception* of surveillance can have a disciplining effect irrespective of the presence of a government authority.

CHAPTER 1. STATES OF INJURY

1 This is similar to the way political movements—in labor, civil rights, and so forth—have been neutralized in the United States through criminalization and incarceration.

2 On January 27, 2017 (six days after his inauguration), President Trump signed an executive order banning foreign nationals from seven Muslim-majority countries from visiting the country for 90 days, suspended all Syrian refugees' entry indefinitely, and prohibited any other refugees entering the country for 120 days

(American Civil Liberties Union 2019). Also, as I mentioned in the book's introduction, this "zero-tolerance" policy, announced on April 6, 2018, directed federal prosecutors to criminally prosecute all adult migrants entering the country without authorization. Because of the 1997 *Flores v. Reno* settlement, this led to the separation of adults from their children and generated widespread public outcry. It later emerged that not only were families being separated, but the administration was unable to keep track of those it had separated, and thus unable to reunite many families (Catholic Legal Immigration Network 2018).

3   This interview took place several months before clashes between white supremacists and counter-protesters in Charlottesville, Virginia, on August 11 and 12, 2017, captured the nation's attention. White nationalist and self-styled "alt-right" groups had planned "Unite the Right" rallies in conjunction with protests against the removal of a Confederate statue from a local park, and confrontations with counter-protesters turned violent. After the Virginia governor declared a state of emergency and the August 12 rally was suspended, a white supremacist drove his vehicle through a crowd of counter-protesters, leaving one woman dead and several wounded. In the wake of these troubling events, President Trump drew widespread criticism for condemning violence "on many sides" and refusing to explicitly denounce white supremacists (Sotomayor, McCausland, and Brockington 2017).

4   All cases of "diabetes" mentioned in this chapter refer to Type 2 diabetes, which, like many chronic illnesses, is disproportionately prevalent among low-income people of color in the United States, including the Latinx community (Centers for Disease Control and Prevention 2017). The links between structural violence and diabetes among Latinx individuals are well documented (e.g., Montoya 2011; Mendenhall 2012; Horton 2016).

5   Such insurance eligibility dilemmas affect not only noncitizens but also other US citizens who are disproportionately subjected to structural violence. I focus here on the particular aspects of structural and symbolic violence that are related to legal status, but similar embodied effects among US citizens are comprehensively detailed by Eubanks in her book *Automating Inequality* (2018).

6   For more discussion of the gender distribution in this study sample, see appendix 4.

7   As defined in section 1905(l)(2)(B) of the Social Security Act (see 42 U.S.C. 1396d), federally qualified health centers (FQHCs) are community-based health care organizations—including community health centers, migrant health centers, health care for the homeless, and health centers for residents of public housing—that receive funds from the Health Resources and Services Administration (HRSA) to provide primary care services in underserved areas. These health centers must meet strict federal criteria to maintain their FQHC status, including providing care on a sliding-fee scale and being accountable to a governing board (which includes patients).

8   Ambulance transport costs are notoriously opaque and remarkably expensive, but it is difficult to state an average due to high variation (Bailey 2017).

CHAPTER 2. HOSTILE TERRAIN

1 In certain cases of clear medical need, such as childbirth or trauma surgery, noncitizens could qualify for federally funded Emergency Medicaid (just as in the blue state county).

2 Prior to this time, immigration policy in relation to Latin American migration alternated between periods of greater and lesser exclusion, including a temporary "amnesty" in 1986 that enabled approximately 2.7 million migrants to adjust their status (get a green card) within an eighteen-month period (Plumer 2013).

3 Anthropologist Jason De León has documented the geographic contours of this assemblage in brutal detail (De León 2015). De León analyzes the human and nonhuman actants whose "complex relationships at different moments across time and space . . . sometimes create things or make things happen" (39). He stresses the way the desert has become a key actant in US immigration policy as avenues to legal residence and naturalization diminish, particularly for Latin American immigrants. De León uncovers the human cost of driving people through dangerous landscapes as a strategy that both effectively limits the number of successful "illegal" border crossers (in that thousands die each year en route) and—as in the case of Jakelin Caal Maquin—absolves federal immigration agencies from blame over those deaths.

4 The term "public charge" first appeared in section 2 of the Immigration Act of 1882, which barred admission to the United States of any "convict, lunatic, idiot, or any person unable to take care of himself or herself becoming a public charge." These exclusions were subsequently expanded through legislation, including the 1952 Immigration and Nationality Act and its 1965 amendments. These declared "any alien likely at any time to become a public charge" inadmissible to the country, as well as making deportable any alien who has received public benefits within their first five years in the United States. Federal guidance in 1999 included Supplemental Security Income (SSI), cash assistance from the Temporary Assistance for Needy Families (TANF) program, and state or local cash assistance programs (often called "general assistance") among disqualifying benefits, but Medicaid, food stamps, WIC, unemployment insurance, housing benefits, childcare subsidies, or other non-cash benefits were explicitly excluded from the "public charge" criteria (see "Field Guidance on Deportability and Inadmissibility on Public Charge Grounds," 64 Fed. Reg. 28689, May 26, 1999). In October 2018 the Trump administration proposed to expand the grounds for inadmissibility under the public charge rule, including any "alien" who receives one or more public benefits for more than twelve months in the aggregate within any thirty-six-month period and adding cash benefits for income maintenance, SNAP (food stamps), most forms of Medicaid, Section 8 Housing Assistance, Section 8 Project-Based Rental Assistance, and certain other forms of subsidized housing to the list of inadmissibility criteria (83 Fed. Reg. 51114). The rule was finalized in August 2019 (84 Fed. Reg. 4192), but due to ongoing litigation it remained enjoined until Janu-

ary 27, 2020, when the US Supreme Court voted 5–4 in *Department of Homeland Security v. New York* to uphold it. The rule became effective on February 24, 2020, but a federal district court vacated the implementation decision in November 2020. On March 15, 2021, the Biden administration declined to challenge the vacatur, thus reverting to prior inadmissibility criteria (86 Fed. Reg. 14221).

5 An omnibus bill encompasses a wide range of (often unrelated) issues, all packaged into one document that the legislature considers as a single vote. For example, Alabama's HB 56 (signed in June 2011) "addressed a range of topics including law enforcement, employment, education, public benefits, harbor/transport/rental housing, voting and REAL ID" (National Conference of State Legislatures 2012).

6 The Minutemen are vigilantes who organized in 2004 to oppose "illegal" immigration through direct action at the border and political lobbying for intensive immigration enforcement measures (Doty 2007).

7 These activities contravened DHS's 2011 memorandum on "sensitive locations," which held that immigration enforcement activities would occur near locations such as schools, churches, and hospitals only in exceptional cases. Reports from communities suggest that such "sensitive locations" are increasingly subject to immigration enforcement activity (Burnett 2017). In October 2021, DHS secretary Mayorkas announced new guidance regarding enforcement actions at "protected locations," which superseded and rescinded "previous sensitive locations guidance" and established that "enforcement actions should not be taken in or near a location that would restrain people's access to essential services or engagement in essential activities" (US Department of Homeland Security 2021). Among such locations were schools and daycare centers, health care facilities (including COVID-19 vaccination locations), religious institutions and ceremonies, playgrounds, disaster/emergency response centers, social service establishments, and public demonstrations.

8 While *Plyler v. Doe* (1982) ensures the right to public education for all students regardless of their (or their parents') immigration status, many states and municipalities continue to discriminate against immigrant students and those in mixed-status families (Lind 2014).

9 See also Asad (2020) on federal legibility and "system embeddedness" and Jimenez (2021) on "legible" versus "illegible" illegality.

10 In the United States, treatment of end-stage renal disease (ESRD) is provided through Social Security Disability (SSDI) coverage—for which undocumented immigrants are ineligible. Some states have elected to define outpatient dialysis as an emergency service, which can therefore be covered through Emergency Medicaid (Rodriguez 2015). This was the case for Guillermo. See also Melo (2017).

11 See, for example, then DHS secretary Kirstjen Nielsen's response to the death of seven-year-old Jakelin Caal Maquin, who perished from septic shock after crossing the border with her family and being apprehended by DHS officials (US Department of Homeland Security 2018; Romero 2018). Nielsen stressed that the responsibility lay not with her agency but with the migrants themselves. "This

family chose to cross illegally," she said. "They were about 90 miles away from where we could process them. . . . We cannot stress how dangerous the journey is when migrants come illegally" (Oprysko and Hesson 2018).

CHAPTER 3. IMMIGRATION FEDERALISM AND HEALTH CARE SURVEILLANCE IN A PROGRESSIVE JURISDICTION

1 This assurance supposes a separation between paper records and automated eligibility systems that rely upon electronic recordkeeping in interoperable government databases. Given the ubiquity of electronic recordkeeping in both health and immigration databases, this assumption is open to question.

2 See "Inadmissibility on Public Charge Grounds," 84 Fed. Reg. 41292.

3 See also the work of Novak, Geronimus, and Martinez-Cardoso (2017) and Torche and Sirois (2018) that demonstrates how aggressive anti-immigrant measures negatively affected birth outcomes among immigrants, even when the implementation and/or persistence of those measures was in reality rather limited. The *perception* of intensive immigration enforcement was as powerful, if not more so, than the measures themselves.

4 The Fourth Amendment of the US Constitution protects people's right to privacy and freedom from government intrusion into "their persons, houses, papers, and effects." It establishes legal safeguards against "unreasonable searches and seizures" and requires warrants indicating probable cause and "particularly describing the place to be searched, and the persons or things to be seized." An important factor in upholding Fourth Amendment protections, and one particularly relevant in relation to immigration enforcement activities in health care spaces, is determining whether a space is considered "private" or "public."

5 Olivia said the italicized words in English, which gave them particular emphasis among the non-English phrases.

CHAPTER 4. "NO SAFE ZONES"

1 That is not to say that the blue state did not in practice enact similarly criminalizing policies through institutions such as local police and sheriff's departments. Rather, I speak here to the state-level policies that explicitly included or excluded Latinx immigrants and members of Latinx communities.

2 I say "relatively" recent in comparison to traditional immigrant destinations like California, Texas, or New York. That said, the so-called New South has by now experienced substantial Latinx immigration for multiple decades, and many of the Latinx residents of the region are US-born children of immigrants. This demographic shift will likely portend political changes throughout the region, as recently incorporated immigrant individuals and families begin to outnumber those who have only recently arrived. For example, in 2020 Ricky Hurtado, the US-born son of Salvadoran immigrants, was the first Latinx representative elected to the North Carolina House of Representatives. Importantly,

he represents the Sixty-Third District, which includes Alamance County, historically one of the most notorious 287(g) partners in the country (US Department of Justice 2012b).

3 For more on visible or "legible" (versus illegible) illegality, see Jimenez (2021).

4 As I mention in the book's introduction, and as De Genova (2002) and others elaborate, immigrant "illegality" is a socially constructed condition that stigmatizes and criminalizes immigrants and immigrant-adjacent families and communities in a superficially race-neutral way while disproportionately discrediting immigrants of color, especially those from Latin America.

5 It's telling that Jorge specifically signaled "American" as tacitly white when he said, "es raro el americano o el moreno que trabaje ahí." (In the context of our conversation, *moreno* clearly referred to African Americans rather than a general term for someone with a relatively dark complexion.) Without Jorge having to say so explicitly, it suggests the internalized symbolic violence of full US citizenship casually imagined as the province of white people.

6 Multiple patient participants in the purple state site mentioned living in a mobile home (*trailer* or *traila*), which may be associated with socioeconomic and environmental precarity but also symbolic of upward mobility in some cases (Kusenbach 2017).

7 Eventually I was able to resolve some of these issues and was put in touch with a free clinic that did not fear government surveillance because it received no government funds. This clinic facilitated my ethnographic fieldwork and interviews, for which I am grateful.

8 The Tea Party movement emerged from the Republican Party in the wake of the 2008 recession and beginning of the Obama administration. With an ostensible focus on fiscal conservatism and small government and strong elements of right-wing populism and racial resentment, the movement supported the rise of formerly unlikely political candidates such as Donald Trump (among others). See, for example, Arceneaux and Nicholson (2012); Zeskind (2012); and Van Dyke and Meyer (2014).

9 For a detailed account of the Criminal Alien Program, see Macías-Rojas (2016).

CHAPTER 5. MEDICAL LEGAL CONSCIOUSNESS IN THE "CRIMMIGRATION" AGE

1 The conceptualization of medical legal consciousness that I present here is related to but broader than that which is briefly described by Diana Hernández (2016) in her discussion of medical legal partnerships as a health and housing intervention. Hernández defines "medical-legal consciousness" as a "vital shift in consciousness that occurs in the partnership between doctors and lawyers" wherein the sharing of their respective expertise enables "exciting prospects for viewing and tackling the problems of poverty more holistically" (887). While I sometimes refer to doctors and lawyers—and medical legal partnerships—

within my conceptualization of medical legal consciousness, when I use this term, I am specifically conveying how criminalization through the law (i.e., legal violence) impacts the health care decision making of (1) noncitizen patients and their families, and (2) various healthcare workers who are also subject to surveillance while facilitating that care. In this chapter, I particularly focus on those who occupy multiply surveilled social positions (e.g., as members of immigrant communities and clinic workers). Thus, while both approaches to the term identify the positive potential of legal expertise to address health inequalities, I emphasize the various subjectivities and reactions that arise through diverse participants' experiences of medical legal violence.

2 Regarding public charge, see the following 2019 rules: "Inadmissibility on Public Charge Grounds" (84 Fed. Reg. 41292); "Visas: Ineligibility Based on Public Charge Grounds" (84 Fed. Reg. 54996); and "Suspension of Entry of Immigrants Who Will Financially Burden the United States Healthcare System, in Order to Protect the Availability of Healthcare Benefits for Americans" (84 Fed. Reg. 53991). Regarding asylum, see, for example, "Asylum Eligibility and Procedural Modifications" (85 Fed. Reg. 38532); "Implementing Bilateral and Multilateral Asylum Cooperative Agreements under the Immigration and Nationality Act" (84 Fed. Reg. 63994); and "Procedures for Asylum and Bars to Asylum Eligibility" (86 C.F.R. 6940).

3 Young and Wallace (2019) identify four categories of immigrant integration and criminalization contexts: "deportable inclusion" (high integration/high criminalization—e.g., Arizona, Florida, New York, Texas); "proactive inclusion" (high integration/low criminalization—e.g., California, New Mexico, Washington); "enhanced deportability" (low integration/high criminalization—e.g., Georgia, North Carolina, Mississippi); and "excluded deportability" (low integration/low criminalization—e.g., Alaska, Delaware, New Hampshire).

4 Noncitizens in every US state are eligible for Emergency Medicaid, which applies to labor and delivery care and other acute emergency care, if they meet general Medicaid financial eligibility criteria. Noncitizens and lawful permanent residents who have lived in the United States for less than five years are ineligible for full-scope Medicaid, even if they would otherwise meet the means-tested eligibility criteria.

5 This was before the Trump administration officially announced the public charge rule change in October 2018.

6 I place "myths" in quotation marks here because some of these are merely rumors, while some have roots in statute and regulations. For example, on May 23, 2019, President Trump signed an executive memo enforcing Section 421 of the 1996 Personal Responsibility and Work Opportunity Reconciliation Act (8 U.S.C. 1631)—which holds that "when an alien receives certain forms of means-tested public benefits, the government or non-government entity providing the public benefit must request reimbursement from the alien's financial sponsor." The 1993 Omnibus Budget Reconciliation Act (PL 103–66, §13612) also includes provisions

for Medicaid estate recovery in certain cases (meaning, yes, the government can sometimes repossess someone's home).

7 Regarding federal public charge inadmissibility guidelines, see 64 Fed. Reg. 28689, which includes (1) Supplemental Security Income (SSI); (2) Temporary Assistance for Needy Families (TANF) cash assistance (part A of Title IV of the Social Security Act—the successor to the AFDC program); (3) state and local cash assistance programs that provide benefits for income maintenance (often called "General Assistance" programs); and (4) programs (including Medicaid) supporting aliens who are institutionalized for long-term care, e.g., in a nursing home or mental health institution. Regarding the Priority Enforcement Program (PEP), there were three tiers of removal priorities: Priority 1 (threats to national security, border security, and public safety), Priority 2 (misdemeanants and new immigration violators), and Priority 3 (other immigration violations). The Trump administration suspended this program in 2017 in order to roll out a zero-tolerance immigration enforcement program.

8 This was in June 2016, before the Trump administration ended the Priority Enforcement Program (PEP) and reinstated the Secure Communities (S-COMM) program through its zero-tolerance immigration enforcement policy (Trump 2017).

9 There is some truth to the myth that certain government benefits must be paid back by an immigrant's sponsor. While this is technically true, prior to the Trump administration, the law was seldom enforced. On May 23, 2019, the Trump administration issued a "Presidential Memorandum on Enforcing the Legal Responsibilities of Sponsors of Aliens," and subsequent USCIS documents emphasized that "if the sponsored immigrant receives any federal means-tested public benefits, the sponsor will be expected to reimburse the benefits-granting agency for every dollar of benefits received by the immigrant" (Cuccinelli 2019a).

10 It is unclear to what degree such separation actually exists. Public charge surveillance means that there is a way for USCIS to review public benefits utilization, including Medicaid, so it is reasonable to assume some level of systems interoperability across agencies.

11 In August 2019 DHS announced that decisions about medical deferrals would no longer be made by USCIS (a relatively administrative arm of immigration processing) but by ICE (an enforcement agency), and it sent out letters notifying beneficiaries of medical exemptions that they must leave the country within thirty-three days to avoid deportation (US Citizenship and Immigration Services 2019; Dooling 2019a). After public outcry and an emergency congressional investigation, DHS reversed course and resumed consideration of medical deferrals (Dooling 2019b).

CONCLUSION

1 Systemic neglect is a feature of structural violence that allows people to fall through the cracks in institutional practices and infrastructures, particularly

in safety net settings that are meant to prevent such harms (see Van Natta et al. 2018).

2 See Coronavirus Economic Stabilization (CARES Act), 15 U.S.C. Ch. 116.

3 "Inadmissibility on Public Charge Grounds; Implementation of Vacatur," 86 Fed. Reg. 14221 (March 15, 2021), www.federalregister.gov.

BIBLIOGRAPHY

Abrego, Leisy J. 2011. "Legal Consciousness of Undocumented Latinos: Fear and Stigma as Barriers to Claims-Making for First- and 1.5-Generation Immigrants." *Law and Society Review* 45 (2): 337–70.

Agamben, Giorgio. 1998. *Homo Sacer: Sovereign Power and Bare Life*. Translated by Daniel Heller-Roazen. Meridian: Crossing Aesthetics.

———. 2005. *State of Exception*. Translated by K. Attell. Chicago: University of Chicago Press.

Alexander, Michelle. 2010. *The New Jim Crow: Mass Incarceration in the Age of Color-blindness*. New York: New Press.

American Civil Liberties Union (ACLU). 2019. "Timeline of the Muslim Ban." Accessed April 2, 2019. www.aclu-wa.org.

———. 2021. "Immigration Detainers." Accessed May 12, 2021. www.aclu.org.

American Immigration Council. 2020. "The 287(g) Program: An Overview." July 2, 2020. www.americanimmigrationcouncil.org.

Arceneaux, Kevin, and Stephen P. Nicholson. 2012. "Who Wants to Have a Tea Party? The Who, What, and Why of the Tea Party Movement." *Political Science and Politics* 45 (4): 700–10. https://doi.org/10.1017/S1049096512000741.

Arizona State Senate. 2010. "Fact Sheet for S.B. 1070." January 15, 2010. www.azleg.gov.

Armenta, Amada. 2012. "From Sheriff's Deputies to Immigration Officers: Screening Immigrant Status in a Tennessee Jail." *Law and Policy* 34 (2): 191–210.

———. 2017. *Protect, Serve, and Deport: The Rise of Policing as Immigration Enforcement*. Berkeley: University of California Press.

Artiga, Samantha, and Maria Diaz. 2019. "Health Coverage and Care of Undocumented Immigrants." Kaiser Family Foundation, July 15, 2019. www.kff.org.

Asad, Asad L. 2020. "On the Radar: System Embeddedness and Latin American Immigrants' Perceived Risk of Deportation." *Law & Society Review* 54(1): 133–67. https://doi.org/10.1111/lasr.12460

Asad, Asad L., and Matthew Clair. 2017. "Racialized Legal Status as a Social Determinant of Health." *Social Science and Medicine* 19: 19–28. http://dx.doi.org/10.1016/j.socscimed.2017.03.010.

Bacon, David, and Bill Ong Hing. 2010. "The Rise and Fall of Employer Sanctions." *Fordham Urban Law Journal* 38 (1): 77–105.

Bailey, Melissa. 2017. "$3,660 for a Four-Mile Ride? Ambulances Are Hitting Patients with Surprise Bills." *Los Angeles Times*, November 29, 2017. www.latimes.com.

Bergeron, C. 2013. "Issue Brief: Going to the Back of the Line: A Primer on Lines, Visa Categories, and Wait Times." Migration Policy Institute Issue Brief, March 2013.

Berlant, Lauren. 2007. "Slow Death (Sovereignty, Obesity, Lateral Agency)." *Critical Inquiry* 33 (4): 754–80.

Bernstein, Hamutal, Dulce Gonzalez, Michael Karpman, and Stephen Zuckerman. 2019. "One in Seven Adults in Immigrant Families Reported Avoiding Public Benefit Programs in 2018." Urban Institute, May 22, 2019. www.urban.org.

Bertakis, Klea D., Rahman Azari, Edward J. Callahan, and John A. Robbins. 2000. "Gender Differences in the Utilization of Health Care Services." *Journal of Family Practice* 49 (2): 147–52.

Bloemraad, Irene, Will Kymlicka, Michèle Lamont, and Leanne S. Son Hing. 2019. "Membership without Social Citizenship? Deservingness and Redistribution as Grounds for Equality." *Daedalus* 2019 (Summer): 73–104. https://doi.org/10.1162/DAED_a_01751.

Bosniak, Linda. 2006. *The Citizen and the Alien: Dilemmas of Contemporary Membership*. Princeton: Princeton University Press.

Bourdieu, Pierre. 2000. *Pascalian Meditations*. Translated by Richard Nice. Palo Alto, CA: Stanford University Press.

Bowker, Geoffrey C., and Susan Leigh Star. 1999. *Sorting Things Out: Classification and Its Consequences*. Cambridge, MA: MIT Press.

Boyd-Barrett, Claudia. 2018. "Fear Pushes More Immigrants to Avoid Seeking Medical Care." *California Health Report*, February 5, 2018. www.calhealthreport.org.

British Broadcasting Company (BBC). 2018. "Why the US Is Separating Migrant Children from Their Parents." June 15, 2018. www.bbc.com.

Brotherton, David, and Luis Barrios. 2011. *Banished to the Homeland: Dominican Deportees and Their Stories of Exile*. New York: Columbia University Press.

Budiman, Abby, Christine Tamir, Lauren Mora, and Luis Noe-Bustamante. 2020. "Facts of US Immigrants, 2018." Pew Research Center Hispanic Trends, August 20, 2020. www.pewresearch.org.

Burnett, John. 2017. "DHS under Pressure over Alleged Violation of Policies on Sensitive Locations." *All Things Considered* (NPR), October 20, 2017. www.npr.org.

Campbell, Colin, and Chiara Vercellone. 2020. "North Carolina Has No Latino Legislators. That's About to Change." *News and Observer*, December 21, 2020. www.newsobserver.com.

Castañeda, Heide. 2009. "Illegality as Risk Factor: A Survey of Unauthorized Migrant Patients in a Berlin Clinic." *Social Science and Medicine* (2009): 1–9.

———. 2017. "Is Coverage Enough? Persistent Health Disparities in Marginalised Latino Border Communities." *Journal of Ethnic and Migration Studies* 43 (12): 2003–19. https://doi.org/10.1080/1369183X.2017.1323448.

———. 2019. *Borders of Belonging: Struggle and Solidarity in Mixed-Status Immigrant Families*. Palo Alto, CA: Stanford University Press.

Castañeda, Heide, Seth M. Holmes, Daniel S. Madrigal, Maria-Elena DeTrinidad Young, Naomi Beyeler, and James Quesada. 2015. "Immigration as a Social Determinant of Health." *Annual Review of Public Health* 36: 1.1–1.18.

Catholic Legal Immigration Network. 2018. "Timeline: Family Separations under the 'Zero-Tolerance' Policy." Accessed April 1, 2019. https://cliniclegal.org.

Centers for Disease Control and Prevention (CDC). 2017. "National Diabetes Statistics Report, 2017: Estimates of Diabetes and Its Burden in the United States." www.cdc. gov.

Centers for Medicare and Medicaid Services (CMS). 2014. "Eligibility for Non-Citizens in Medicaid and CHIP." Accessed December 16, 2014. www.healthcare.gov.

———. N.d. "Eligibility." Accessed March 10, 2021. www.medicaid.gov.

Chacón, Jennifer. 2009. "Managing Immigration through Crime." *Columbia Law Review* 109: 135–48.

———. 2012. "Overcriminalizing Immigration." *Journal of Criminal Law and Criminology* 102 (3): 613–52.

Charmaz, Kathy. 2014. *Constructing Grounded Theory.* 2nd ed. Introducing Qualitative Methods series. Thousand Oaks, CA: Sage.

Clarke, Adele. 2005. *Situational Analysis: Grounded Theory after the Postmodern Turn.* Thousand Oaks, CA: Sage.

Clarke, Adele, Janet K. Shim, Laura Mamo, Jennifer R. Fosket, and Jennifer R. Fishman. 2003. "Biomedicalization: Technoscientific Transformations of Health, Illness and US Biomedicine." *American Sociological Review* 68 (2): 161–94.

Cohn, D'vera, Jeffrey S. Passel, and Kristen Bialik. 2019. "Many Immigrants with Temporary Protected Status Face Uncertain Future in US." Pew Research Center, November 27, 2019. www.pewresearch.org.

Correal, Annie, and Luis Ferré-Sadurní. 2021. "$2.1 Billion for Undocumented Workers Signals New York's Progressive Shift." *New York Times*, April 8, 2021. www.nytimes.com.

COVID Tracking Project. 2021. "Racial Data Dashboard." Accessed March 20, 2021. https://covidtracking.com.

Cuadros, Paul. 2009. *A Home on the Field: How One Championship Team Inspires Hope for the Revival of Small Town America.* New York: HarperCollins.

Cubanski, Juliette, Tricia Neuman, and Anthony Damico. 2016. "Medicare's Role for People under Age 65 with Disabilities." Kaiser Family Foundation, August 12, 2016. www.kff.org.

Cuccinelli, Ken. 2019a. "Presidential Memorandum on Enforcing the Legal Responsibilities of Sponsors of Aliens." US Citizenship and Immigration Services, June 14, 2019. www.uscis.gov.

———. 2019b. "Press Briefing by USCIS Acting Director Ken Cuccinelli." August 12, 2019. www.whitehouse.gov.

Davies, Anita A., Anna Basten, and Chiara Frattini. 2010. "Migration: A Social Determinant of the Health of Migrants." *Eurohealth* 16 (1): 10-12.

Deeb-Sossa, Natalia. 2016. "'Why Do Your People Do Things That Just Aren't Right'? Latinas/os and Race Relations at a Community Clinic in el Nuevo South." *Journal of Ethnic and Migration Studies* 43 (6): 1009–25. https://doi.org/10.1080/13691 83X.2016.1220291.

De Genova, Nicholas P. 2002. "Migrant 'Illegality' and Deportability in Everyday Life." *Annual Review of Anthropology* 31: 419–47. https://doi.org/10.1146/annurev. anthro.31.040402.085432.

———. 2013. "Spectacles of Migrant 'Illegality': The Scene of Exclusion, the Obscene of Inclusion." *Ethnic and Racial Studies* 36 (7): 1180–98. https://doi.org/10.1080/014198 70.2013.783710.

———. 2014. "Immigration 'Reform' and the Production of Migrant 'Illegality.'" In *Constructing Immigrant "Illegality": Critiques, Experiences, and Responses*, edited by Cecilia Menjívar and Daniel Kanstroom. New York: Cambridge University Press.

De León, Jason. 2015. *The Land of Open Graves: Living and Dying on the Migrant Trail*. Oakland: University of California Press.

Dickerson, Caitlin, and Miriam Jordan. 2020. "South Dakota Meat Plant Is Now Country's Biggest Coronavirus Hot Spot." *New York Times*, May 4, 2020. www.nytimes. com.

Dooling, Shannon. 2019a. "Trump Administration Ends Protection for Migrants' Medical Care." NPR, August 27, 2019. www.npr.org.

———. 2019b. "After a Month of Public Outcry, Immigration Officials Resume Medical Deferrals for Deportation." WBUR, September 19, 2019. www.wbur.org.

Doty, Roxanne Lynn. 2007. "States of Exception on the Mexico-US Border: Security, 'Decisions,' and Civilian Border Patrols." *International Political Sociology* 1 (2): 113–37.

Dunn, Timothy J. 2009. *Blockading the Border and Human Rights: The El Paso Operation That Remade Immigration Enforcement*. Austin: University of Texas Press.

Esparza, Marcia, Henry R. Huttenbach, and Daniel Feierstein, eds. 2010. *State Violence and Genocide in Latin America: The Cold War Years*. New York: Routledge.

Eubanks, Virginia. 2018. *Automating Inequality: How High-Tech Tools Profile, Police, and Punish the Poor*. New York: St. Martin's.

Ewick, Patricia, and Susan S. Silbey. 1998. *The Common Place of Law: Stories from Everyday Life*. Chicago: University of Chicago Press.

———. 2003. "Narrating Social Structure: Stories of Resistance to Law." *American Journal of Sociology* 108 (6): 1328–72.

Farmer, Paul. 2003. *Pathologies of Power: Health, Human Rights, and the New War on the Poor*. Berkeley: University of California Press.

Fassin, D. 2009. "Another Politics of Life Is Possible." *Theory, Culture, and Society* 26: 44–60.

Feere, Jon. 2012. "An Overview of E-Verify Policies at the State Level." Center for Immigration Studies Backgrounder, July 26, 2012. https://cis.org.

Findley, Sally E., and Sergio E. Matos. 2015. *Bridging the Gap: How Community Health Workers Promote the Health of Immigrants*. New York: Oxford University Press.

Fink, Leon. 2003. *The Maya of Morganton: Work and Community in the Nuevo New South*. Chapel Hill: University of North Carolina Press.

Foucault, Michel. 1977. *Discipline and Punish: The Birth of the Prison*. New York: Random House.

———. 1978. *The History of Sexuality*. Vol. 1, *An Introduction*. New York: Random House.

———. 2004. *Security, Territory, Population: Lectures at the Collège de France, 1977–1978.* New York: Picador.

Fragomen, Austin T. 1997. "The Illegal Immigration Reform and Immigrant Responsibility Act of 1996: An Overview." *International Migration Review* 31 (2): 438–60.

Furuseth, Owen J., and Heather A. Smith. 2006. "From Winn-Dixie to Tiendas: The Remaking of the New South." In *Latinos in the New South*, edited by Heather A. Smith and Owen J. Furuseth, 1–17. Aldershot, UK: Ashgate.

Galtung, Johan. 1969. "Violence, Peace, and Peace Research." *Journal of Peace Research* 6 (3): 167–91.

García, Angela S. 2019. *Legal Passing: Navigating Undocumented Life and Local Immigration Law.* Oakland: University of California Press.

García Hernández, César Cuauhtémoc. 2015. *Crimmigration Law.* Chicago: American Bar Association Publishing.

Gilens, Martin. 1999. *Why Americans Hate Welfare: Race, Media and the Politics of Antipoverty Policy.* Chicago: University of Chicago Press.

Gill, Hannah. 2018. *The Latino Migration Experience in North Carolina: New Roots in the Old North State.* 2nd ed. Chapel Hill: University of North Carolina Press.

Golash-Boza, Tanya Maria. 2015. *Deported: Immigrant Policing, Disposable Labor, and Global Capitalism.* New York: New York University Press.

———. 2016. "Feeling Like a Citizen, Living as a Denizen: Deportees' Sense of Belonging." *American Behavioral Scientist* 60 (13): 1575–89.

Goldring, Luin, Carolina Berenstein, and Judith K. Bernhard. 2009. "Institutionalizing Precarious Migratory Status in Canada." *Citizenship Studies* 13 (3): 239–65.

Gómez Cervantes, Andrea, and Cecilia Menjívar. 2020. "Legal Violence, Health, and Access to Care: Latina Immigrants in Rural and Urban Kansas." *Journal of Health and Social Behavior* 61 (3): 307–23. https://doi.org/10.1177/0022146520945048.

González-Barrera, Ana, and Jens Manuel Krogstad. 2016. "US Immigrant Deportations Declined in 2014, but Remain Near Record High." *Pew Research Center*, August 31, 2016. www.pewresearch.org.

Grinberg, Emanuella, and Mariano Castillo. 2018. "US Authorities Fire Tear Gas to Disperse Migrants at Border." CNN, November 26, 2018. www.cnn.com.

Guerrero, Alma, Rodrigo Dominguez-Villegas, and Arturo Vargas Bustamante. 2021. "Forgoing Healthcare in a Global Pandemic: The Chilling Effects of the Public Charge Rule on Health Access among Children in California." UCLA Latino Policy and Politics Initiative, April 6, 2021. https://latino.ucla.edu.

Gulasekaram, Pratheepan, and Karthick Ramakrishnan. 2015. *The New Immigration Federalism.* Cambridge: Cambridge University Press.

Gusmano, Michael K. 2012. "Undocumented Immigrants in the United States: US Health Policy and Access to Care." Hastings Center. Accessed March 6, 2015. www.undocumentedpatients.org.

Hagan, Jacqueline, David Leal, and Néstor Rodríguez. 2015. "Deporting Social Capital: Implications for Immigrant Communities in the United States." *Migration Studies* 3 (3): 370–92.

Haley, Jennifer M., Genevieve M. Kenney, Hamutal Bernstein, and Dulce Gonzalez. 2020. "One in Five Adults in Immigrant Families with Children Reported Chilling Effects on Public Benefit Receipt in 2019." Urban Institute, June 18, 2020. www.urban.org.

Han, Hahrie, and Liz McKenna. 2021. "To Learn about the Democratic Party's Future, Look at What Latino Organizers Did in Arizona." *Washington Post*, February 9, 2021. www.washingtonpost.com.

Healthinsurance.org. 2018. "Medicaid Coverage in Your State." March 24, 2018.

Hernández, Diana. 2016. "'Extra Oomph': Addressing Housing Disparities through Medical Legal Partnership Interventions." *Housing Studies* 31 (7): 871-890. https://doi.org/10.1080/02673037.2016.1150431.

Herndon, Astead W. 2020. "Georgia Was a Big Win for Democrats. Black Women Did the Groundwork." *New York Times*, December 5, 2020. www.nytimes.com.

Holmes, Seth. 2013. *Fresh Fruit, Broken Bodies: Migrant Farmworkers in the United States*. Berkeley: University of California Press.

Horton, Sarah B. 2004. "Different Subjects: The Health Care System's Participation in the Differential Construction of the Cultural Citizenship of Cuban Refugees and Mexican Immigrants." *Medical Anthropology Quarterly* 18: 472–89.

———. 2016. *They Leave Their Kidneys in the Field: Illness, Injury, and Illegality among US Farmworkers*. Berkeley: University of California Press.

———. 2020. Introduction to *Paper Trails: Migrants, Documents, and Legal Insecurity*, edited by Sarah B. Horton and Josiah Heyman, 1–26. Durham: Duke University Press.

Hu, Margaret. 2017. "Algorithmic Jim Crow." *Fordham Law Review* 86 (2): 633–96.

Ibarra, Ana. 2017. "Fearing Deportation, Parents Worry about Enrolling Undocumented Kids in Medi-Cal." KQED California Healthline, May 16, 2017. www.kqed.org.

Immigrant Legal Resource Center (ILRC). 2019. "National Map of Local Entanglement with ICE." November 13, 2019. www.ilrc.org.

———. 2020. "National Map of 287(g) Agreements." October 21, 2020. www.ilrc.org.

Immigration and Customs Enforcement (ICE). 2018. "Secure Communities." March 20, 2018. www.ice.gov.

Ingber, Sasha, and Rachel Martin. 2019. "Immigration Chief: 'Give Me Your Tired, Your Poor Who Can Stand on Their Own 2 Feet.'" NPR, August 13, 2019. www.npr.org.

Jerome-D'Emilia, Bonnie, and Patricia D. Suplee. 2012. "The ACA and the Undocumented." *American Journal of Nursing* 112 (4): 21–27.

Jimenez, Anthony. 2021. "The Legal Violence of Care: Navigating the US Health Care System While Undocumented and Illegible." *Social Science and Medicine* 270 (2021): 113676. https://doi.org/10.1016/j.socscimed.2021.113676.

Johnson, Tae D. 2021. "Interim Guidance: Civil Immigration Enforcement and Removal Priorities." US Department of Homeland Security—Immigration and Customs Enforcement. February 18, 2021. www.ice.gov.

Jones, Jennifer A. 2019. *The Browning of the New South*. Chicago: University of Chicago Press.

Joseph, Tiffany D. 2016a. "What Health Care Reform Means for Immigrants: Comparing the Affordable Care Act and Massachusetts Health Reforms." *Journal of Health Politics, Policy, and Law* 41 (1): 101–16.

———. 2016b. "The Growing Citizen-Noncitizen Divide: Life along the Documentation Status Continuum." American Dilemmas Seminar, Political Science Department, Brown University, Providence, RI, February 24, 2016.

———. 2020. "The Documentation Status Continuum: Citizenship and Increasing Stratification in American Life." Preprint on *SocArXiv*, March 13, 2020. https://doi.org/10.31235/osf.io/2x6hq.

Kaiser Family Foundation (KFF). 2013. "Summary of the Affordable Care Act." April 25, 2013. https://kff,org.

———. 2015. "Key Facts about the Uninsured Population." Accessed December 1, 2015. http://kff.org.

———. 2016. "Key Facts about the Uninsured Population." Accessed January 19, 2017. http://kff.org.

———. 2020a. "Health Coverage of Immigrants." March 18, 2020. www.kff.org.

———. 2020b. "Medicaid/CHIP Coverage of Lawfully-Residing Immigrant Children and Pregnant Women." Accessed February 10, 2021. www.kff.org.

———. 2020c. "Status of State Medicaid Expansion Decisions: Interactive Map." Accessed June 10, 2021. www.kff.org.

———. 2021. "Status of State Action on Medicaid Expansion Decision." June 24, 2021. www.kff.org.

Kalhan, Anil. 2013. "Immigration Policing and Federalism through the Lens of Technology, Surveillance, and Privacy." *Ohio State Law Journal* 74 (2013): 1105–65.

———. 2014. "Immigration Surveillance." *Maryland Law Review* 74 (1): 1–78.

Kaur, Harmeet. 2020. "California Is Now Offering Support to Undocumented Immigrants, in the First Relief Fund of Its Kind." CNN, May 18, 2020. www.cnn.com.

Kennedy, Kelly. 2018. "Deportation Fears Have Legal Immigrants Avoiding Health Care." Associated Press, January 22, 2018. https://apnews.com.

Kennedy, Merritt. 2016. "Clinton-Trump Showdown Was the Most-Watched Presidential Debate Ever." NPR, September 27, 2016. www.npr.org.

Kline, Nolan. 2019. *Pathogenic Policing: Immigration Enforcement and Health in the US South*. New Brunswick: Rutgers University Press.

Krogstad, Jens Manuel. 2016. "Key facts about immigrants eligible for deportation relief under Obama's expanded executive actions." Pew Research Center, January 19, 2016. www.pewresearch.org.

Kurzban, Ira J. 2008. "Criminalizing Immigration Law." 2008 Immigration Law Conference, University of Texas.

Kusenbach, Margarethe. 2017. "'Look at My House!' Home and Mobile Home Ownership among Latino/a Immigrants in Florida." *Journal of Housing and the Built Environment* 32 (1): 29–37. https://doi.org/10.1007/s10901-015-9488-8.

Light, Donald W. 2000. "The Sociological Character of Health-Care Markets." In *Handbook of Social Studies in Health and Medicine*, edited by Gary L. Albrecht, Ray Fitzpatrick, and Susan C. Scrimshaw. Thousand Oaks, CA: Sage.

Lind, Dara. 2014. "Public Schools Are Required to Accept Immigrants—but They Keep Finding Ways Not To." *Vox*, May 9, 2014. www.vox.com.

López-Sanders, Laura. 2017a. "Changing the Navigator's Course: How the Increasing Rationalization of Healthcare Influences Access for Undocumented Immigrants under the Affordable Care Act." *Social Science and Medicine* 178 (2017): 46–54. http://dx.doi.org/10.1016/j.socscimed.2017.01.066.

———. 2017b. "Navigating Health Care: Brokerage and Access for Undocumented Latino Immigrants under the 2010 Affordable Care Act." *Journal of Ethnic and Migration Studies* 43 (12). https://doi.org/10.1080/1369183X.2017.1323452.

Lowrey, Annie. 2017. "Trump's Anti-Immigrant Policies Are Scaring Eligible Families Away from the Safety Net." *Atlantic*, March 24, 2017. www.theatlantic.com.

Macías-Rojas, Patrisia. 2016. *From Deportation to Prison: The Politics of Immigration Enforcement in Post–Civil Rights America*. New York: New York University Press.

Makhlouf, Medha D. 2020. "Laboratories of Exclusion: Medicaid, Federalism and Immigrants." *New York University Law Review* 95 (6): 1680–1777.

Manuel, Jennifer I. 2018. "Racial/Ethnic and Gender Disparities in Health Care Use and Access." *Health Services Research* 53 (3): 1407–29. https://doi.org/10.1111/1475-6773.12705.

Marrow, Helen B. 2011. *New Destination Dreaming: Immigration, Race, and Legal Status in the Rural American South*. Palo Alto, CA: Stanford University Press.

———. 2012. "Deserving to a Point: Unauthorized Immigrants in San Francisco's Universal Access Healthcare Model." *Social Science and Medicine* 74 (6): 846–54.

Marrow, Helen B., and Tiffany D. Joseph. 2015. "Excluded and Frozen Out: Unauthorised Immigrants' (Non)Access to Care after US Health Care Reform." *Journal of Ethnic and Migration Studies* 41 (14): 2253–73.

Marshall, Thomas Humphrey. 1950. *Citizenship and Social Class*. Cambridge: Cambridge University Press.

Mbembe, Achille. 2003. "Necropolitics." *Public Culture* 15 (1): 11–40.

McAdam, Doug, and Karina Kloos. 2014. "How Did We Get into This Mess?" In *Deeply Divided: Racial Politics and Social Movements in Post-War America*. Oxford: Oxford University Press.

Melo, Milena A. 2017. "Stratified Access: Seeking Dialysis Care in the Borderlands." In *Unequal Coverage: The Experience of Health Care Reform in the United States*, edited by Jessica M. Mulligan and Heide Castañeda, 59–78. New York: New York University Press.

Melossi, Dario. 2015. *Crime, Punishment, and Migration*. Los Angeles: Sage.

Mendenhall, Emily. 2012. *Syndemic Suffering: Social Distress, Depression, and Diabetes among Mexican Immigrant Women*. New York: Routledge.

Menjívar, Cecilia. 2006. "Liminal Legality: Salvadoran and Guatemalan Immigrants' Lives in the United States." *American Journal of Sociology* 111 (4): 999–1037.

——. 2013. "Central American Immigrant Workers and Legal Violence in Phoenix, Arizona." *Latino Studies* 11 (2): 228–52.

——. 2016. "Immigrant Criminalization in Law and the Media: Effects on Latino Immigrant Workers' Identities in Arizona." *American Behavioral Scientist* 60 (5–6): 597–616. https://doi.org/10.1177/0002764216632836.

——. 2017. "Spaces of Legal Ambiguity: Central American Immigrants, 'Street-Level Workers,' and Belonging." In *Within and Beyond Citizenship: Borders, Membership and Belonging*, edited by Roberto G. Gonzales and Nando Sigona, 36–52. Oxfordshire: Routledge.

——. 2021. "The Racialization of 'Illegality.'" *Daedalus* 150 (2): 91–105. https://doi.org/10.1162/daed_a_01848.

Menjívar, Cecilia, and Leisy Abrego. 2012. "Legal Violence: Immigration Law and the Lives of Central American Immigrants." *American Journal of Sociology* 117 (5): 1380–1421.

Menjívar, Cecilia, and Daniel Kanstroom, eds. 2014. *Constructing Immigrant "Illegality": Critiques, Experiences, and Responses*. New York: Cambridge University Press.

Menjívar, Cecilia, and Néstor Rodríguez, eds. 2005. *When States Kill: Latin America, the US, and Technologies of Terror*. Austin: University of Texas Press.

Merry, Sally Engel. 1985. "Concepts of Law and Justice among Working Class Americans." *Legal Studies Forum* 9 (1): 59–71.

Miller, Teresa A. 2003. "Citizenship and Severity: Recent Immigration Reforms and the New Penology." *Georgetown Immigration Law Journal* 17: 611–66. https://digitalcommons.law.buffalo.edu/.

Mohl, Raymond A. 2003. "Globalization, Latinization, and the Nuevo New South." *Journal of American Ethnic History* 22: 31–66.

Montoya, Michael J. 2011. *Making the Mexican Diabetic: Race, Science, and the Genetics of Inequality*. Berkeley: University of California Press.

Morgen, Sandra, and Jeff Maskovsky. 2003. "The Anthropology of Welfare 'Reform': New Perspectives on US Urban Poverty in the Post-Welfare Era." *Annual Review of Anthropology* 32 (3): 15–38. https://doi.org/10.1146/annurev.anthro.32.061002.093431.

Motomura, Hiroshi. 2007. *Americans in Waiting: The Lost Story of Immigration and Citizenship in the United States*. Oxford: Oxford University Press.

Musumeci, MaryBeth. 2019. "Explaining *Texas v. US*: A Guide to the 5th Circuit Appeal in the Case Challenging the ACA." Kaiser Family Foundation, July 3, 2019. www.kff.org.

National Conference of State Legislatures (NCSL). 2012. "State Omnibus Immigration Legislation and Legal Challenges." August 27, 2012. www.ncsl.org.

National Immigration Law Center (NILC). 2014. "Major Benefit Programs Available to Immigrants in California." Accessed May 14, 2015. www.nilc.org.

——. 2018. "Trump Executive Order Makes Border Crisis Worse." June 20, 2018. www.nilc.org.

——. 2021a. "Biden Administration Day One Immigration Actions." January 2021. www.nilc.org.

———. 2021b. "Litigation Related to Deferred Action for Childhood Arrivals (DACA)." January 14, 2021. www.nilc.org.

Neubeck, Kenneth J., and Noel A Cazenave. 2001. *Welfare Racism: Playing the Race Card against America's Poor*. New York: Routledge.

New York Lawyers for the Public Interest (NYLPI). 2012. "Discharge, Deportation, and Dangerous Journeys: A Study on the Practice of Medical Repatriation." Seton Hall University Center for Social Justice Report. https://medicalrepatriation.files.

Novak, Nicole L., Arline T. Geronimus, and Aresha M. Martinez-Cardoso. 2017. "Change in Birth Outcomes among Infants Born to Latina Mothers after a Major Immigration Raid." *International Journal of Epidemiology* 46 (3): 839–49. https://doi.org/10.1093/ije/dyw346.

Nwadiuko, Joseph, Jashalynn German, Kavita Chapla, Frances Wang, Maya Venkata-ramani, Dhananjay Vaidya, and Sarah Polk. 2021. "Changes in Health Care Use among Undocumented Patients, 2014–2018." *JAMA Netw Open* 4 (3): e210763. https://doi.org/10.1001/jamanetworkopen.2021.0763.

Omi, Michael, and Howard Winant. 2014. *Racial Formation in the United States*. New York: Routledge.

Oprysko, Caitlin, and Ted Hesson. 2018. "Trump Administration Rejects Responsibility for Death of 7-Year-Old Girl in Border Patrol Custody." *Politico*, December 14, 2018. www.politico.com.

Page, Kathleen R., and Alejandra Flores-Miller. 2021. "Lessons We've Learned—COVID-19 and the Undocumented Latinx Community." *New England Journal of Medicine* 384: 5–7. https://doi.org/10.1056/NEJMp2024897.

Park, Lisa Sun-Hee. 2011. *Entitled to Nothing: The Struggle for Immigrant Health Care in the Age of Welfare Reform*. New York: New York University Press.

Patel, Leigh. 2015. "Deservingness: Challenging Coloniality in Education and Migration Scholarship." *Association of Mexican-American Educators* 9 (3): 11–21.

Philbin, Morgan M., Morgan Flake, Mark L. Hatzenbuehler, and Jennifer S. Hirsch. 2018. "State-Level Immigration and Immigrant-Focused Policies as Drivers of Latino Health Disparities in the United States." *Social Science and Medicine* 199: 29–38.

Pinderhughes, Howard, Rachel A. Davis, and Myesha Williams. 2016. *Adverse Community Experiences and Resilience: A Framework for Addressing and Preventing Community Trauma*. Oakland, CA: Prevention Institute.

Plumer, Brad. 2013. "Congress Tried to Fix Immigration Back in 1986. Why Did It Fail?" *Washington Post*, January 30, 2013. www.washingtonpost.com.

Portes, Alejandro, and Rubén G. Rumbaut. 2014. *Immigrant America: A Portrait*. 4th ed. Berkeley: University of California Press.

Provine, Doris Marie, and Monica W. Varsanyi. 2020. "Documenting Membership: The Divergent Politics of Migrant Driver's Licenses in New Mexico and Arizona." In *Paper Trails: Migrants, Documents, and Legal Insecurity*, edited by Sarah B. Horton and Josiah Heyman, 74–108. Durham: Duke University Press.

Quesada, James, Laurie Kain Hart, and Philippe Bourgois. 2011. "Structural Vulnerability and Health: Latino Migrant Laborers in the United States." *Medical Anthropology* 30 (4): 339–62. https://doi.org/10.1080/01459740.2011.576725.

Rhodes, Scott D., Lilli Mann, Florence M. Simán, Eunyoung Song, Jorge Alonzo, Mario Downs, Emma Lawlor, Omar Martinez, Christina J. Sun, Mary Claire O'Brien, Beth A. Reboussin, and Mark A. Hall. 2015. "The Impact of Local Immigration Enforcement Policies on the Health of Immigrant Hispanics/Latinos in the United States." *American Journal of Public Health* 105 (2): 329–37.

Ribas, Vanesa. 2015. *On the Line: Slaughterhouse Lives and the Making of the New South.* Berkeley: University of California Press.

Robinson, Cedric J. 1983. *Black Marxism.* Chapel Hill: University of North Carolina Press.

Rodríguez, Néstor, and Cristian Paredes. 2014. "Coercive Immigration Enforcement and Bureaucratic Ideology." In *Constructing Immigrant "Illegality": Critiques, Experiences, and Responses,* edited by Cecilia Menjívar and Daniel Kanstroom. New York: Cambridge University Press.

Rodriguez, Rudolph. 2015. "Dialysis for Undocumented Immigrants in the United States." *Advances in Chronic Kidney Disease* 22 (1): 60–65.

Romero, Simon. 2018. "Father of Migrant Girl Who Died in US Custody Disputes Border Patrol Account." *New York Times,* December 15, 2018. www.nytimes.com.

Sainsbury, Diane. 2012. *Welfare States and Immigrant Rights: The Politics of Inclusion and Exclusion.* Oxford: Oxford University Press.

Salami, Amanda. 2017. "Immigrant Eligibility for Health Care Programs in the United States." National Conference of State Legislatures, October 19, 2017. www.ncsl.org.

Salsberg, Edward, Leo Quigley, Nicholas Mehfoud, Kimberley Acquaviva, Karen Wyche, and Shari Sliwa. 2017. "Profile of the Social Work Workforce: A Report to Council on Social Work Education and National Workforce Initiative Steering Committee." October 2017. www.cswe.org.

Sigona, Nando. 2012. "'I Have Too Much Baggage': The Impacts of Legal Status on the Social Worlds of Irregular Migrants." *Social Anthropology/Anthropologie Sociale* 20 (1): 50–65. https://doi.org/10.1111/j.1469-8676.2011.00191.x.

Silbey, Susan S. 2005. "After Legal Consciousness." *Annual Review of Law and Society* 1 (2005): 323–68. https://doi.org/10.1146/annurev.lawsocsci.1.041604.115938.

Smith, Robert Courtney, and Andrés Sebastián Besserer Rayas. 2020. "Disrupting the Traffic Stop to Deportation Pipeline in New York State: How Greenlight Laws Will Reduce Harm to Children." Paper presented at the American Sociological Association Annual Meeting, virtual conference, August 8, 2020.

Snow, David, Daniel Cress, Liam Downey, and Andrew Jones. 1998. "Disrupting the 'Quotidian': Reconceptualizing the Relationship between Breakdown and the Emergence of Collective Action." *Mobilization* 3 (1): 1–22.

Sommers, Benjamin D. 2013. "Stuck between Health and Immigration Reform—Care for Undocumented Immigrants." *New England Journal of Medicine* 369 (7): 593–95.

Sontag, Deborah. 2008. "Immigrants Facing Deportation by US Hospitals." *New York Times*, August 3, 2008. www.nytimes.com.

Soss, Joe, Richard C. Fording, and Sanford F. Schram. 2011. *Disciplining the Poor: Neoliberal Paternalism and the Persistent Power of Race*. Chicago: University of Chicago Press.

Sotomayor, Marianna, Phil McCausland, and Ariana Brockington. 2017. "Charlottesville White Nationalist Rally Violence Prompts State of Emergency." Reuters/NBC News, August 12, 2017. www.nbcnews.com.

Striffler, Steve. 2005. *Chicken: The Dangerous Transformation of America's Favorite Food*. New Haven: Yale University Press.

Stuart, Forrest, Amada Armenta, and Melissa Osborne. 2015. "Legal Control of Marginal Groups." *Annual Review of Law and Social Science* 11 (2015): 235–54.

Stuesse, Angela. 2016. *Scratching Out a Living: Latinos, Race, and Work in the Deep South*. Oakland: University of California Press.

Stuesse, Angela, and Mathew Coleman. 2014. "Automobility, Immobility, Altermobility: Surviving and Resisting the Intensification of Immigrant Policing." *City and Society* 26 (1): 51–72.

Stuesse, Angela, and Laura E. Helton. 2013. "Low-Wage Legacies, Race, and the Golden Chicken in Mississippi: Where Contemporary Immigration Meets African American Labor History." *Southern Spaces*, December 31, 2013. https://southernspaces.org.

Stumpf, Juliet. 2006. "The Crimmigration Crisis: Immigrants, Crime, and Sovereign Power." *American University Law Review* 56: 367–419.

———. 2013. "The Process Is the Punishment in Crimmigration Law." In *The Borders of Punishment: Migration, Citizenship, and Social Exclusion*, edited by K. Franko Aas and M. Bosworth, 58–75. Oxford: Oxford University Press.

Taylor, Charles A., Christopher Boulos, and Douglas Almond. 2020. "Livestock Plants and COVID-19 Transmission." *PNAS* 117 (50): 31706–15. https://doi.org/10.1073/pnas.2010115117.

Torche, Florencia, and Catherine Sirois. 2018. "Restrictive Immigration Law and Birth Outcomes of Immigrant Women." *American Journal of Epidemiology* 188 (1): 24–33. https://doi.org/10.1093/aje/kwy218.

Torres, Lourdes. 2018. "Latinx?" *Latino Studies* 16 (3): 283–85.

Trump, Donald J. 2017. Executive Order 13768: "Enhancing Public Safety in the Interior of the United States." January 25, 2017. www.whitehouse.gov.

———. 2019. "President Donald J. Trump's Address to the Nation on the Crisis at the Border." January 8, 2019. www.whitehouse.gov.

Turner, Bryan. 1997. "From Governmentality to Risk: Some Reflections on Foucault's Contribution to Medical Sociology." In *Foucault, Health and Medicine*, edited by Alan Petersen and Robin Bunton, ix–xxi. London: Routledge.

US Bureau of Labor Statistics (BLS). 2020. "Employment Recovery in the Wake of the COVID-19 Pandemic." Monthly Labor Review, December 2020. www.bls.gov.

———. 2021. "Labor Force Statistics from the Current Population Survey." January 22, 2021. www.bls.gov.

US Census Bureau. 2021. "QuickFacts." July 1, 2021. www.census.gov.

US Citizenship and Immigration Services (USCIS). 2008. "DNA-Sample Collection and Biological Evidence Preservation in the Federal Jurisdiction [73 FR 74932] [FR 100–08]." December 10, 2018. www.uscis.gov.

———. 2013. "Questions and Answers: Reasonable Fear Screenings." June 18, 2013. www.uscis.gov.

———. 2014. "Executive Actions on Immigration." Accessed June 4, 2015. www.uscis.gov.

———. 2015. "Questions and Answers: Credible Fear Screening." July 15, 2015. www.uscis.gov.

———. 2019. "Decision [Individual Letters from USCIS to Immigrants Seeking Medical Deferrals]." August 2019. https://d279m997dpfwgl.cloudfront.net.

US Department of Agriculture (USDA). 2020. "Rural-Urban Continuum Codes." Economic Research Service. Accessed April 2, 2021. www.ers.usda.gov.

US Department of Homeland Security (DHS). 2013. "Clarification of Existing Practices Related to Certain Health Care Information." October 25, 2013. www.ice.gov.

———. 2014. "Policies for the Apprehension, Detention and Removal of Undocumented Immigrants." Agency memorandum, November 20, 2014. www.dhs.gov.

———. 2017. "Immigration Data and Statistics." Accessed January 20, 2017. www.dhs.gov.

———. 2018. "DHS Statement on Tragic Death of Minor at Border." Facebook, December 14, 2018. www.facebook.com.

———. 2019. "Yearbook of Immigration Statistics" (2008–2016). www.dhs.gov.

———. 2021. "Secretary Mayorkas Issues New Guidance for Enforcement Action at Protected Areas." October 27, 2021. www.dhs.gov.

US Department of Justice (DOJ). 2011. "United States' Investigation of the Maricopa County Sheriff's Office." Letter from Assistant Attorney General Thomas E. Perez to Maricopa County Attorney Bill Montgomery, December 15, 2011. www.justice.gov.

———. 2012a. "Statement of Attorney General Eric Holder on Supreme Court's Ruling *Arizona v. United States*." June 25, 2012. www.justice.gov.

———. 2012b. "United States' Investigation of the Alamance County Sheriff's Office." Letter from Assistant Attorney General Thomas E. Perez to Alamance County Attorney Clyde B. Albright and Chuck Kitchen, September 18, 2012. www.justice.gov.

Vaidya, Varun, Gautam Partha, and Monita Karmakar. 2012. "Gender Difference in Utilization of Preventive Care Services in the United States." *Journal of Women's Health* 21 (2): 140–5. https://doi.org/10.1089/jwh.2011.2876.

Van Dyke, Nella, and David S. Meyer, eds. 2014. *Understanding the Tea Party Movement*. New York: Routledge.

Van Natta, Meredith. 2019. "First Do No Harm: Medical Legal Violence and Immigrant Health in Coral County, USA." *Social Science and Medicine* 235. https://doi.org/10.1016/j.socscimed.2019.112411.

Van Natta, Meredith, Nancy J. Burke, Irene H. Yen, Mark D. Fleming, Christoph L. Hanssmann, Maryani Palupy Rasidjan, and Janet K. Shim. 2019. "Stratified Citizenship, Stratified Health: Examining Latinx Legal Status in the US Healthcare Safety Net." *Social Science and Medicine* 220: 49–55. https://doi.org/10.1016/j. socscimed.2018.10.024.

Van Natta, Meredith, Nancy J. Burke, Irene H. Yen, Sara Rubin, Mark D. Fleming, Ariana Thompson-Lastad, and Janet K. Shim. 2018. "Complex Care and Contradictions of Choice in the Safety Net." *Sociology of Health and Illness* 40 (3): 538–51. https://doi.org/10.1111/1467-9566.12661.

Varsanyi, Monica W., Paul G. Lewis, Doris Marie Provine, and Scott Decker. 2012. "A Multilayered Jurisdictional Patchwork: Immigration Federalism in the United States." *Law and Policy* 34 (2): 138–58.

Vásquez, Tina. 2020. "'I'm Afraid to Go Back': Poultry Workers Fear Returning to Work as COVID-19 Spreads through Plants." *Prism*, May 4, 2020. https://prismreports.org.

Viladrich, Anahí. 2012. "Beyond Welfare Reform: Reframing Undocumented Immigrants' Entitlement to Health Care in the United States; A Critical Review." *Social Science and Medicine* 74: 822–29.

Weheliye, Alexander G. 2014. *Habeas Viscus: Racializing Assemblages, Biopolitics, and Black Feminist Theories of the Human.* Durham: Duke University Press.

Western New York Law Center (WNYLC). 2021. "NY Health Access: Emergency Medicaid in New York State—Limited Medicaid Coverage for Undocumented Immigrants." March 9, 2021. www.wnylc.com.

Wiley, Dinah. 2014. "For DACA Grantees, Health Insurance Is (Only) a Dream." Georgetown University Healthy Policy Institute, Center for Children and Families, April 11, 2014. https://ccf.georgetown.edu.

Willen, Sarah S. 2007. "Toward a Critical Phenomenology of 'Illegality': State Power, Criminalization, and Abjectivity among Undocumented Migrant Workers in Tel Aviv, Israel." *International Migration* 45 (3): 8–38.

———. 2012a. "Migration, 'Illegality,' and Health: Mapping Embodied Vulnerability and Debating Health-Related Deservingness." *Social Science and Medicine* 74 (6): 805–11. https://doi.org/10.1016/j.socscimed.2011.10.041.

———. 2012b. "How Is Health-Related Deservingness Reckoned? Perspectives from Unauthorized Im/migrants in Tel Aviv." *Social Science and Medicine* 74 (6): 812–21. https://doi.org/10.1016/j.socscimed.2011.06.033.

Yoo, Grace J. 2008. "Immigrants and Welfare: Policy Constructions of Deservingness." *Journal of Immigrant and Refugee Studies* 6: 490–507.

Young, Maria-Elena de Trinidad, and Steven P. Wallace. 2019. "Included, but Deportable: A New Public Health Approach to Policies That Criminalize and Integrate Immigrants." *American Journal of Public Health* 109 (9): 1171–6.

Zepeda-Millán, Chris. 2017. *Latino Mass Mobilization: Immigration, Racialization, and Activism.* Cambridge: Cambridge University Press.

Zeskind, Leonard. 2012. "A Nation Dispossessed: The Tea Party Movement and Race." *Critical Sociology* 38 (4): 495–509. https://doi.org/10.1177/0896920511431852.

Zimmerman, Cathy, Ligia Kiss, and Hossain Mazeda. 2011. "Migration and Health: A Framework for 21st Century Policy-Making." *PLoS Med* 8 (5): e1001034. https://doi.org/10.1371/journal.pmed.1001034.

INDEX

Abrego, Leisy J., 14, 19
ACA. *See* Affordable Care Act
administrative records, 98–99
AEDPA. *See* Antiterrorism and Effective Death Penalty Act
Affordable Care Act (ACA), 6–7, 65, 106–7, 111; attacks on, 7–8; in blue states, 118; EHRs under, 157–58; Medicaid and, 18, 63–64, 122; in purple states, 122; in red states, 63–64
Alejandra (patient), 127, 128, 134–35, 143
Alicia (clinic attendee), 100–103
alt-right, 209n3
ambulances, 49, 209n8
American flag, 88
American Immigration Lawyers Association, 91
amnesty, 210n2
anonymity, 70
anti-immigrant rhetoric, 89, 103–4; avoidance of care caused by, 114; codification of, 163; openness of, 113; of Republicans, 4–5, 7; symbolic violence of, 25, 185; of Trump, 25, 36–37, 42–43, 57, 62–63, 88
Antiterrorism and Effective Death Penalty Act (AEDPA), 206n10
anxiety, patient, 74
Arizona, 64
Armenta, Amada, 22
Asad, Asad L., 14
assemblages: defining, 60–61; dynamic nature of, 75–76; in red states, 26, 59–60, 185–86; across state-level political landscapes, 18; symbolic violence of, 70

asylum-free zones, 122
asylum hearings, 1–3
audits, health department, 146–47
Automating Inequality (Eubanks), 209n5
autonomy, patient, 160–61
avoidance of care: anti-immigrant rhetoric leading to, 114; as medical legal violence, 83–84

Barrio 18, 205n3
Beatriz (community organization leader), 98, 99
Beckett, Dr., 142–47
Bentham, Jeremy, 208n21
Biden, Joe, 11; immigration law under, 187–88
biometric data, 64–65
biopolitics: immigration law and, 20; surveillance at clinics, 140–49
Black Lives Matter, 121
blindness, 138
blood pressure, 47
blood transfusions, 101
blue states, 18, 26–27; ACA resources in, 118; anxieties over Trump in, 110–11; clinic workers in, 150–51, 191–92; demographics of, 121; fieldwork in, 158–59; immigration federalism and, 186; immigration law in, 113; integration in, 123–24; Medicaid in, 38, 107; medical legal violence in, 118–19; surveillance in, 89, 100
border crisis, Trump on, 33, 84, 86. *See also* US-Mexico border
Border Patrol, US, funding of, 61–62

Borders of Belonging (Castañeda), 22
Bowker, Geoffrey C., 60–61
bureaucratic hurdles: for noncitizens, 72–73; Trump creating, 73
bureaucratic inscription, 21
Bush, George W., 11, 190, 206n11

Caitlyn (administrative assistant), 146–47
Camila (counselor), 167
CAP. *See* Criminal Alien Program
capitalism, 15–16. *See also* racial capitalism
CARES. *See* Coronavirus Aid, Relief, and Economic Security Act
Carina (patient), 125, 131–34, 140
Dr. Carrera, 113–15, 117
Castañeda, Heide, 22
Catholic Legal Immigration Network, 91
CBP. *See* Customs and Border Protection
Central American immigrants, 40, 50, 52, 88, 104, 126, 168; criminalization of, 10, 12; destabilization fled by, 205n3; violence fled by, 165
Certificate of Confidentiality, 25
Chacón, Jennifer, 10
charity care, 138–39
Charlottesville, 209n3
chemotherapy, 162
Chinese Exclusion Act of 1882, 205n5
chronic illness, 30, 75
citizenship, 8–9; defining, 13; exclusion from, 38, 100–104; historical limitations to, 205n5; legal consciousness shaping, 14; through marriage, 95; Medicaid and compromising, 134–35; under racial capitalism, 13–16; as racialized construction in the South, 141
Clair, Matthew, 14
clinic networks, 110–11
clinic resistance, surveillance and, 108–18
clinic safety plans, 117
clinic values, 170–76
clinic workers: in blue states, 150–51, 191–92; deputization of, 154; documenta-

tion of stories of, 24–28; as facilitators, 170–76; federal policy resisted by, 90; on immigration enforcement, 97–98, 123; immigration federalism and, 111–13; on Law X, 69; medical legal consciousness of, 154, 161, 177–78; medical legal violence navigated by, 58; myths dispelled by, 159–60; non-medical, 152; on patient security, 111–12; on public charge issues, 174–75; in purple states, 122–23, 150–51, 191–92; in red states, 150–51, 191–92; surveillance and, 142; under Trump, 174; trust of, 163–70
Clinton, Bill, 11, 190
Clinton, Hillary, 4–5
colon cancer, 50
colonialism, white supremacy and, 6
community clinics, 29, 43, 94; frontline workers at, 103
community engagement, 93–94
community organizing, 96
community service, 129
compounded harms, 45–50
Confederate flags, 120
Constitution, US, immigration law and, 10–11
coronavirus. *See* COVID-19 pandemic
Coronavirus Aid, Relief, and Economic Security (CARES) Act, 189
COVID-19 pandemic, 6, 28, 148, 178; burden of, for nonwhite people, 184–85; EMR in, 182–83; inclusion/exclusion dialectic in, 184–85; isolation in, 180; Latinx immigrants in, 180; legal violence and, 183; in poultry plants, 180–82; in purple states, 179–80; spread of, 179–81; state of exception and, 184–85; testing, 181, 183
credible fear, 205n2
Criminal Alien Program (CAP), 144
criminalization, 15, 27, 79, 154; of Central American immigrants, 10, 12; DACA and, 171–72; driver's license issues and,

ABOUT THE AUTHOR

MEREDITH VAN NATTA is Assistant Professor of Sociology and a medical sociologist at the University of California, Merced. Her current research focuses on how immigration, health, and welfare policies shape health care for noncitizens in the United States, as well as the biometric surveillance of immigrant individuals and communities.

Printed in the United States
by Baker & Taylor Publisher Services